A HISTORY OF ANTHROPOLOGY

Anthropology, Culture and Society

Series Editors:
Professor Thomas Hylland Eriksen, University of Oslo
Dr Katy Gardner, University of Sussex
Dr Jon P. Mitchell, University of Sussex

A
HISTORY
OF
ANTHROPOLOGY

Thomas Hylland Eriksen
and Finn Sivert Nielsen

Pluto Press

LONDON • STERLING, VIRGINIA

First published 2001
by PLUTO PRESS
345 Archway Road, London N6 5AA
and 22883 Quicksilver Drive,
Sterling, VA 20166–2012, USA

www.plutobooks.com

British Library Cataloguing in Publication Data
A catalogue record for this book is available from
the British Library

ISBN 0 7453 1390 6 hardback
ISBN 0 7453 1385 X paperback

Library of Congress Cataloging in Publication Data
applied for

10   9   8   7   6   5   4   3

Designed and produced for Pluto Press by
Chase Publishing Services, Fortescue, Sidmouth EX10 9QG
Typeset from disk by Stanford DTP Services, Towcester
Printed and bound in the European Union by
Antony Rowe, Chippenham and Eastbourne, England

CONTENTS

PREFACE

This is an ambitious book, but not a pretentious one. It is ambitious in that it tries, within the space of relatively few pages, to make sense of the diverse history of anthropology. Our priorities, omissions and interpretations are bound to be contested, since there can be no single authoritative history of anything, least of all a sprawling, dynamic and disputed field like anthropology. Still, the book is unpretentious, since our aim throughout has been to offer a sober and balanced account of the historical growth of anthropology as a discipline, not to propose a radical re-interpretation of it.

There exists a growing scholarly literature on the history of anthropology, which this textbook does not try to compete with. Nevertheless, we know of no existing book with exactly the same scope as this one. The scholarly literature is often specialised, and existing textbooks on anthropological history are either more theoretically oriented or more committed to one or a few professional traditions. Although we may not always have succeeded, we have strived to give an impression of the parallel, convergent and interdependent developments of all major traditions in social and cultural anthropology.

The book is chronologically ordered. Beginning with the 'proto-anthropologies' from ancient Greece to the Enlightenment, it continues with the creation of academic anthropology and the growth of classical sociology during the nineteenth century. The third chapter concentrates on the four men who, by general consensus, are considered the founding fathers of twentieth-century anthropology, and the fourth chapter indicates how their work was continued, and diversified, by their students. The fifth and sixth chapters both deal with the same period – from about 1946 to about 1968, but concentrate on different trends: Chapter 5 discusses the theoretical controversies surrounding concepts of society and social integration, while Chapter 6 covers concepts of culture and symbolic meaning. In Chapter 7, the intellectual and political upheavals of the 1960s and 1970s are presented, with emphasis on the impulses emanating from Marxism and feminism. Chapter 8 deals with the 1980s, concentrating on the postmodernist movement and its close cousin, postcolonialism, two critical trends, which seriously challenged the discipline's self-confidence; while the ninth and final chapter presents a few of the major post-postmodern trends that emerged during the 1990s.

We do not consider the history of anthropology to be a linear tale of progress. Some 'modern' controversies, for example, have occupied scholars since the Enlightenment and even earlier. At the same time, we believe that there has been a steady, cumulative growth in knowledge and understanding within the subject, not least with regard to method. Moreover, as anthropology responds to changes in the outside world, its substantial focus changes accordingly. Thus, the movement from the early industrial and colonial age to the information age of global modernities has led the subject through a series of transformations, yet essentially it continues to raise the same questions that were asked 50, 100 or even 200 years ago.

Oslo/Copenhagen, July 2001
THE & FSN

1 BEGINNINGS

How long have anthropologists existed? Opinions are divided on this issue. The answer depends, largely, on what one means by an anthropologist. People have always been curious about their neighbours and more remote people. They have gossiped about them, fought them, married them and told stories about them. Some of these stories or myths have been written down. Some writings were later criticised as inaccurate or ethnocentric (or flatly racist). Some stories were compared with others, about other peoples, leading to more general assumptions about 'people elsewhere'. In this sense, we start an anthropological inquiry the moment a foreigner moves into the neighbouring flat.

If we restrict ourselves to anthropology as a scientific discipline, some would trace its roots back to the European Enlightenment during the eighteenth century; others would claim that anthropology did not arise as a science until the 1850s, yet others would argue that anthropological research in its present-day sense only commenced after the First World War. Nor can we avoid such ambiguities.

It is beyond doubt, however, that anthropology, considered as the science of humanity, originated in the region we commonly but inaccurately call 'the West', notably in three or four 'Western' countries: France, Great Britain, the USA and, until the Second World War, Germany. Historically speaking, this is a European discipline, and its practitioners, like those of all European sciences, occasionally like to trace its roots back to the ancient Greeks.

HERODOTUS AND OTHER GREEKS

Thanks to research carried out by anthropologists, historians and archaeologists, we today believe that 'the ancient Greeks' probably differed fairly radically from ourselves. In the classical, 'democratic' city-states, more than half the population were slaves; free citizens regarded manual labour as degrading, and democracy (which was also 'invented' by the Greeks) was probably more similar to the competitive *potlatch* feasts of the Kwakiutl (Chapter 4), than to the institutions described in modern constitutions (see Finley 1973; P. Anderson 1974).

Going back to the Greeks is thus a long journey, and we peer into their world through cracked and smoky glass. We catch sight of little city-states surrounded by traditional Iron Age farmland, and connected to the outside world through a network of maritime trade relationships between urban settlements all along the Mediterranean and Black Sea coasts. The trade in luxury goods and the slavery brought considerable wealth to the cities, and the citizens of the *polis*, with their distaste for physical labour, had at their disposal a large surplus, which they used, among other things, to build temples, stadiums, baths and other public buildings, where male citizens could meet and engage in philosophical disputes and speculations about how the world was put together.

It was in such a community that Herodotus of Halicarnassus (*c.* 484–425 BC) lived. Born in a Greek colonial town on the south-west coast of present-day Turkey, Herodotus began to travel as a young man and gained an intimate knowledge of the many foreign peoples that the Greeks maintained contacts with. Today, Herodotus is mainly remembered for his history of the Persian Wars, but he also wrote detailed travel narratives from various parts of western Asia and Egypt, and from as far away as the land of the Scythians on the northern coast of the Black Sea. In these narratives, far removed as they are from our present world, we recognize a problem that has followed anthropology, in various guises, up to this very day: how should we relate to 'the others'? Are they basically like ourselves, or are they basically different? Much anthropological theory has tried to strike a balance between these positions, and this is exactly what Herodotus did too. Sometimes he is simply a prejudiced and ethnocentric 'civilized man', who disdains everything foreign. At other times he acknowledges that different people have different values because they live under different circumstances, not because they are morally deficient. Herodotus' descriptions of language, dress, political and judicial institutions, crafts and economics are highly readable today. Although he sometimes clearly got the facts wrong, he was a meticulous scholar, whose books are often the only written sources we have about peoples of a distant past.

Many Greeks tested their wits against a philosophical paradox that touches directly on the problem of how we should relate to 'the others'. This is the paradox of *universalism* versus *relativism*. A present-day universalist would try to identify commonalities and similarities (or even universals) between different societies, while a relativist would emphasise the uniqueness and particularity of each society or culture. The Sophists of Athens are sometimes described as the first philosophical relativists in the European tradition (several almost contemporary thinkers in Asia, such as Gautama Buddha, Confucius and Lao-Tze, were concerned with similar questions). In Plato's (427–347 BC) dialogues *Protagoras* and *Gorgias*, Socrates argues with the Sophists. We may picture them in dignified intellectual battle, surrounded by colourful temples and solemn public buildings, with their slaves scarcely visible in the shadows between the columns. Other citizens stand as spectators, while Socrates' faith in a universal reason, capable of ascertaining universal truths, is confronted by the relativist view that truth will always vary with experience and what we would today call culture.

Plato's dialogues do not deal directly with cultural differences. But they bear witness to the fact that cross-cultural encounters were part of everyday life in the city-states. The Greek trade routes stretched from the Straits of Gibraltar to present-day Ukraine, they fought wars with Persians and many other 'barbarians'. The very term barbarian is Greek and means 'foreigner'. To a Greek ear it sounded as if these aliens were only able to say 'bar-bar, bar-bar'. Similarly, in Russian, Germans are to this day called *nemtsy* (the mute ones): those who speak, but say nothing.

Aristotle (384–322 BC) also indulged in sophisticated speculations about the nature of humanity. In his philosophical anthropology he discusses the differences between humans in general and animals, and concludes that although humans have several needs in common with animals, only man possesses reason, wisdom and morality. He also argued that humans are fundamentally social by nature. In anthropology and elsewhere, such a universalistic style of thought, which seeks to establish similarities rather than differences between groups of people, plays a prominent role to this day. Furthermore, it seems clear that anthropology, up through history, has vacillated between a universalistic and a relativistic stance, and that central figures in the discipline are also often said to lean either towards one position or the other.

AFTER ANTIQUITY

In the classical Greek city-state, conditions were perhaps particularly favourable for the development of systematic science. But in the ensuing centuries as well, 'civilized' activities such as art, science and philosophy were cultivated all around the Mediterranean: first, in the Hellenistic period, after the Macedonian, Alexander the Great (356–323 BC) had led his armies to the northern reaches of India, spreading Greek urban culture wherever he went; then later, during the several centuries when Rome dominated most of Europe, the Middle East and North Africa, and impressed on its population a culture deriving from Greek ideals. In this complex, multinational society, it is not surprising to find that the Greek interest in 'the other' was also carried on. Thus, the geographer Strabo (c. 63–4 BC–c. AD 21) wrote several voluminous tomes about strange peoples and distant places, which sparkle with curiosity and joy of discovery. But when Christianity was established as state religion and the Roman Empire started falling apart in the mid-fourth century AD, a fundamental change took place in European cultural life. Gone were the affluent citizens of Antiquity, who could indulge in science and philosophy, thanks to their income from trade and slave labour. Gone, indeed, was the entire city culture, the very glue that held the Roman Empire together as an (albeit loosely) integrated state. In its place, countless local

European cultures manifested themselves, carriers of Germanic, Slavic, Finno-Ugric and Celtic traditions that were as ancient as those of pre-urban Greece. Politically, Europe fell apart into hundreds of chiefdoms, cities and autonomous local enclaves, which were only integrated into larger units with the growth of the modern state, from the sixteenth century onwards. Throughout this long period, what tied the continent together was largely the Church, the last lingering trustee of Roman universalism. Under the aegis of the Church, international networks between monks and clergymen arose and flourished, connecting the pockets of learning in which the philosophical and scientific traditions of Antiquity survived.

Europeans like to see themselves as linear descendants of Antiquity, but throughout the Middle Ages, Europe was a periphery. During the 600s to 700s, the Arabs conquered territories from Spain to India and, for at least the next seven centuries, the economic, political and intellectual centres of the Mediterranean world lay in sophisticated metropolises such as Baghdad and Córdoba, not in the ruins of Rome or Athens, not to mention such glorified villages as London or Paris. The greatest historian and social philosopher of this period was Ibn Khaldun (1332–1406), who lived in present-day Tunisia. Khaldun wrote, among other things, a massive history of the Arabs and Berbers, furnished with a long, critical introduction on his use of sources. He developed one of the first non-religious social theories, and anticipated Émile Durkheim's ideas about social solidarity (see Chapter 2), which are today considered a cornerstone of sociology and anthropology. In line with Durkheim and the first anthropologists who utilized his theories, Khaldun stresses the importance of kinship and religion in creating and maintaining a sense of solidarity and mutual commitment among the members of a group.

There are nevertheless a few European writings from the late medieval period, which may be considered precursors of latter-day anthropology. Most famous is Marco Polo's (1254–1323) account of his expedition to China, where he allegedly spent seventeen years. Another example is the great journey through Western Asia described in *The Voyage and Travels of Sir John Mandeville, Knight*, written by an unknown Englishman in the fourteenth century. Both of these books stimulated the European interest in alien peoples and customs. Then, with the advent of mercantilist economies and the contemporaneous Renaissance in the sciences and arts, the small, but rich European city-states of the late Middle Ages began to develop rapidly, and the earliest signs of a capitalist class emerged. Fired by these great social movements and financed by the new entrepreneurs, a series of grand exploratory sea voyages were now launched by European rulers. These journeys – to Africa, Asia and America – are often described in the West as 'the great discoveries', though the 'discovered' peoples themselves may often have had reason to question their greatness (see, for example, Wolf 1982).

THE IMPACT OF THE EUROPEAN CONQUESTS

The 'great discoveries' were of crucial importance for later developments in Europe and the world, and – on a lesser scale – for the development of anthropology. From Henry the Navigator's exploration of the West coast of Africa in the early fifteenth century, via Columbus's five journeys to America (1492–1506), to Magellan's circumnavigation of the world (1519–22), the travels of this period fed the imaginations of the Europeans with vivid descriptions of places whose very existence they had hitherto been unaware of. These travelogues, moreover, reached unusually wide audiences, since the printing press, invented in 1448, soon made books a common and relatively inexpensive commodity all over Europe.

Many travelogues were obviously full of factual errors and marred by deep-seated Christian prejudices. A famous example is the work of the cartographer Amerigo Vespucci, who published many popular accounts from the continent that still bears his name. His books were reprinted and translated many times, but his descriptions of the Americans (who were called Indians, since Columbus believed he had found a route to India), reveal a much less scrupulous attitude to facts than in Herodotus' or Khaldun's writings. Vespucci seems to use the Indians as mere literary effect, to underpin the statements he makes about his own society. Native Americans are, as a rule, represented as distorted or, frequently, inverted reflections of Europeans: they are godless, promiscuous, naked, have no authority or laws, they are even cannibals! Against this background, Vespucci argues effectively for the virtues of absolutist monarchy and papal power, but his ethnographic descriptions are virtually useless as clues to native life at the time of the Conquest.

There were contemporaries of Vespucci, such as the French Huguenot Jean de Léry, who gave more truthful accounts of Indian life, and such books also sold well. But then, the market for adventure stories from distant climes seems to have been insatiable in Europe at this time. In most of the books, a more or less explicit contrast is drawn between the Others (who are either 'noble savages' or 'barbarians') and the existing order in Europe (which is either challenged or defended). As we shall see in later chapters, the legacy of these early, morally ambiguous accounts still rests heavily on contemporary anthropology, and to this day, anthropologists are often accused of distorting the reality of the peoples they write about – in the colonies, in the Third World, in subcultures or marginal areas. And, as in Vespucci's case, these descriptions are often denounced as telling us more about the anthropologist's own background than about the people under study.

The conquest of America contributed to a veritable revolution among European intellectuals. Not only did it provoke thought about cultural differences, it soon became clear that an entire continent had been discovered that was not even mentioned in the Bible! This blasphemous insight

stimulated the ongoing secularisation of European intellectual life, the
liberation of science from the authority of the Church, and the relativisation
of concepts of morality and personhood. As Todorov (1984) argues, the
Indians struck at the very heart of the European idea of what it means to be
human. The Indians were humans, but they did not behave in ways that
Europeans considered 'natural' for human beings. What was then human?
What was natural? During the Middle Ages, philosophers assumed that God
had created the world once and for all and given its inhabitants their
particular natures, which they had since retained. Now it was becoming
possible to ask whether the Indians represented an *earlier stage* in the
development of humanity. This in turn led to embryonic notions of progress
and development, which heralded a radical break with the static world-view
of the Middle Ages. In the later history of anthropology, notions of
development and progress have at times played an important role. But if
progress is possible, it follows that progress is brought about by the activity
of human beings, and this idea, that people shape their own destinies, is an
even more enduring notion in anthropology.

Thus, when the Europeans examined themselves in the mirror held up by
the Indians, they discovered themselves as free, modern individuals. Among
the most striking expressions of this new-found, subjective freedom, are the
Essais (1580) of the French philosopher Michel de Montaigne (1533–92).
With an open-mindedness and in a personal style that were unheard of at
the time, Montaigne speculates about numerous issues large and small.
Unlike nearly all his contemporaries, Montaigne, in his writings about
remote peoples, appears as what we today would call a cultural relativist. In
the essay 'Of Cannibals', he even concludes that if he had been born and
raised in a cannibal tribe, he would in all likelihood himself have eaten
human flesh. In the same essay, which would later inspire Rousseau,
Montaigne also coined the term *le bon sauvage*, 'the noble savage', an idea
that has later been much debated in anthropology.

In the following centuries, the European societies expanded rapidly in scale
and complexity, and intercultural encounters – through trade, warfare,
missionary work, colonialisation, migration and research – became increasingly common. At the same time, 'the others' became increasingly visible in
European cultural life – from Shakespeare's plays to Rameau's librettos.
Every major philosopher from Descartes (1596–1650) to Nietzsche
(1844–1900) developed his own doctrine of human nature, his own philosophical anthropology, often basing it directly on current knowledge and
beliefs about non-European peoples. But in most of these accounts 'the
others' still play a passive role: the authors are rarely interested in their
lifeways as such, but rather in their usefulness as rhetorical ammunition in
European debates about Europe itself.

A famous example of this was the great philosophical controversy between
empiricists and *rationalists* during the seventeenth and eighteenth centuries.
The former position was held by British philosophers such as John Locke

(1632–1704). Locke considered the human mind to be blank slate at birth, a *tabula rasa*. All our ideas, values and assumptions are the result of our experiences – or 'sense impressions' – of the world. People are not born different, but become different through differing experiences. Here Locke is laying the epistemological groundwork of a science of society that combines a universalistic principle (we are all born the same) and a relativistic principle (our differing experiences make us different). But seventeenth-century philosophers were less specialised than in our day, and it was therefore quite *comme il faut* for a man like Locke to step directly from a discussion of ontology to contemporary political commentary. Locke's empiricism thus had direct repercussions for his political argument in favour of a principle of 'natural law' (*jus naturel*) – which is the basis of the modern idea of universal human rights. The notion that all humans are born with certain intrinsic rights goes back to the Middle Ages, when Thomas Aquinas (1225–74) held that the rights of Man were given by God. But in the seventeenth century, philosophers like Locke and Thomas Hobbes (1588–1679) argued that natural law was not 'given' from above, but implicit in the biological needs of the individual. Thus, the argument is turned on its head: it is by being human that one has rights, not by divine (or royal) grace. This was a radical position in its time, and even when used explicitly to justify autocracy (as Hobbes does), it has revolutionary potential. All over Europe, kings and princes were confronted by the demands of an increasingly restive, and increasingly powerful, liberal bourgeoisie: demands that the Ruler be bound by law to respect the rights of individuals to property, personal security and rational public debate. It seems safe to assume that these issues mattered more to Locke than the lifeways of distant people, and that his philosophical anthropology was heavily influenced by this fact.

The legacy of British empiricism, which reached its most sophisticated form in the Scottish Enlightenment, notably in David Hume's philosophy, is still evident in contemporary British anthropology, as we will see later on in this book. Similarly, French and German anthropology still bear the stamp of Continental rationalism, a position that was perhaps most forcefully argued by René Descartes, a man of many talents, who made substantial contributions to mathematics and anatomy, and is often considered the founder of modern philosophy. In anthropology he is particularly noted for the sharp distinction he drew between consciousness and spiritual life on the one hand, and the material world and the human body on the other. While the British empiricists assumed that the sensory apparatus of the body was the only source of valid knowledge about the external world, Descartes distrusted the senses. Our images of the outside world are just that – images – and as such they are deeply marked by the perceiving subject's pre-existing *ideas* about the world. We can only see the world through a filter of ideas. The primary task of philosophy must therefore be to ascertain whether true ideas exist, that might form an incontrovertible basis for positive knowledge. With this aim in mind, Descartes assumed an attitude of 'radical methodological doubt'. All ideas that may be doubted are uncertain and therefore unsuitable as a foundation for science. Not many ideas survived Descartes' acid test. His dictum *Cogito, ergo sum* ('I think, therefore I am'), expresses his primary certainty: I can be sure that I exist since I know that I think. But Descartes spent a great deal of energy on deriving two other certainties from this one: the certainty of God's existence, and the certainty of mathematical statements.

Unlike Locke, Descartes was not a social philosopher. Still, he was a child of his times. Although his rationalist epistemology was explicitly opposed to that of the empiricists, Descartes – like Locke and Hobbes – places the individual at the centre of his inquiry. After all, his proof of God's existence followed from the individual's self-recognition. The empiricists also shared Descartes' faith in the human faculty of reason, and both rationalists and empiricists were key actors in defining the premises of a secular science, as representatives of the new, bourgeois social order that was soon to emerge throughout Western Europe.

WHY ALL THIS IS NOT QUITE ANTHROPOLOGY YET

This brief review of the pre-history of anthropology has suggested that a number of issues that would later attain prominence in anthropology, had already been the subject of extensive debate ever since Antiquity. Exotic peoples had been described normatively (ethnocentrism) or descriptively (cultural relativism). The question had repeatedly been raised whether people everywhere and at all times are basically similar (universalism) or profoundly different (relativism). There had been attempts to define the differences between animals and humans, nature and culture, the inborn and the learned, the sensual body and the conscious mind. Many detailed descriptions of foreign peoples had also been published, and some of these were based on meticulous scholarship.

In spite of these deep-going historical continuities, we maintain that anthropology as a science only appeared at a later stage, though it is true that its birth was a more gradual process than is sometimes assumed. Our reasons for this are, first, that all the work mentioned so far belongs to one of two genres: travel writing and social philosophy. It is only when these two aspects of anthropological inquiry are fused, i.e. when data and theory are integrated, that anthropology appears. Second, and perhaps more controversially, we call attention to the fact that all the writers mentioned so far are influenced by their times and their society. This is of course true of contemporary anthropologists as well. But modern anthropologists live in a modern world, and we argue that anthropology makes no sense at all outside a modern context. The discipline is a product, not merely of a series of singular thoughts such as those we have mentioned above, but of wide-ranging changes in European culture and society, that in time would lead to the formation of capitalism, individualism, secularised science, patriotic nationalism and extreme cultural reflexivity.

On the one hand, then, certain topics have constantly followed us throughout the time we have dealt with so far. On the other hand, from the fifteenth century onwards, a range of new ideas and new forms of social life had appeared, which would form the groundwork on which anthropology and the other social sciences would be built.

Two of these new ideas have been discussed above. First, we have seen that the encounter with 'the other' stimulated European intellectuals to see society as an entity undergoing change and growth, from relatively simple, small-scale, local communities, to large, complex, industrial nations. But the idea of development or progress was not confined to notions of social change. The individual, too, could develop, through education and career, by refining his personality and finding his 'true self'. As Bruno Latour (1991) points out, the idea of the autonomous individual was a prerequisite for the idea of society. Only when the free individual was established as 'the measure of all things', could the idea of society as an association of individuals put down roots and become an object of systematic reflection. And only when society had emerged as an object to be continuously improved and reshaped into more advanced forms, could the independent, rational individual change into something new and different, and even 'truer to herself'. And without an explicit discourse about these ideas, a subject such as anthropology could never arise. The seeds were sown in early modern philosophy, important advances were made in the eighteenth century, but it was only in the nineteenth century that anthropology became an academic discipline, and only in the twentieth century that it attained the form in which it is taught to students today. We shall now turn to the intellectual currents of the eighteenth and early nineteenth centuries, before recounting – in the next chapter – how anthropology came of age as an academic discipline.

THE ENLIGHTENMENT

The eighteenth century saw a flowering of science and philosophy in Europe. During these years, the self-confidence of the bourgeoisie increased, citizens reflected on the world and their place in it, and would soon make political demands for a rational, just, predictable and transparent social order. The key word was *enlightenment* (*Aufklärung, illumination*). As Hobbes, Locke and Descartes had argued, the free individual was to be the measure of all things – of knowledge and of the social order – the authority of God and Ruler was no longer taken for granted. But the new generations of intellectuals developed these ideas further. They met in informal clubs and salons to discuss art, philosophy and social issues. Private letters and diaries evolved into newspapers, periodicals and novels, and although censorship was still common in most places in Europe, the new media soon gained greater freedom and wider circulation. The bourgeoisie sought to free itself from the power of Church and nobility, and to establish in their stead a secular democracy. Traditional religious beliefs were increasingly denounced as superstitions – roadblocks on the way to a better society, governed by reason. The idea of progress also seemed to be confirmed by the development of technology, which made its first great advances at this time. New technologies made scientific measurements more accurate. Industrial machinery began to appear. Descartes' purely theoretical attempt to prove the universal truth of mathematics suddenly became a practical issue of burning relevance. For if mathematics, the language of reason, could reveal such fundamental natural truths as Newton's laws, did it not follow that nature was itself reasonable, and that any reason-driven enterprise was bound to succeed? All of these expectations culminated abruptly in the French Revolution, which attempted to realise the dream of a perfectly rational social order in practice, but was quickly superseded by its irrational opposite: the revolution devoured its children. And then all the dreams, the disappointments, the paradoxes of the Revolution spread during the Napoleonic Wars in the early 1800s to all of Europe and deeply influenced the ideas of society that later generations would develop.

But we are still in the eighteenth century, the 'age of reason', when the first attempts were made at creating an anthropological science. An important early work was Giambattista Vico's (1668–1744) *La scienza nuova* (1725; *The New Science*, 1999). This was a grand synthesis of ethnography, history of religion, philosophy and natural science. Vico proposed a universal scheme of social development, in which all societies went through four phases, with particular, formally-defined characteristics. The first stage was a 'bestial condition' without morality or art, followed by the 'Age of Gods', an age of nature worship and rudimentary social structures. Then came the 'Age of Heroes', with widespread social unrest due to great social inequality, and the 'Age of Man', when class differences disappeared and equality reigned. This epoch, however, was in its turn threatened by internal corruption and degeneration to 'bestiality'. Here, for the first time, we see a theory of social development that not only contrasts barbarianism and civilization, but specifies a number of transitional stages. Vico's theory would become a model for later evolutionists from Marx to Frazer. But Vico has an element that most of his followers lacked. Societies do not necessarily develop linearly towards constantly improved conditions, but go through cycles of degeneration and growth. This gives Vico's enlightenment work a critical and romantic subtext, as in Rousseau (see below).

Vico was an Italian pioneer, but it was in France that the first steps were taken towards the establishment of anthropology as a science. In 1748, Baron de Montesquieu (1689–1755) published his *De l'esprit des loix* (*The Spirit of Laws*, 1977). This is a comparative, cross-cultural study of legislative systems which Montesquieu had first- or second-hand knowledge of, and from which he attempts to derive the general principles that underlie legal systems cross-culturally. Montesquieu pictures the legal system as an aspect of the wider social system, intimately entwined with many other aspects of the larger whole (politics, economy, kinship, demography, religion, etc.) – a view that has led many to describe him as a proto-functionalist (Chapter 3). According to Montesquieu, polygamy, cannibalism, paganism, slavery and other barbarous customs could be explained by the functions they fulfilled within society as a whole. Montesquieu also wrote the remarkable *Lettres persanes* (1722; *Persian Letters*, 1973), a collection of fictitious letters from two Persians describing France to their countrymen. Montesquieu here exploits the 'strangeness' of cultural difference to parody France at the time of Louis XIV. The book is thought-provoking. Even today it remains controversial, since Montesquieu has recently been accused of being a proto-*Orientalist* (Said 1978, 1993), who unduly emphasised the exoticism of the Persians. This critique is undoubtedly justified, and Montesquieu's primary aim is clearly not to describe Persia but to criticise France. But the Persian letters also reveal a sophisticated understanding of a problem that is at times referred to as *homeblindness* in contemporary anthropology: our inability to see our own culture 'objectively', 'from the outside'. Montesquieu employed a particular technique to overcome this problem: he described his own society from the point of view of an outsider. This is a technique that critical anthropologists still use today.

Yet another step towards a science of anthropology was taken by a group of young, idealistic French intellectuals. These were the Encyclopaedists, led by the philosopher Denis Diderot (1713–84) and the mathematician Jean Le Rond d'Alembert (1717–83). Their aim was to collect, classify and systematise as much knowledge as possible in order to further the advance of reason, progress, science and technology. Diderot's *Encyclopédie* was published in 1751–72, and included articles by illustrious intellectuals like Rousseau, Voltaire and Montesquieu. The encyclopaedia quickly established itself as a model for later projects of its kind. It was a liberal and wide-ranging, not to say a revolutionary work, which was censored in many parts of Europe for its crude criticism of the Church. But the 17 volumes of text and 11 volumes of illustrations also contained other controversial material, such as detailed descriptions of mechanical devices developed by ordinary farmers and craftsmen. The fact that such matters were taken seriously in an academic work was unheard of at the time, and hinted that it would soon be legitimate to study the everyday life of ordinary people. The encyclopaedia also contained detailed descriptions of culture and social customs all over the world. One of its youngest contributors, Marquis de Condorcet (1743–94), who was to die prematurely in a Jacobin jail, wrote systematic comparisons between different social systems, and tried to develop a synthesis of mathematics and social science that would allow him to formulate objective laws of social development.

The most influential contributor to the *Encyclopédie* was undoubtedly Jean-Jacques Rousseau (1712–78). Contrary to most of his contemporaries,

Rousseau argued that development was not progressive, but degenerative, and that the source of this decline was society itself. Starting from an initial, innocent state of nature, where each individual lived by herself in harmony with her surroundings, people went on to found institutions of marriage and kinship, and settled in small, sedentary groups. Eventually, these groups grew in complexity, and invented priests and chiefs, kings and princes, private property, police and magistrates, until the free and good soul of man was crushed under the weight of social inequality. All human vices were the product of the growth in social inequality, and Rousseau traced the original fall from grace back to the coming of envy into the world. 'Man was born free, but is everywhere in chains', he declares in *Du contrat social* (1762; *On the Social Contract*, 1978); but he also promises that the 'false social contract' of his day may be replaced by another, true, contract based on freedom and democracy. In spite of his scepticism with regard to the current situation, Rousseau thus carried on the same utopian dreams as Vico or Condorcet.

The model for Rousseau's ideal society was to be found among the 'noble savages', the free, stateless peoples. This re-evaluation of simple societies was obviously a significant step towards true cultural relativism. But Rousseau's relativism went only skin deep. For him as well, the 'primitives' were mainly of interest as the opposite of his own time. They were symbols of the rational man who would be reborn in the ideal society of the future. Man was thus either free and rational or unfree and corrupted, and with this as a premise, hands-on investigations of empirical cultural differences were deemed irrelevant. Still, Rousseau has been an important source of inspiration for later social scientists – from Marx to Lévi-Strauss – and he is often considered an intermediary between French Enlightenment and Germanic Romanticism, which emerged during the late 1700s, in part as a reaction to Enlightenment philosophy. Here, Rousseau's celebration of 'authentic man' was carried further still, and the first concepts of *culture* were presented explicitly.

ROMANTICISM

The Enlightenment believed in the individual and the rational mind. Romantic thought, in contrast, shifted its attention from the individual to the group, from reason to emotion. In politics there was a similar move, from a universalistic discourse about free individuals and democracy, to a particularistic discourse about nation-building and national sentiment. It is common to view Romanticism as a trend that displaced the Enlightenment during the years of reaction after the French Revolution. But perhaps it is more accurate, as Ernest Gellner (1991) suggests, to see the two movements as parallel flows, at times diverging or competing, at times intersecting and blending together. The latter is especially common in anthropology, which aims not only to understand cultural wholes (a Romantic enterprise), but also to dissect, analyse and compare them (an Enlightenment project).

Germany, the heartland of Romantic thought, was in the eighteenth century still a political patchwork of independent principalities and autonomous cities, loosely united under the aegis of the 'Holy Roman Empire' – about which Voltaire once said that it was neither holy, nor Roman, nor an empire. The notion of a German nation was thus, unlike the French ideas of society and citizenship, based on language and culture rather than politics. France was a large and powerful state, whose fashion, poetry and royalty dominated the Western world. To speak French was everywhere seen as the mark of a cultivated mind. One of the most popular German Romantics (Friedrich Richter) even took a French pen name: Jean Paul. It was only natural that the politically fragmented, but culturally articulate Germans would eventually react to the French domination. The Germans also had greater reason to speculate about the qualities that unified their nation than the centralised French. In 1764, the young Johann Gottfried von Herder (1744–1803) published his *Auch eine Philosophie der Geschichte* ('Yet another Philosophy of History', 1993), which was a sharp attack on the French universalism championed, for example, by Voltaire (1694–1778). Herder proclaimed the primacy of emotions and language, and defined society a deep-seated, mythical community. He argued that every *Volk* (people) had its own values, customs, language and 'spirit' (*Volksgeist*). From this perspective, Voltaire's universalism was nothing but provincialism in disguise. His universal civilisation was, in fact, nothing but French culture.

The Voltaire–Herder debate continues to challenge us today. Herder's attack on the open-ended, transnational universalism of Voltaire is reminiscent of twentieth-century anthropologists' critique of missions, development aid, minority policies and globalisation. It also reminds us of the criticism levelled at anthropology itself, as an agent of cultural imperialism. A distinction between culture and civilisation, further, was later developed in the German-speaking world, albeit with limited success in academia: culture was seen as experiential and organic, while civilisation was cognitive and superficial.

Herder's concept of the *Volk* was refined and politicised by later philosophers, including Fichte (1762–1814) and Schelling (1775–1854), in whose hands it was transformed into a tool for the burgeoning nationalist movements that spread through Europe in the wake of the Napoleonic Wars. But the same concept also entered academia, where it reappeared, early in the twentieth century, as the doctrine of cultural relativism. Thus, the opposed doctrines of relativism and nationalism both trace their roots back to the same concept of culture, which originated in German Romanticism.

The greatest philosopher of the time was undoubtedly Immanuel Kant (1724–1804). Kant's philosophy is too fundamental to fit into a clear-cut philosophical school. Indeed, Kant is often said to have brought an end to many venerable philosophical debates, among them the controversy between empiricists and rationalists. In his *Kritik der reinen Vernunft* (1781; *Critique of Pure Reason*, 1991), Kant concurred with Locke and Hume that true knowledge derived from sense impressions, but he also stressed (with Descartes) that sensory data were filtered and shaped by the faculties of the mind. Knowledge was both sensual and mathematical, positive and speculative, objective and subjective. Kant's great achievement was to demonstrate that thought and experience were dynamically related, and that the acquisition of knowledge is a creative process. To know the world is to *create* a world that is accessible to knowledge. Man is therefore in a sense unable to know the world as it is in itself (*Ding an Sich*). But he gains access to the world as it represents itself to him (*Ding für Mich*), and is able to acquire true knowledge about this world.

To know the world is to contribute to its creation, as any anthropologist on fieldwork knows. We sample, shape and interpret reality as we go along, and this process, which Kant was the first to recognise explicitly, continues to generate major debates in anthropology today. But in Kant's formulation, his idea was still not directly applicable to the social sciences. It fell to his successor, Georg Wilhelm Friedrich Hegel (1770–1831), to complete his line of reasoning. For Kant, knowledge was a process, a never-ending movement. The fixed point around which this movement flowed was the individual. With Hegel, the fixed point vanishes. The individual, too, is a part and a result of the process of knowing. Thus, by knowing the world, we create not only a knowable world, but a knowing Self. But if there is no fixed point, how is knowledge attainable at all? Who shall be the measure of all things, if not the individual? Hegel answers to this that we are not alone in the world. The individual participates in a communicative fellowship with other people. The world created through knowing is therefore fundamentally collective, and the individual is not its cause, but one of its effects.

Thus, through Hegel's complex and often obscure formulations, we see the principle of *methodological collectivism* emerge – the notion that society is more fundamental than the individual. The opposite view, *methodological individualism*, follows Kant and takes the single person as its starting-point. Even today, these positions are relatively well-defined in anthropology. But with Hegel, collectivism reaches an apogee. He describes a *Weltgeist*, a 'world-spirit' that evolves independently of individuals but manifests itself through them. The *Geist* has its centres and peripheries, and spreads according to specific evolutionary laws. With this idea, Geana (1995) has suggested, Hegel was the first philosopher to envision a truly global humanity.

By now, the epistemological foundations of modern social theory have been laid. If knowledge is a collective process, which creates a collective world that can be known by individuals, it becomes possible to envision this world as a more or less systematic pattern of communication between persons. Theorists have later described this pattern variously, with concepts such as structure, function, solidarity, power, system and aggregate. Hegel himself was concerned with the development of the *Weltgeist*, and described its unfolding as a dialectical process of conflict and synthesis, that led society on to new evolutionary stages. But although dialectics have later acquired prominence among social theorists inspired by Marx, the 'social construction of reality' remains the most important idea that social science has inherited from Hegel and Kant.

But this idea also perfectly suited the nationalist movements that Herder had inspired, which had spread throughout Europe in the decades after 1800. Nations were precisely such socially constructed realities and communicative fellowships as Hegel had described, each with its own unique style and character. Ideally, the nation was a collectivity of the people, ruled by the people, in accordance with the people's deepest collective longings and needs. Nationalism was thus inspired by Romantic philosophy, but it was also a product of underlying historical processes: the political upheavals in the wake of the Napoleonic wars, the sense of alienation brought about by industrialisation, the spread of revolutionary ideals of freedom, equality and brotherhood.

It was in this world of upheaval and transition that anthropology first emerged as an academic discipline. An important precondition for this development was the establishment of the first ethnographic museums. Collections of exotica had long existed at the European courts. One of the earliest, founded by the Danish king, Frederick III, dates back to 1650 and would later form the basis of the Danish National Museum. But systematic collection of ethnographica only started in the 1800s. Large national museums were established in London (1753), Paris (1801) and Washington, DC (1843), and all of these would eventually develop influential ethnographic departments. Still, the first specialised ethnographic museums were established in German-speaking areas, notably Vienna (1806), Munich (1859) and Berlin (1868). This may seem surprising, as Germany and Austria had no colonial empires. Nevertheless, German academics had, in accordance with Herder's programme, begun to carry out empirical studies of the customs of 'the people'. They collected data on peasant life – on folktales and legends, dress and dance, crafts and skills. The earliest museums were thus primarily concerned with *Volkskunde* (the study of peasant cultures at home) rather than *Völkerkunde* (the study of remote peoples). In any case, we should note that the institutionalisation of anthropology commenced in German-speaking areas, rather than in France or Britain – a fact that is often neglected in historical accounts of anthropology.

As the next chapter will indicate, the German contribution to anthropology remained important throughout the nineteenth century, while at the same time a peculiar 'Victorian' anthropology developed in Great Britain.

2 VICTORIANS, GERMANS AND A FRENCHMAN

Between the Napoleonic wars (1792–1815) and the First World War (1914–18), we see the rise of modern Europe – and of the modern world. This was, perhaps above all, the age of the Industrial Revolution. In the 1700s, profound transformations had taken place in agriculture and manufacturing, particularly in Britain. Steam power and spinning machines had become widespread, and a growing class of landless peasants and urban labourers began to make themselves heard. But the greatest changes were still ahead. In the 1830s, the first major railways were built; a decade later, steamships crossed the Atlantic on a regular basis; and in 1846, the telegraph was introduced. It was becoming possible, on a scale that the world had never seen before, to move vast quantities of information, raw materials, commodities and people across global distances. This, in turn, meant that production could be increased both in agriculture and manufacturing. Europe was able to feed more people, in part through increased production, in part through expanding imports. As a result, population grew. In 1800, Britain had 10.5 million people. By 1901, there were 37 million, 75 per cent of whom lived in cities. Peasants deserted the countryside, forced out by population pressure and the rationalisation of agriculture, and moved to urban centres like London or Paris, where they were re-socialised as workers. Conditions in the rapidly growing cities were hardly optimal: epidemics were common, and when the first British law against child labour was introduced in 1834 it affected only children under the age of 9.

In time, protests against these changes increased in frequency and scale. The most dramatic example was the French Revolution, but the Chartist revolt in Britain in the 1840s, the French, Austrian and Italian revolutions in 1848–9, the Paris Commune of 1870, also clearly indicate the potential for violence that industrialisation unleashed. And along with the protests, a new, socialist ideology grew. Its roots go back to social philosophers such as Rousseau and Henri de Saint-Simon (1760–1825), and to the German neo-Hegelians, but its decisive formulation came with Karl Marx, to whom we shall return later.

The success of the labour movement during the nineteenth century would hardly have been possible without the train and the steamship. Millions of migrants were transported by rail and ship to the USA, Australia, Argentina,

South Africa, Siberia and elsewhere, relieving population pressure in Europe, and permitting a long-term rise in standards of living for all. Meanwhile, in the colonies, administrations disseminated European culture and institutions. This grand process of diffusion had variable effects. New power relations arose – between colonial administrator and Indian merchant, between plantation owner and black slave, between Boer, Englishman and Bantu, between settler and Australian aborigine. In the wake of these new relations of dominance and dependence, new philosophies, ideologies and myths arose to defend or attack them. The campaign against slavery is an early example, and slavery was successfully abolished in the British and French dependencies in the 1830s. But racism, which first emerged as an organised ideology during the nineteenth century, was a response to the same processes. Finally, an internationalised science emerged. The global researcher becomes a popular figure – the prototype naturally being Charles Darwin (1809–82), whose *Origin of Species* (1859) was based on data collected during a six-year circumnavigation of the globe.

It is hardly surprising that anthropology arose as a discipline at this time. The anthropologist is a prototypical global researcher, dependent on detailed data about people all over the world. Now that these data had suddenly become available, anthropology could be established as an academic discipline. So could sociology. If anthropology grew from imperialism, sociology was a product of the changing class relations brought about by industrialisation in Europe itself – all the founding fathers of sociology discuss the meaning of 'modernity', and contrast it with 'pre-modern' conditions.

BIOLOGICAL AND SOCIAL EVOLUTIONISM – MORGAN

While most major nineteenth-century sociologists were German or French, the leading anthropologists were based either in Britain (the greatest colonial power, with plentiful access to 'others') or the USA (where 'the others' were close at hand). Theoretical developments in the two traditions also differed markedly. The *evolutionism* typical of nineteenth-century anthropology built on ideas of development from the eighteenth century, bolstered by the experience of colonialism, and (starting in the 1860s) by the influence of Darwin and his most famous supporter, the social philosopher Herbert Spencer (1820–1903), who founded Social Darwinism, a social philosophy extolling the virtues of individual competition. But anthropology did not develop into a racist pseudo-science. All the leading anthropologists of the time supported the principle of *the psychic unity of mankind* – humans were everywhere born with roughly the same potentials, and inherited differences were negligible. Indeed, theories of social evolution presupposed this principle. For if racial differences were held to be fundamental, the cultural comparisons on which these theories were based would be unnecessary.

Meanwhile, Continental sociologists followed the lead of Kant and Hegel, and explored the socially constructed reality discovered by the two Germans. Various sociologists realised this project in various ways, but they shared the idea of society as an autonomous reality that must be studied on its own terms, not with the methods of natural science. Like the anthropologists, the sociologists asserted the psychic unity of mankind and deferred to evolutionist theory. Unlike the anthropologists, who classified and compared the external characteristics of societies all over the globe, sociologists were concerned with the internal dynamics of Western, industrial society. The sophisticated theories that were thus developed were to have a fundamental impact on anthropology as well, starting in the early twentieth century.

Here we shall illustrate the differences between these two emerging traditions with the work of two of their most prominent pioneering figures: the American anthropologist Lewis Henry Morgan (1818–81) and the German sociologist Karl Marx (1818–83).

Morgan's life in many ways embodied the America of equal opportunity that the French sociologist Alexis de Tocqueville had described in 1835. He grew up on a farm in New York State, was educated as a lawyer, and became a prosperous and active participant in local politics. An early champion of the political rights of Native Americans, he had been fascinated by Indians since his youth. In the 1840s, he lived with the Iroquois for some time, and was adopted into one of their clans and given the name *Tayadaowuhkuh*: 'he who builds bridges'.

Morgan realised that most of the complexity of Native American culture would soon be irretrievably destroyed as a result of the influx of Europeans, and considered it a crucial task to document traditional culture and social life before it was too late. This attitude, often referred to as *urgent anthropology*, was shared by the second great American anthropologist, Franz Boas (Chapter 3), and has since been widespread in research on indigenous peoples.

Morgan had close contact with the people he studied, sympathised with their problems, and published detailed accounts of their culture and social life. But he also made substantial theoretical contributions, particularly in his pioneering work on kinship. Morgan's interest in kinship dated back to his stay with the Iroquois. Later, he discovered surprising similarities and differences between their kinship system and others in North America. He then devised a large-scale comparative study of Native American kinship, eventually including other groups as well. Morgan created the first typology of kinship systems (cf. Holy 1996), and introduced a distinction between *classificatory* and *descriptive* kinship which is still in use. To simplify greatly – descriptive systems (like our own) differentiate kinsmen of the direct ascending or descending line (linear kin) from kinsmen 'to the side' (collateral kin, such as siblings, cousins and in-laws). Classificatory kinship (as with the Iroquois) does not differentiate these two categories. Here the same term might be used, for example, for all linear and collateral male kin on the father's side (father, father's brother, father's brother's son, etc.). But Morgan did more than formulate a theory; he grounded it in years of intensive study of existing kinship systems around the world. In his influential *Systems of Consanguinity and Affinity of the Human Family* (1870), the results of this research are presented, defining kinship, once and for all, as a primary anthropological concern.

For Morgan, kinship was primarily a point of entry to the study of social evolution. He argued that primitive societies were organised on the basis of kinship, and that terminological variations among kinship systems correlated with variations in social structure. But he also supposed that kinship terminology changed slowly, and that it therefore contained clues to an understanding of earlier stages of social evolution.

In his magnum opus *Ancient Society* (1877), Morgan attempts a grand synthesis of all this work. He distinguishes three major stages of cultural evolution: savagery, barbarism and civilisation (with three sub-stages each for savagery and barbarism). His criteria for these divisions were mostly technological: his 'savages' were hunters and gatherers, 'barbarism' was associated with agriculture, 'civilisation' with state formation and urbanisation. In hindsight, it seems clear that Morgan's synthesis did not succeed. Even if his basic evolutionary scheme is accepted, the details are often hazy. At times, isolated technological features are accorded unreasonable weight – for example, pottery is *the* criterion of the transition between two stages. Where would that leave the Polynesian chiefdoms, with their complex political systems, but no trace of pottery? It is only fair to add that Morgan himself was conscious that his conclusions were often speculative, and critical of the quality of his (mostly secondary) data.

Morgan had considerable influence on later anthropology, particularly on kinship studies, but also on American cultural materialists and other evolutionist anthropologists in the twentieth century (Chapter 5). But Morgan was read by sociologists as well. When Marx discovered Morgan towards the end of his life, he and his partner, Friedrich Engels, attempted to integrate Morgan's ideas in his own, post-Hegelian, evolutionary theory. The unfinished results of this work were published by Engels in *The Origin of the Family, Private Property, and the State*, in 1884, the year after Marx's death.

MARX

The scope and aims of Marx's work contrast sharply with Morgan's, despite their shared commitment to materialist explanations. Marx's writings on non-industrial societies are scattered and tentative. It was through his analysis of capitalist society in his masterwork, *Das Kapital* (vols 1–3, 1867, 1885, 1896; *Capital*, 1906), that he made his lasting contribution to social theory. Though Marxism collapsed as a political movement late in the 1980s, it has remained an important academic influence.

Born in the same year as Morgan, into a wealthy Jewish family in an incon-spicuous German town, Marx completed a university education in philosophy before embarking on a career as social theorist, pamphleteer, editor, journalist, labour organiser and agitator. He was actively involved in the revolutionary wave that left the European establishment in shock in 1848–9, and in the Paris Commune in 1870. After the Commune, he became known as one of the leading figures of the international labour movement.

Marx's influence on social theory is manifold and complex, and may be traced in many anthropological analyses to this day (though his influence on sociology, history and economics is even greater). The confluence of social theory and political activism runs deep in Marx, and gives his entire project a paradoxical and thought-provoking character (see Berman 1982). In a sense, Marx tried throughout his life to reconcile an idealist impulse from German philosophy (particularly Hegel) with a materialist world-view. It is sometimes said that he 'placed Hegel on his feet': he retained Hegel's dialectical principle, but argued that the movement of history took place on a material, not a spiritual, level. Society, according to Marx, consists of infra-structure and superstructure. The former comprises the conditions for existence – material resources and the division of labour; the latter includes all kinds of ideational systems – religion, law and ideology. In all societies, the primary contradiction runs through the infrastructure: between the relations of production (that organise labour and property) and the forces of production (e.g. technology or land). When technological advances render previous relations of production obsolete, class conflict ensues, and the relations of production are changed – e.g. from slavery to feudalism to capitalism. Marx predicted that the capitalist system would itself give way to socialism (ruled by a dictatorship of the proletariat), and finally to classless communism – a utopia, where everything is owned by all.

The theory is so ambitious, and in many respects so ambiguous, that it was bound to raise many problems when confronted with real-world com-plexities. An example is Marxian class analysis. Marx postulated, roughly, that property-holders and the propertyless constitute discrete classes with particular interests. The objective interest of the working class consists in overthrowing the ruling class through revolution. But the working class is only partly conscious of being exploited, since the true power relations are concealed by an *ideology* that justifies the existing order. Superstructural phenomena such as law, religion or kinship are typically infused with a 'false consciousness' that pacifies the population.

But, asks the anthropologist, is this model applicable to non-Western contexts? How does it fit with Morgan's dictum that kinship is the primary organising principle in primitive societies? Is kinship part of the infrastruc-ture? But how can that be, if kinship is an ideology which conceals the infrastructure? Must the entire distinction between infra- and superstruc-ture, the material and the spiritual, be abandoned? In what sense, if any, is ideology 'less real' than power? Such issues have attained greater and greater prominence in anthropology, and a significant part of Marx's attraction today lies in his ability to generate questions such as these.

Marx himself was not oblivious to these problems. His extensive discussion of value formation is proof enough of this. The value of an object in itself, its concrete *use value*, its correspondence to real human needs, is transformed, under capitalism, into an abstract *exchange value*, its value *as compared to* other objects. 'Material' objects are transformed into 'spiritual' commodities, and the further this continues, the more abstract, absurd and alienated does the world seem. In such passages, 'value' becomes a deeply ambiguous concept, in which power and ideology, the material and the spiritual merge seamlessly. Nevertheless, it remains doubtful whether Marx actually solved the problem he posed for himself. We might note, for example, that his difficulties with bringing materialism and (Hegelian) idealism together are reminiscent of Morgan's problem with the materialist causes of kinship terminology. Only in the 1980s did we see a concerted effort at solving the paradox.

BASTIAN, TYLOR AND OTHER VICTORIANS

Morgan and Marx belonged to the first generation of social scientists, who were active in the 1850s to 1870s. But although their contribution overshadows that of most of their contemporaries, they were far from alone: In the 1860s, while Morgan was still at work on his great volume on kinship, a series of books were published in Europe which in part complemented Morgan, in part raised altogether different questions. In 1860, the prolific German anthropologist Adolf Bastian (1826–1905) published his three-volume *Der Mensch in der Geschichte* ('Man in History', see Koepping 1983). Bastian, originally a medical doctor, was trained as an ethnographer under the influence of the brothers Wilhelm and Alexander von Humboldt, the linguist and the geographer who revolutionised humanistic and social thought in Germany during the first half of the 1800s. Bastian travelled extensively, indeed it has been estimated that he spent twenty years outside of Germany (Koepping 1983: 8). In between his travels he wrote his books, was appointed Professor of Ethnology at the University of Berlin and Director of the Imperial Museum, founded the important Berliner Museum für Völkerkunde in 1868, and contributed generously to its collections. Like the Humboldt brothers before him and Boas after him (Chapter 3), Bastian continued the German tradition of research on *Volkskultur* that had been inspired by Herder, and sharply criticised the simplistic evolutionist schemes that were on the rise in his day. As the only major nineteenth-century anthropologist, Bastian was an energetic and articulate critic of evolutionism. His view was that all cultures have a common origin, from which they have branched off in various directions – a view later developed with great sophistication by Boas and his students. He was keenly aware of the historical connections between cultures, and thus anticipated a later development in German anthropology, namely diffusionism. Bastian even anticipated structuralism and Jungian psychology, when he argued that all humans share certain elementary patterns of thought: *Elementärgedanken*. It was chiefly in German anthropology, and largely through Bastian's work, that the embryonic principle of cultural relativism, evident in Herder but absent from Enlightenment thought and nineteenth-century Anglo-American anthropology, asserted its presence in anthropology during the nineteenth century. In France, for example, the sociological school of Auguste Comte (1798–1857) was anything but relativist, operating with a rigid system of three stages of social evolution.

The year after the publication of *Der Mensch in der Geschichte*, the Scottish lawyer Henry Maine (1822–88) published *Ancient Law*. This was primarily an inquiry into cultural history based on written sources. Maine tried to demonstrate how changes in legislation reflect wider social changes, and distinguished traditional societies based on *status* from modern societies based on *contract*. In status-based societies, rights are distributed through personal relationships, kinship and inherited rank. Contract society, in contrast, is based on formal, written principles which function independently of actual persons. The distinction between status and contract is still in use today, and many scholars have followed Maine's lead in distinguishing between two 'ideal types' – simple and complex societies – and have, in turn, been criticised for oversimplification.

An evolutionist idea that influenced Morgan, Engels and others, but has since been discarded, was the theory of original matriarchy. This was first launched by the Swiss lawyer Johann Jakob Bachofen (1815–87), in *Das Mutterrecht* (1861; 'Mother's Right', see Bachofen 1968). Bachofen argued in favour of an evolutionary theory that moved from an initial stage of general promiscuity (*Hetarismus*) to the first organised form of social life – matriarchy – where women held political power. Real matriarchies, Bachofen admitted, no longer existed, but their traces were found in matrilineal kinship systems, where descent chiefly follows the mother's line. This idea, which implied that humanity progressed as female leaders were replaced by males, gained many followers, and was almost taken for granted by the next generation of anthropologists. In Britain it was promoted by another lawyer interested in social evolution, John Ferguson McLennan (1827–81). Though no ethnographic evidence exists for this idea, it has remained so resilient that it was felt that it needed to be demolished as late as the 1970s, among feminist anthropologists (Bamberger 1974).

Thus, Morgan did not work in an intellectual vacuum. Interest in comparative studies of culture and society was on the rise, particularly in Britain and Germany, and access to reliable empirical data was rapidly improving due to colonialism. Still, the only nineteenth-century anthropologist to rival Morgan in influence was Edward Burnett Tylor (1832–1917).

E.B. Tylor grew up as a Quaker, and was barred by his faith from a university education. But during a convalescence in Cuba, he discovered an interest in archaeology and was invited to take part in an expedition to the Toltec ruins in Mexico. In an era dominated by evolutionism, the step from prehistory to anthropology was short, and Tylor's work as an anthropologist would soon gain him (and the discipline) considerable prestige. In 1896, he was appointed the first British professor of anthropology, at the University of Oxford. In 1912, he was knighted. Tylor was still a young man when he published his first great evolutionist synthesis, *Researches into the Early History of Mankind and the Development of Civilization* (1865); and his major work, *Primitive Culture* (1871), followed just a few years later. Tylor here proposed an evolutionary scheme reminiscent of Morgan's in *Ancient Society* (the two books were published in the same year). He shared Morgan's faith in the primacy of material conditions. Like Morgan, too, his knowledge of cultural variation was vast (Darwin refers to Tylor several times in his work on human evolution from the 1870s). But Tylor did not share Morgan's interest in kinship terminology, and instead developed a theory of *cultural survivals*. Survivals were cultural traits that had lost their original functions in society, but had continued, for no particular reason, to survive. Such traits were of crucial importance to the effort to reconstruct human evolution. Tylor advocated a trait-by-trait comparative method, which allowed him to isolate survivals from the larger social system. Though influential at the time, this method was abandoned by the next generation of anthropologists. Curiously, it reappeared in the mid-1970s, when the sociobiologist Edward O. Wilson, in an intellectual venture comparable to Tylor's, attempted to reconcile cultural variation and Darwinist evolutionism (see Ingold 1986).

But Tylor's most significant contribution to modern anthropology is his definition of culture. The definition appears on the first page of *Primitive Culture*, and reads like this:

Culture, or civilization, taken in its broad, ethnographic sense, is that complex whole which includes knowledge, belief, art, morals, law, custom, and any other capabilities and habits acquired by man as a member of society. (Tylor 1958 [1871]: 1)

On the one hand, culture is thus a general term that cross-cuts evolutionary stages. Where evolution differentiates societies in qualitative terms, culture unites mankind. Tylor, like Bastian, was an explicit proponent of the 'psychic unity of humanity'. And the similarity to Bastian goes deeper than this. Tylor was well versed in German anthropology and philosophy, and had read both Bastian himself and several of his teachers (see Koepping 1983). On the other hand, Tylor equates culture with civilisation, a qualitative term. Culture thus, at least implicitly, becomes a matter of degree: everyone has it, but not in equal amount. This concept of culture starkly contradicts Bastian and the entire Herderian notion of *Volk*. For Herder and his successors, humanity consisted of autonomous, bounded *cultures*. For Tylor and other Victorian evolutionists, humanity consisted of groups that were cultured to various degrees, and distributed on the rungs of a ladder of cultural evolution.

In the years between 1840 and 1880, a whole range of new problems was raised by sociologists and anthropologists. While Marx developed the first grand theory in sociology, comprising modernisation, value formation, power and ideology, and while Darwin formulated the principles of biological evolution, anthropologists were engaged in a dual project. In part they were busy devising grand evolutionary schemes – unilineal in intent and universalistic in pretensions; in part they were documenting the immense range of human socio-cultural variation – and out of the knowledge thus accumulated grew the first low-level theories, pertaining to specific ethnographic domains, such as kinship, and rooted in specific and detailed empirical descriptions.

It was still uncommon for the anthropologist himself to carry out field studies, although Morgan and Bastian were prominent exceptions. Another, less well-known exception was the Russian ethnographer Nicolai Nicolaievich Miklukho-Maklai (1846–88), who in 1871, 40 years before Malinowski, carried out a 15-month intensive field study on the New Guinea coast, and laid the groundwork for a rich ethnographic tradition in Russia that is virtually unknown in the West (see Plotkin and Howe 1985). But the vast majority of anthropologists gathered their data through correspondence with colonial administrators, settlers, officers, missionaries and other 'whites' living in exotic places. Given the uneven quality of these data and the authors' vast theoretical ambitions, such studies were almost always full of the kind of speculation that Radcliffe-Brown (Chapter 3) would later dismiss as *conjectural history*. But in spite of these shortcomings, the learned books of the Victorians were theoretically focused and empirically grounded to an extent that had never been seen before.

The importance of kinship in this phase of the discipline's evolution cannot be overstated. Kinship terminology was a limited empirical field. Nevertheless, mapping and understanding it was a humbling experience. The closer one looked at these strangely formal systems, the more complex they seemed. True, to the first practitioners of kinship studies, mostly lawyers by profession, the task seemed fairly simple. They looked for a 'legal system' that would regulate behaviour in primitive societies, and kinship was the obvious candidate – an empirical system of formalised, verbalised norms. At the end of the century, it was widely held that kinship was a kind of anthropologist's Rosetta Stone, that allowed primitive customs to be understood and translated into rational terms.

THE GOLDEN BOUGH AND THE TORRES EXPEDITION

For a couple of decades after the prolific 1860s and 1870s, little of importance was published in anthropology. In sociology too, there seems to have been a dearth – a notable exception being Ferdinand Tönnies' *Gemein-schaft und Gesellschaft* (1887; *Community and Society*, 1963), which proposed a dichotomy of the traditional and modern that was similar to McLennan's, but with a less judicial accent. In the course of these years a new generation appeared. Many of the leading figures discussed so far, including Marx, Morgan, Bachofen and Maine, were dead. In anthropology, we see the first institutionalisation of the discipline in Britain, Germany, France and the USA. Independent national traditions were starting to crystallise, and separate sets of issues were being raised in each of the four countries. The Germans followed the lead of Bastian and the comparative linguists, whose success in untangling the history of the Indo-European languages was almost as sensational, in its time, as Darwin's evolutionism. A research programme for the study of human prehistory was established that mimicked the spread and movement of languages in much the same way as evolutionism mimicked biology. This programme, *diffusionism*, studied the origin and dissemination of cultural traits. The challenge posed by these concrete historians to the abstract histories of evolutionism, made diffusionism a truly radical innovation around the turn of the century. In the USA and Britain, evolutionism remained dominant, but scholars were becoming increasingly specialised, focusing on particular subfields, such as kinship, religion, magic or law. In France, meanwhile, a unique blend of sociology and anthropology was under way. Each of these research programmes, however, was seriously hampered by a lack of accurate and detailed data. This gap had become increasingly evident throughout the nineteenth century, and there was by now a near-universal consensus in the field that more and better data were needed. As early as 1857, British anthropologists published the first edition of what was to become *the* authoritative work on field methods for nearly a century – *Notes and Queries on Anthropology*, which was re-issued in four revised, and ever more detailed, editions. But the methodological breakthrough that everyone was waiting for did not arrive before a radically new conception of anthropological fieldwork was established.

The last great Victorian evolutionist was James George Frazer (1854–1941), a student of Tylor who was celebrated, far beyond anthropological circles, for his masterpiece *The Golden Bough*, which was first published as a two-volume set in 1890, and later expanded to fill twelve gigantic tomes. *The Golden Bough* is a vast, comparative investigation of the history of myth, religion and other 'exotic beliefs', with examples drawn from all over the world. Like so many of the evolutionists, Frazer believed in a three-step model of cultural evolution: a 'magical' stage is replaced by a 'religious' stage, which gives way to a 'scientific' stage. This general scheme can be traced through Comte all the way back to Vico. Though Frazer clearly considered magical rites irrational, and assumed that 'primitives' based their lives on a completely mistaken understanding of nature, his main concern was to identify patterns and universal traits in mythical thought. With a few notable exceptions (Lévi-Strauss being one of them), modern anthropologists rarely refer to Frazer as anything but an historical figure. But his influence was greatest outside of anthropology; two of his warmest admirers were the poet T.S. Eliot and the psychologist Sigmund Freud. Yet Frazer's fascinating and ponderous work was never followed up by later research. It stands alone, a majestic monument to the insecure empirical basis of Victorian evolutionism.

Another British turn-of-the-century enterprise, less noticed at the time and far less well known outside anthropology, namely the Torres Expedition, organised from the University of Cambridge in 1898 to the Torres Straits, between Australia and New Guinea, has fared better in hindsight. The expedition was to collect detailed data about the traditional population of the islands in the area, and included several anthropologists – though all were originally trained in other disciplines, since academic training in anthropology was still very rare. Alfred C. Haddon (1855–1940) was originally a zoologist, William H.R. Rivers (1864–1922) a psychologist, and Charles G. Seligman (1873–1940) a medical doctor. In contrast to the individualist ideal of later British fieldwork, the Torres expedition was a collective effort where scholars from various disciplines explored different aspects of the local culture. Nevertheless, due to the high quality and the impressive volume of the data they collected, many have seen these anthropologists as the first true fieldworkers. 'Through their work', writes one commentator, 'British social anthropology was born' (Hynes 1999).

Haddon, a colleague of Frazer's at the University of Cambridge, had planned the Torres expedition as an 'ideal' field project, where the participants would cover all aspects of native life: ethnography, psychology, linguistics, physical anthropology and musicology. He himself would take care of sociology and folklore, as well as material culture. For Seligman, who in later years became a central figure at the influential anthropology department at the London School of Economics, the expedition was the beginning of a career which, after work in Melanesia and Sri Lanka, would culminate in several major field studies in the Sudan. He thus contributed decisively to moving the focus of British anthropology from the Pacific islands (where it remained until well into the 1920s) to Africa (which would soon become an ethnographic gold mine). Seligman's major work from the Sudan, co-authored with his wife Brenda Seligman (Seligman and Seligman 1932), is still regarded as a classic in its field.

Rivers was the most unusual member of the expedition. Until his early death in 1922, he was a professor at the University of Cambridge, where he invested much effort in developing a psychological anthropology, a project that was too far ahead of its time to succeed. Towards the end of his life, Rivers came under the influence of Sigmund Freud's psychology. During the Torres expedition, Rivers concentrated particularly on the mental abilities of the natives, especially their use of the senses. In 1908, he published a descriptive monograph, *The Todas*, based on work among a tribe in South India; and in 1914 *The History of Melanesian Society*, a comprehensive work which outlined the immense cultural variation of Melanesia and explained it as a result of repeated waves of migration, an hypothesis which is still accepted, with due modifications, among present-day archaeologists. With this work, Rivers started to move away from evolutionism, towards the new school of diffusionism, which was the subject of his last works.

DIFFUSIONISM

Diffusionists studied the geographical distribution and migration of cultural traits, and posited that cultures were patchworks of traits with various origins and histories. All parts of a culture are therefore not necessarily linked into a larger whole. In contrast, most evolutionists held that societies were coherent, functional systems. True, evolutionists also recognised the existence of isolated, non-functional cultural traits (Tylor's *survivals*) and, in practice, these received a disproportionate amount of analytical attention (considering that they were atypical), since they were the key to recon-structing the social forms of the past. But when the evolutionist perspective collapsed, the idea of societies as coherent wholes was also discredited (though it remained strong in sociology, and would soon reappear with renewed force in British social anthropology). Now *all* cultural traits were potential 'survivals'. Diffusionists still used them to reconstruct the past, but 'the past' was no longer a unilineal movement through well-defined stages. Cultural history was a fragmented story of cultural encounters, migrations and influences, each instance of which was unique. In the early decades of the twentieth century, diffusionism was an attractive alternative to evolu-tionism, because it had greater respect for the facts on the ground and more modest theoretical pretensions.

The fact that technology and ideas could travel was not a new discovery. In the eighteenth century, German philologists had shown that European and North Indian languages had shared origins. Archaeologists had discovered that pottery and other artefacts had spread from cultural centres to peripheries. Europeans were conscious of the fact that the dominant religion of their own continent had Middle Eastern origins. What was new about anthropological diffusionism was its systematic comparative effort and its emphasis on detailed empirical knowledge. Like Rivers, many diffusion-ists worked in limited regions, where it was possible to demonstrate convincingly that specific cultural traits had an identifiable history.

Diffusionism was chiefly a Germanic specialisation, with centres in the great museum cities of Berlin and Vienna. Apart from Rivers, it had little direct influence on British and French anthropology (but as we shall see, it had important repercussions in the USA). Like their colleagues elsewhere, the German anthropologists of the nineteenth century tended to subscribe to some kind of evolutionist framework. But the influence from Herder, with its emphasis on the unique and local, along with the relativism we have noted in Bastian's work, counteracted this tendency, and when evolutionism was challenged at the turn of the century, this tradition again came to the fore. Scholars like Friedrich Ratzel (1844–1904), Fritz Graebner (1877–1934), Leo Frobenius (1873–1938) and Wilhelm Schmidt (1868–1954) followed the lead of Herder (and Bastian), emphasising the uniqueness of each people's cultural heritage. They argued that cultural evolution was not unilineal, and that there was no simple determinist link between, say, technological complexity and complexity in other areas. A people with a simple technology might perfectly well have a highly sophisticated religious system.

The diffusionists aimed at a comprehensive survey of the spread of cultural traits from the earliest times until today. They developed complex (sometimes, it must be said, rather arcane) classifications of 'culture circles' (*Kulturkreise*) and surveyed their possible dissemination from an original centre. In certain cases, as in Graebner's studies from Oceania, they could identify as many as seven historically discrete sediments or *Kulturkreise* in each society.

It is worth noting that diffusionism did not shed its evolutionist background overnight. Most diffusionists still believed that social change generally led to progress and increased 'sophistication'. What they objected to in Victorian evolutionism was its unilineal and deterministic character; the idea, found in Tylor and others, that all societies must pass through certain stages that were more or less the same all over the world. The diffusionist world-view was less tidy than this, and more sensitive to local variation.

As we shall see in the next chapter, both evolutionism and diffusionism were thoroughly thrashed by the following generations of social and cultural anthropologists. But diffusionist research was often far more sophisticated than later anthropologists were willing to admit, and in the German-language area, particularly in Austria, the *Kulturkreise* programme remained vigorous until the 1950s.

Diffusionism was also important for East European anthropologists, not least for the large group of Russian anthropologists who followed the lead of Miklukho-Maklai. Three prominent names were Vladimir Ilich Jochelson (1855–1937), Vladimir Germanovich Bogoraz (1865–1936) and Lev Yacovlevich Shternberg (1861–1927), all of whom were exiled to Eastern Siberia by the Czar and used the opportunity to carry out long-term fieldwork among the indigenous peoples of the region. Around the turn of the century, they participated in a major Russo-American expedition to the indigenous peoples around the Bering Strait, organised by a German-American by the name of Franz Boas. These scholars were diffusionist in their orientation, and indeed diffusionism is even today a respectable theory in Russia, with long traditions and high analytical and methodological standards. In the West, diffusionism survives in the tradition of *imperialism studies* that ultimately stems from Marx and Lenin, but which has been resurrected under such headings as 'dependency studies', 'global system studies' and, most recently, 'globalisation studies' (see Chapters 7 and 9). The Marxian influence here adds power to the diffusionists' Herderian brew, with a more potent and violent result.

THE NEW SOCIOLOGY

The new generations of anthropologists, who will be introduced in the following chapters, had good reason to distance themselves from evolutionism and diffusionism. They were convinced that they had discovered a theoretical alternative with greater potential than any previous theory of socio-cultural variation. British (and to a lesser extent, American) anthropologists had discovered Continental sociology.

What is called 'classical sociology' in textbooks and undergraduate courses, usually refers to the *oeuvre* of a handful of (mostly German or French) theorists, who produced most of their work between the 1850s and the First World War. The leading lights of the first wave were Marx, Comte and Spencer, though the latter two are nearly forgotten today. The second generation included Ferdinand Tönnies (1855–1936), Emile Durkheim (1858–1917), Georg Simmel (1858–1918) and Max Weber (1864–1920). Like Marx, all of these authors are still read for the intrinsic interest of their work (rather than as expressions of an historical *Zeitgeist*). Tönnies explored the simple/complex society dichotomy in sociology, adding complexity and nuance to the simple schemes that had gone before him; Simmel (who is experiencing a renaissance today) is admired for his studies of modernity, the city and money. Both Durkheim and Weber are still considered important enough to generate frequent book-length commentaries. But of all the classical sociologists, Durkheim has been most significant for anthropology, in part because he himself was concerned with many anthropological themes, in part because of his direct and immediate influence on British and French anthropology. In the USA, the influence of 'classical sociology' only made itself felt many years later, and was never as strong as in Europe. The main influence here was rather from Bastian and the *Völkerkunde* school, which was brought into American anthropology by its (German) founding father, Franz Boas. The leading American anthropologists of the early twentieth century were therefore oriented towards cultural history, linguistics and even psychology rather than sociology.

DURKHEIM

Like Marx, Durkheim grew up in a Jewish family (in a small town near Strasbourg), and his parents wanted him to become a rabbi. He did so well in school, however, that he was admitted to the prestigious École Normale Supérieure in Paris, which secured a later academic career. During his education he had lost his religious faith, and become part of a dynamic and critical intellectual milieu. Throughout his life, Durkheim was deeply concerned with moral issues, and he was a committed promoter of social and educational reforms. In 1887, he was appointed lecturer in pedagogy and sociology at the University of Bordeaux, becoming the first French social scientist to hold an academic post. During this period, which lasted until his move to Paris in 1902, Durkheim wrote two of his most important works, *De la division du travail social* (1893; *The Division of Labour in Society*, 1964) and *Le Suicide* (1897; *Suicide*, 1951). He also founded the influential journal *L'Année Sociologique*, which he continued to edit after moving to Paris. As professor at the Sorbonne from 1906 till his death in 1917, Durkheim's influence on later French sociology and anthropology was immense. With his nephew and intellectual successor Marcel Mauss, he wrote extensively on non-European peoples; a notable work in this regard is *Classification Primitive* (1900; *Primitive Classification*, 1963), a study of the social origins of knowledge systems, which draws on ethnographic data, particularly from Australia. This book, which posits an intrinsic connection between classification and social structure, is still a point of reference for anthropological studies of classification.

Unlike both diffusionists and evolutionists, Durkheim was not particularly interested in origins. He was concerned with *synchronic* rather than *diachronic* explanations. Like the diffusionists, but unlike the evolutionists, he was deeply committed to basing his anthropology on observable, often quantifiable data. Unlike the diffusionists, however, he was convinced that societies were logical, integrated systems, in which all parts were dependent on each other and worked together to maintain the whole. In this, he approached the evolutionists, who, like him, drew analogies between the functional systems of the body and society. Indeed, Durkheim often described society as a *social organism*. Like Tönnies and Maine, but unlike Marx and Morgan, Durkheim subscribed to a dichotomous division of societal types – dropping all talk of 'stages' and 'evolution', he juxtaposed traditional and modern societies without postulating that the former would ever evolve into the latter. Primitive societies were neither 'survivals' from a dim past nor 'steps' towards progress, but social organisms that deserved to be studied on their own terms. Finally, unlike Bastian and the *Völkerkunde* school, Durkheim was concerned, not with culture, but with society, not with symbols and myths, but with organisations and institutions.

The book on the division of labour delves into the difference between simple and complex social organisations. In Durkheim's view, the former are based on *mechanical solidarity*. People support the existing social order and each other because they share the same everyday life, carry out the same tasks and perceive each other as similar. In complex societies, in contrast, *organic solidarity* prevails. Here, society and mutual commitment are maintained by people's perception of each other as different, with *complementary* roles. Each carries out a different task that contributes to the whole.

Durkheim adds that the two forms of solidarity must be understood as general principles of social integration rather than societal types. Most societies have elements of both. Moreover, the distinction does more than posit a contrast between 'ourselves' and 'the other'. Both Durkheim and many of his successors, right up to Louis Dumont (see Chapter 6), were intrigued by the complexities of traditional Indian society, and maintained that its caste system expressed an advanced form of organic complexity.

Durkheim's last, and perhaps greatest work, *Les Formes élémentaires de la vie réligieuse* (1915; *The Elementary Forms of Religious Life*, 1995) was published just two years before his death. Here, he attempts to grasp the meaning of 'solidarity' itself, of the very force that keeps society together. Solidarity, Durkheim argues, arises from *collective representations* – then as now a controversial term. These are symbolic 'images' or 'models' of social life that are shared by a group. Such 'images' develop through interpersonal relationships, but attain a supra-individual, objective character. They make up an all-embracing, virtual, 'socially constructed' reality that echoes Kant and Hegel, and which to the people who live in the society appear just as real as material world. But they are not objective images of this world. They are moral entities, with power over the emotions. Religion becomes an important object of inquiry for Durkheim, because it is here, more than anywhere else, that the emotional attachment of individuals to collective representations is established and strengthened. This attachment is primarily formed in *ritual*, in which religion is expressed through physical interaction and solidarity becomes a direct, bodily experience. Ritual hedges itself off from *profane* daily life, drawing a protective magic circle around its own, forbidden, *sacred* domain. This demarcation allows the experience of ritual to be intensified until an almost mystical union is achieved. Bringing the memory of this experience back into everyday life, we remember how the world truly is.

Religion and ritual had long attracted the interest of anthropologists, who had documented it in a wide range of empirical forms. The problem of understanding social integration in stateless societies had been an important (though often implicit) concern in evolutionism. And bewilderment at the exotic symbols and customs of 'the others' was the point of departure of all anthropological inquiry. Now Durkheim seemed to offer an analytical tool that would bring all these interests together. 'The exotic' could be understood as an integrated system of collective representations, whose function was to create social solidarity. And religion, the most mystifyingly 'exotic' phenomenon of all, turned out to be the rational dynamo driving this entire process.

When British anthropologists embraced Durkheim early in the twentieth century (Chapter 3), they found countless applications for his theory, in the study of religion, legal systems and – not least – kinship. Indeed, Durkheim is therefore often described as the founder of structural-functionalism, though properly this was a purely British school, developed by Radcliffe-Brown and his students. But Durkheim and the 'British School' agreed that social phenomena and their attendant collective representations were objectively existing entities. In Durkheim's *Règles de la méthode sociologique* (1895; *Rules of Sociological Method*, 1982), he argues that social phenomena should be studied 'as things' (*comme des choses*) – and describes individuals more as the products of society than as its producers. His contemporary, Max Weber, the last great, classical sociologist with a place in the anthropological pantheon, presents a contrast in more than one way.

WEBER

Max Weber grew up in a prosperous and authoritarian Prussian family, was educated at the universities of Berlin, Heidelberg and Göttingen, and rose rapidly in the German academic world. He was appointed professor at age 31 (in 1895), and in the course of a few years, published learned works about topics as diverse as the fall of the Roman Empire and agricultural problems in contemporary eastern Germany. From his mother, who was raised in a strict, Calvinist home, he had inherited ideals of ascetism and strict work discipline, which he put into practice in his academic life. In 1898, after only three active years, he suffered a mental breakdown, and was able to resume work only after another five years had passed. Immediately after his recovery, Weber wrote the book that many consider his finest: *Die protestantische Ethik und der 'Geist' der Kapitalismus* (1904–5; *The Protestant Ethic and the Spirit of Capitalism*, 1976). This is a work of cultural and economic history which explores the roots of European modernity. Weber argues that the Calvinists (and other puritan Christians of the sixteenth and seventeenth centuries) formulated a view of life that corresponded closely to the image of the perfect capitalist. The Calvinists believed that human life was predestined, that a few were singled out by God for salvation, but it was impossible for human beings to comprehend who or why this should be. The God of Calvin was cold and stern. He demanded obedience, but would not explain his reasons. According to Weber (and we sense that he may here be speaking from personal experience), this ambiguity, coupled to the merciless doctrine, created an unbearable tension in the life of Calvinists. Looking for solutions, it occurred to them that hard work coupled with a frugal lifestyle could only bring them closer to God's grace. They were enjoined to produce results, but forbidden to taste the fruits of their labour. Instead, they reinvested them in their enterprise, generating a spiral of increasing profits to the glory of God.

Weber's point is not necessarily that Calvinism was the *cause* of capitalism. There were many reasons why capitalism arose, and re-investment was by no means an invention of Calvin's. The point was rather that Calvinism (and in a broader sense, Protestantism as a whole) formulated an explicit ideology that justified and even glorified the capitalist ethic.

In Weber's Germany the humanities or, literally, 'spiritual sciences' (*Geisteswissenschaften*), had great prestige, and hermeneutics was considered a natural component of a cultured education. And it was hermeneutics, the science of understanding and interpreting the viewpoint of an alien culture, person or text, that inspired Weber to search for the *motivations* behind actions, for how a certain way of acting could make sense to individuals. Weber is, in this perspective, an early representative of what would later be called *methodological individualism*. It is not the system or the whole that interests him, but the fact that when individuals *do* things, they have *reasons* for doing them. Weber's sociology is therefore associated with the German word *Verstehen* (understanding). It is an 'understanding' and 'empathic' sociology, which seeks to 'put itself in the other's shoes', by grasping her motives, the choices she confronts and the responses that would be natural for her, given the concrete circumstances of her life. *Verstehen*, in other words, implies a focus on what the world means for individuals, and what kind of meaning it has.

What Weber himself sought to understand, however, was above all, power. Power was a major theme in Marx also (in Durkheim it plays a minor role), but the two men gave the word very different meanings. Marx had described power as based on control of the means of production, and therefore associated with property. Power is contested, overthrown, and society is changed – so far Marx and Weber agreed perfectly. But according to Marx, change does not arise from individuals pursuing values and striving for goals, but from slow-moving structural conflicts in the hidden depths of the social system. Marx saw power as an anonymous force, concealing its true face behind the veil of ideology. Weber focused on the effects of individual strategies to achieve power.

Like his contemporaries, the diffusionists, Weber was opposed to abstract, 'experience-distant' theoretical schemes. What mattered was the particular, the historical coincidence. Weber saw nothing unreasonable in supposing that power and property were often linked, but he declined to generalise further. Power, as he defines it, is the ability to get someone to do something that he would not otherwise have done. *Legitimate power* (or *authority*) is power based on a minimum of physical coercion and violence, that has been accepted as a legal, moral, natural or God-given fact of life by a populace that has been taught to believe that this is so. In his second great work, *Wirtschaft und Gesellschaft* (published posthumously in 1922; *Economy and Society*, 1968), Weber goes on to describe three *ideal types* of legitimate power. The 'ideal type' is another important Weberian neologism: it refers to simplified models that may be applied to the real world, to reveal specific aspects of its functioning – thus, the 'ideal types' themselves have no empirical reality. Weber's three ideal types of legitimate power may briefly be described as follows: *traditional authority* is power legitimised by ritual and kinship; *bureaucratic authority* is power legitimised through formalised administration; *charismatic authority* is the power of the prophet or the revolutionary to 'sway the masses'. The three types, Weber emphasises, may well coexist within a single society. Now, the first two types look suspiciously similar to the primitive/modern dichotomies proposed by Maine, Tönnies or Durkheim. But the third type is an innovation. It bears witness to the fact that Weber, towards the end of his life, had read Nietzsche and Freud, two contemporary thinkers from the German-language area, who argued the primacy of the individual with great force. There is a kind of power, Weber is telling us, that is unpredictable and individual, that is based on the seductive abilities of the exceptional individual, rather than on property (Marx) or stable norms (Durkheim).

Thus, for Weber, society was a more individual and less collective endeavour than for Marx or Durkheim. Society is not, as in Durkheim, a moral order that is given once and for all. Neither is it, as in Marx, a product of ponderous collective forces that individuals can neither understand nor influence. It is an ad hoc order, that is generated when different people with different interests and values meet, quarrel, and try (ultimately by force) to convince one another and arrive at some kind of agreement. Thus, Weber sees competition and conflict as potential sources of constructive change. Here he is in agreement with Marx, and in opposition to Durkheim, who assumed that change and disaster were practically synonymous. But in Weber, conflicts are not, as in Marx, vast and impersonal, but enacted by individuals. Thus, while Marx and Durkheim each developed a distinct brand of *methodological collectivism*, which studies society primarily as an integrated whole – Weber announced a *methodological individualism* that accepted that societies could be confusing, inconsistent and unpredictable.

The influence of Weber's legacy on anthropology was less direct than that of Durkheim, who himself was instrumental in founding modern French anthropology. Although he quickly became a key figure in international sociology, Weber's impact on anthropology came largely after the Second World War. It is a testimony to his great breadth as a theorist that otherwise very different anthropologists, such as hermeneutician Clifford Geertz and methodological individualist Fredrik Barth, are both deeply indebted to Weber, but for different reasons.

By the turn of the twentieth century, the Continental sociologists were engaged in a lively discourse on issues of social theory, attaining levels of sophistication that anthropologists could not pretend to. In our own day, Marx, Durkheim and Weber are far more frequently cited by anthropologists than Morgan, Bastian or Tylor, who would soon be effectively discredited by the followers of Durkheim. Soon, now, the impact of Durkheim would shake anthropology deeply, while Weber and Marx still lurked in the shadows, only appearing as major influences after the Second World War.

Still, the heritage of nineteenth-century anthropology is richer than is often supposed. Evolutionism never disappeared completely, and has had several influential twentieth-century proponents. Diffusionism, is, as we have hinted above, still a force to be reckoned with. Many concepts have survived, and are still used: Maine's distinction between contract and status, Tylor's definition of culture, Bastian's incipient cultural forms are all 'survivals' (to use a native term) of Victorian anthropology. It is nevertheless only with the developments described in the next chapter that social and cultural anthropology appears on the stage as we know it today.

3   FOUR FOUNDING FATHERS

The long years of Queen Victoria's reign, starting two decades after the end of the Napoleonic Wars and ending with the Boer War in South Africa, were a time of relative peace and prosperity in Europe. There had been remarkable technological changes and scientific innovations, the French, British, German and Russian colonial empires had expanded, the economy had been restructured and had grown; there had been massive population increases and important advances in democracy and education. In the last decades of the nineteenth century, a world of intensified exchange (and global exploitation), cultural globalisation (and cultural imperialism) and greatly increased political integration (often in the form of colonialism) emerged under the unquestioned leadership of Great Britain. In this historical setting, evolutionist theories might seem to be stating an obvious fact of nature. The Victorians saw their conquest of the world as tangible evidence that their culture was more evolved than all others.

At the turn of the twentieth century, this optimism had begun to falter, after which it was shattered by the atrocities of the First World War. Sigmund Freud's theory of dreams and the subconscious, published in 1900, and Albert Einstein's theory of general relativity (1905), may be seen as symbolic points of entry into a new, and more ambivalent epoch of modernity. These theories attacked the very substance of the Victorian world: Freud dissolved the free, rational individual, the means and end of progress, into subconscious desires and irrational sexuality. Einstein dissolved physics, the most abstract of the empirical sciences, and the foundation of technological innovation, into uncertainty and flux. In 1907, Arnold Schoenberg wrote the first bars of twelve-tone music and Pablo Picasso began to experiment with non-representational painting. *Modernism* was born in the arts, a movement which – despite its misleading name – offered an ambivalent view on truth, morality and progress. In politics, anarchists proclaimed the destruction of the state and feminists demanded the end of the bourgeois family. Less than two decades into the new century, a devastating war left the old Europe in ruins, and the Russian Revolution established a new, frightening or attractive version of modern rationalism. It was in this turbulent period of decay and renewal, disillusion and new utopias that anthropology was transformed into a modern social science.

Looking back, the history of anthropology until around 1900 had definitely not been a case of 'unilineal evolution'. Questions that had been raised forcefully by Enlightenment and Romantic thinkers of the late eighteenth century, were actively ignored by anthropologists in the 1800s. This is particularly true of the problems of relativism and cultural translation, which would be among the core issues for anthropology throughout the twentieth century. The important discoveries in German comparative philology, notably the relatedness of Indo-European languages, were transformed into airy speculations in the hands of comparative evolutionists. ('Degeneration' was the evolutionists' own term for this.) To the authors of this book, twentieth-century anthropology seems, in its fundamental mindset, more akin to the liberal and tolerant thought of the eighteenth century than to that of the authoritarian, conformist and evolutionist century that followed. We find it significant, too, that both the twentieth and the eighteenth century have been epochs of war in Europe, whereas the nineteenth century, after Napoleon, was uncommonly peaceful. What we have learned from the nineteenth century, in spite of all its faults, is the value of systematic, inductive reasoning, the value of models and 'ideal types' that we can project onto the real world, to ascertain its form.

The discipline of anthropology as we know it today developed in the years around the First World War, and we will uncontroversially describe its growth by focusing on four outstanding individuals – two in Britain, one in the USA and one in France. There are other national traditions and other scholars in the metropolitan countries who seemed just as important at the time, but who failed to leave sufficient intellectual progeny to be treated with the same deference here. It is only with the hindsight offered by the passing of time that we can assess the *historical* importance of past events; their *contemporary* importance may, however, have been different. Consider, for example, that Herbert Spencer was the single most famous European intellectual in the closing decades of the nineteenth century, just as Henri Bergson was the most famous philosopher in the first decades of the twentieth. Neither is considered a player in Premier Division Academia today, a century later.

The men whose work will form the backbone of this chapter were Franz Boas (1858–1942), Bronislaw Malinowski (1884–1942), A.R. Radcliffe-Brown (1881–1955) and Marcel Mauss (1872–1950). Between them, they effected a near-total renovation of three of the four national traditions discussed in the previous chapter – the American, the British and the French. In the fourth, Germanic, tradition, diffusionism retained its hegemony. Terrible things were in store for it, and for the Russian diffusionist tradition. Before long, Boas's books would be burned in Berlin, a generation of Russian ethnographers would die in the Gulag, and after the Second World War, certain German ethnologists would be found guilty of Nazi collaboration. For these and other reasons, German and Russian anthropology developed slowly during most of the twentieth century, and only rarely communicated with the mainstream traditions. However, Boas was a German and Malinowski a Pole, and since both brought along with them an intimate knowledge of the German tradition when they emigrated, to the USA and Britain, German anthropology lived on throughout the twentieth century, albeit in transplanted and 'hybrid' forms.

All of our four players were to some extent socially marginal in the environments they inhabited. Mauss was a Jew, Radcliffe-Brown came from a working-class background, Malinowski was a foreigner, and Boas was both a foreigner and a Jew. Perhaps predictably, the four had no shared programme. There were significant methodological and theoretical differences between the schools they founded, which even today may be traced in French, British and American anthropology. There were (and are) no clear-cut boundaries, as the influence of Durkheim on British anthropology most clearly shows. There was also significant personal contact across the divisions, as witnessed in the lively debate between Rivers and Boas's collaborator Kroeber, about the use of psychological and sociological models in anthropological research. Finally, all four of our heroes had the intellectual legacy of the nineteenth century in common. The near-universal consensus now was that evolutionism had failed. But there was also a silent acknowledgement of the fact that the evolutionists, from Morgan to Tylor, had after all established some of the basic parameters of the discipline.

The transition to a modern, largely non-evolutionist social science occurred in different ways in the three countries. In Great Britain, there was a radical rupture with the past. Radcliffe-Brown and Malinowski proclaimed an intellectual revolution and criticised some of their teachers severely. In the USA and France, continuity appeared to be greater. In the USA, Boas was the widely respected mentor and focal point of academic anthropology throughout the transition. In France, Mauss simply continued his uncle's work after the latter's death, though he emphasised the study of non-European peoples to a greater extent than Durkheim had.

It is sometimes claimed, not least by British social anthropologists, that Radcliffe-Brown and Malinowski more or less single-handedly created modern anthropology. This may have seemed to be the case at mid-century, when American anthropology had diverged out into many specialised strands and Mauss's students had not yet made their mark. British 'kinshipology' (Chapters 4 and 5) seemed, in contrast, to rest securely on a method invented by Malinowski and a theory developed by Radcliffe-Brown, as an established 'science of society'.

BOAS AND HISTORICAL PARTICULARISM

In 1886, the 28-year-old Franz Boas found himself in New York. He was on his way home to Germany, destined for a successful academic career. Boas already held a doctorate from Kiel and an academic position in Berlin, and he had participated in several ethnographic expeditions to northern and western Canada. However, Boas chose to stay in New York, possibly because it was a city where being a Jew was not a major handicap; certainly in part because it brought him closer to the peoples that fascinated him, the North American Indians and Inuit. In New York, Boas was first employed as editor of a scientific journal, then as an academic at a small university. In 1899, he became Professor of Anthropology at the prestigious Columbia University in New York, where he remained until his death in 1942. During the intervening 43 years, Boas would be teacher and mentor to two generations of American anthropologists. His general message to his students was simple. He had received his training from German scholars who were sceptical about evolutionism, and regarded diffusionism with sympathy. He was, like so many others of his generation, convinced that the development of general theory was totally dependent on sufficient empirical grounding. The chief task of the anthropologist, therefore, consisted in collecting and systematising detailed data on particular cultures. Only then could one embark on theoretical generalisations. In these and other respects, Boas was a true child of German romantic humanism as interpreted by Bastian.

In Great Britain, anthropology would be reshaped into *social* anthropology during the interwar years – a sociologically based, comparative discipline with core concepts such as social structure, norms, statuses and social interaction. In the USA, the discipline became known as *cultural* anthropology. Here, Tylor's broad definition of culture, abandoned in Britain in favour of a concept of *society*, was retained. In the American (and Tylorian) sense, culture is a far wider concept than society. If society is made up social norms, institutions and relationships, then culture consists of everything that humans have created, *including* society – material phenomena (a field, a plough, a painting ...), social conditions (marriage, households, the state ...) and symbolic meaning (language, ritual, belief ...). Anthropology – the science of humanity – was, quite literally, concerned with everything human. Boas recognised that no individual could contribute equally to all parts of this subject (though he made heroic attempts to do so himself), and therefore advocated a 'four-field approach' that divided anthropology into linguistics, physical anthropology, archaeology and cultural anthropology. Students were trained in all four fields, later to specialise in one of them. Specialisation was therefore an integral part of American anthropology from its inception, while in both Britain and France a far more generalistic approach remained the ideal. It is symptomatic that, in the 1930s, there already existed established research teams, specialising, for example, in Native North American languages.

Boas's own writings covered a broad field, though with a decided slant towards cultural anthropology. He had carried out individual field research among the Inuit and Kwakiutl of the north-west coast America, but he also worked with assistants who collected material on many other Indian peoples. During fieldwork, he would often make use of linguistically proficient members of the tribe under study, who would record, discuss and interpret the statements of informants. Some of these collaborators, notably the prodigious George Hunt, who co-wrote several of Boas's books on the Kwakiutl, have only recently been recognised as anthropological scholars in their own right.

Fieldwork of Boas's kind was often team-oriented, it did not presuppose a lone individual subjected to long-term, continuous 'immersion' in the field. Stays in the field were often short. It was frequently 'long-term' in another sense, however, in as much as such stays were repeated many times over the years, sometimes by different people, all of whom collaborated on the same project (see Foster et al. 1979). Such a methodological strategy was perhaps only natural, given that 'the field' was close at hand in the USA, not at the antipodes, as in Britain.

Boas was less hostile to historical reconstructions than his younger British contemporaries (see pp. 41–7). Indeed, he retained physical anthropology and archaeology as parts of the holistic anthropological enterprise. He never-theless shared the British critique of evolutionism. In its place, he proposed the principle of *historical particularism*. Like Bastian, he held that each culture contained its own values and its own unique history, which could, in some cases, be reconstructed by anthropologists. He saw intrinsic value in the plurality of cultural practices in the world and was deeply sceptical of any attempt, political or academic, to undermine this diversity. Writing about Kwakiutl dancing, for example, he says it is an example of the culture's approach to rhythm, and therefore it cannot be reduced to a mere 'function' of society (as the British *social* anthropologists seemed to prefer). One must instead ask what this rhythm *is* for the people who dance to it, and the answer can only be found by exploring the emotional states, which generate and are generated by the rhythm (Boas 1927).

Boas was an early and tireless critic of racism and of science that was inspired by it – the latter had supporters among the establishment of Victorian anthropology. Such anthropologists had argued that each 'race' had a distinctive innate potential for cultural development. Boas answered that culture was *sui generis* – its own source – and that inborn differences could not account for the impressive range of cultural variation that anthro-pologists had already documented. The term *cultural relativism*, which we have referred to several times above, was actually coined by Boas. In our own day, it is often asked whether relativism is to be understood as a method-ological or a moral imperative, and it is most often answered that cultural relativism is a method. To Boas, this would no doubt seem to be hair-splitting. Method and morality were for him two sides of the same coin.

Boas dominated American anthropology through four decades, but left no grand theory or monumental work that is read by each succeeding generation of anthropologists. The main reason is perhaps his distrust of lofty generalisations. During his studies with Bastian, he had been warned against the perils of empty theorising, and in his writings, he tried to identify the unique circumstances that had generated particular cultures, rather than jumping to general conclusions. He was also cautious in his use of comparison, which all too easily established artificial similarities between societies that were fundamentally different. Boas was thus an outspoken methodological individualist, in the sense that he sought the particular instance rather than the general scheme, and which explains his life-long scepticism with regard to Durkheim.

Boas's students include almost all the important American anthropologists of the next generation (with some notable exceptions, to which we shall return). Among them were Alfred L. Kroeber (1876–1960), who founded the Department of Anthropology at Berkeley, together with Robert H. Lowie (1883–1957), his long-time colleague and fellow cultural historian; Edward Sapir (1884–1939), founder of the Department of Anthropology at Yale and of the school of 'ethnolinguistics'; Melville Herskovits (1895–1963), founder of Afro-American studies in the United States, and Professor at the Department of Anthropology at Northwestern University; Ruth Benedict (1887–1948), who inherited Boas's Chair at Columbia University, and formed the 'culture and personality' school; and Margaret Mead (1901–78), the runt of the litter, who continued Benedict's work, and became perhaps the most influential public figure in the history of anthropology.

As the above list indicates, the cultural anthropology championed by Boas evolved in several directions during his own lifetime (Chapter 4). Further diversification occurred in the 1950s, when Morgan was rediscovered and Radcliffe-Brown's students at Chicago developed their own brand of British-style social anthropology. Nevertheless, the legacy of Boas remains at the heart of American anthropology to this day.

MALINOWSKI AND THE TROBRIAND ISLANDERS

In 1910, 24 years after Boas made his fateful decision to remain in the USA, a young Polish intellectual moved from Leipzig to London. Bronislaw Malinowski had received a doctoral degree in physics and philosophy a few years earlier in Krakow, part of the Austro-Hungarian Empire (now part of Poland). In Leipzig, he had studied psychology and economics, and had been convinced by the social psychologist Wilhelm Wundt (1832–1920) that society had to be understood *holistically*, as a unity of intertwined parts, and that analysis should be synchronous (not historical). During the same period, Malinowski read *The Golden Bough*, and made his move to study under Seligman at the London School of Economics, which already had a reputation for offering good conditions for exotic fieldwork.

Four years later, Malinowski carried out a six-month field study on an island off the coast of New Guinea, which he regarded as a failure. After a short stay in Australia, spent reflecting over his methods, he set off again, this time for the Trobriand Islands in the same region, where he would spend altogether nearly two years, between 1915 and 1918. After the end of the war, he returned to Europe to write *Argonauts of the Western Pacific* (Malinowski 1984 [1922]), possibly the single most revolutionary work in the history of anthropology. Following the success of *Argonauts*, he attracted a small group of accomplished and enthusiastic students to the LSE, most of whom would leave their mark on the discipline in the coming decades. Malinowski died in the USA, in the middle of a study of social change among Indian peasants in Mexico.

Argonauts, Malinowski's first major work, remains his most famous. The book was prefaced by Sir James Frazer, who lavished praise on the young Pole, clearly unaware that, in an academic sense, he was signing his own death warrant. The voluminous book is fluently written. It leads us through a highly focused and extremely detailed examination of a single institution among the Trobrianders, the *kula* trade, where symbolic valuables circulate over a large area between the islands of Melanesia. Malinowski describes the planning of expeditions, the routes followed, the rites and practices associated with them, and traces the connections between the *kula* trade and other Trobriand institutions, such as political leadership, domestic economics, kinship and rank. A contemporary and countryman of the novelist Joseph Conrad, Malinowski brought home news from 'the heart of darkness', in the form of nuanced and naturalistic images of the Trobrianders, who in the end emerge as neither spectacular, exotic nor 'radically different' from Westerners, but simply as distinctive.

It has been claimed that Malinowski was virtually interned on the Trobriand Islands during the First World War, since, as a citizen of the Habsburg Empire, he was technically an enemy of Britain. This is a distortion of the facts (Kuper 1996: 12). Malinowski was not a flighty romantic who 'just happened' to discover the principle of modern fieldwork. His student, Raymond Firth (1957), describes him as a thorough and systematic ethnographer, with an unusual capacity for acquiring languages and an outstanding faculty of observation. Another common misunderstanding has it that Malinowski 'invented' *fieldwork*. As we have seen, ethnographic expeditions were common long before Malinowski's time, and some of these, like the Torres expedition, had maintained rigorous methodological standards. What Malinowski 'invented' was not fieldwork, but a particular fieldwork method, which he called *participant observation*. The simple, but revolutionary, idea behind this method was to live with the people one studied, and learn to participate as far as possible in their lives and activities. For Malinowski, it was essential to stay long enough in the field to become thoroughly aquainted with the local way of life, and to be able to use the local vernacular as one's working language. Interpreters, formal interviews and social aloofness would no longer do. Malinowski lived alone in a hut in the middle of a Trobriand village for months on end – though he kept his tropical suit and hat immaculately white, and though his posthumously published diaries (Malinowski 1967) reveal that he often felt homesick, despondent, and sick and tired of 'the natives'.

Malinowski's 'participant observation' set a new standard for ethnographic research. No fact was too trivial to be recorded. As far as was practically possible, the ethnographer should take part in the ongoing flow of everyday life, avoiding specific questions that might divert the stream of events, and without restricting attention to particular parts of the scene. But Malinowski did not not restrict himself to unstructured methods. He collected accurate data about yam yields, land rights, gift exchange, trade patterns and political conflicts, among other things, and carried out structured interviews whenever he deemed it necessary. What he did not do to any significant extent was to contextualise the Trobrianders within a wider historical and regional context. In this, he stands in striking contrast to his French colleague, Marcel Mauss, who was a specialist on the Pacific, with a much broader and deeper knowledge of the region's cultural history than Malinowski, but who had never been there.

Virtually everything Malinowski published, from *Argonauts* onwards, drew extensively on his Trobriand data. He wrote about economics and trade, marriage and sex, magic and world-views, politics and power, human needs and social structure, kinship and aesthetics. His descriptions run over several thousand pages, and demonstrate conclusively the potential of long-term intensive fieldwork. The sheer number of Trobriand institutions, beliefs and practices, showed beyond doubt that a 'primitive', 'simple' society, near the bottom of the evolutionist ladder, was in fact a highly complex and multifaceted universe in itself. Malinowski's work revealed, more convincingly than any theoretical argument, the absurdity of a comparative project that compared single traits. From now on, context and interconnections would be essential qualities of any anthropological account.

Malinowski's theoretical views have generally been received less enthusiastically by later anthropologists than his methods and ethnography. His theoretical stance was basically eclectic, but in line with current fashions he named his theoretical programme *functionalism*. All social practices and institutions were functional in the sense that they fit together in a functioning whole, which they contributed to maintaining. But unlike the other functionalists who followed Durkheim, Malinowski saw individuals, not society, as the system's ultimate goal. Institutions existed for people, not vice versa, and it was their needs, ultimately their biological needs, that was the prime motor of social stability and change. This was *methodological individualism* in yet another guise, and in a collectivist academic climate dominated by Durkheimians, it was not very favourably received. For a few decades after his death, Malinowski's star continued to fade, until disillusionment with 'Grand Theory' set in during the 1970s, which led to his rehabilitation in anthropological communities on both sides of the Atlantic – at the expense of his colleague and rival, Radcliffe-Brown. Malinowski emphasised attention to detail and the importance of grasping the native's point of view, and part of his reaction against his immediate predecessors sprang from a deep scepticism towards high-flying theories. We note the similarity to Boas here, as a sign of their common Germanic training. Malinowski differed from Boas, however, in his reluctance to engage in any form of historical reconstruction. With Radcliffe-Brown he waged an anti-evolutionary – and anti-historical – campaign that was so successful that the subject was more or less banned in British anthropology for nearly half a century.

Malinowski called himself a functionalist, but his views differed fundamentally from the rival programme of structural-functionalism. In Malinowski's view, the individual was the foundation of society. For the Durkheimian structural-functionalists, the individual was an epiphenomenon of society and of little intrinsic interest – what mattered was to elicit the elements of social structure. These two lineages of British social anthropology – biopsychological functionalism and sociological structural-functionalism – highlight a basic tension in the discipline, between what has later been referred to as *agency* and *structure*. The individual has agency in the sense that he or she is a creator of society. Society imposes structure on the individual and limits his or her options. The two viewpoints are, as Giddens (1979) points out, complementary. But in interwar British anthropology this was not seen. Malinowski's functionalism and Radcliffe-Brown's structural-functionalism were perceived as diametrical opposites.

RADCLIFFE-BROWN'S 'NATURAL SCIENCE OF SOCIETY'

Alfred Reginald Radcliffe-Brown (1881–1955) belonged to Malinowski's generation, but his family background was not cosmopolitan and intellectual, but English working class. He began his academic career as plain A.R. Brown. Raising funds through his family, he embarked on medical studies at Oxford, but was encouraged by his teachers, notably Rivers, to move to Cambridge and study anthropology. He did fieldwork in 1906–8 on the Andaman Islands east of India, and published a well-received field report in the diffusionist style, but he would soon switch to a different theoretical course. Shortly after its publication, Radcliffe-Brown read Durkheim's masterpiece *The Elementary Forms of Religious Life*. He gave a long lecture series on Durkheim at Oxford, and when his monograph, *Andaman Islanders*, was finally published in 1922, it appeared more than anything else to be a brilliant demonstration of Durkheimian sociology applied to ethnographic material.

Like Boas and Malinowski, Radcliffe-Brown spent the interwar years building a following and developing academic institutions devoted to the new anthropology. Unlike them, however, he spent long periods of his professional life as an academic nomad, building up important anthropological milieux in Cape Town, Sydney and Chicago. During his travels he had built up a widespread international network, through which his influence was felt in Great Britain as well. So when he finally returned to Oxford to accept a Chair in Social Anthropology in 1937, it was as a celebrated exile, rather than an outsider. When Malinowski left for the USA the year after, Radcliffe-Brown quickly gathered the reins in his hands and became the leading figure in anthropology in Britain. Several of the main 'Radcliffe-Brownian' anthropologists, including Evans-Pritchard and Fortes (Chapter 4), had initially been students of Malinowski, and were exhilarated at the return of the long-absent master of theoretical abstraction. British interwar anthropology thus went through two phases: first a period dominated by detailed ethnography with a regional emphasis on the Pacific, then a period focused on Durkheimian structural analysis, with an emphasis on Africa.

Radcliffe-Brown followed Durkheim in seeing the individual chiefly as a product of society. While Malinowski trained his students to go out and look for human motivations and the logic of action, Radcliffe-Brown asked his to discover abstract structural principles and socially integrating mechanisms. Although the contrast is often exaggerated in historical accounts, the result was sometimes strikingly different styles of inquiry.

The 'mechanisms' that Radcliffe-Brown hoped to identify, were of Durkheimian origin, akin, perhaps to the latter's collective representations. But Radcliffe-Brown had explicit hopes of transforming anthropology into a 'real' science, which Durkheim probably did not share. In *A Natural Science of Society*, his last book (based on a lecture series held in Chicago in 1937 and posthumously published in 1957), he indicates the tenor of this hope. Society is bound together by a *structure* of juridical rules, social statuses and moral norms, which circumscribe and regulate behaviour. Social structure exists, in Radcliffe-Brown's work, independently of the individual actors who reproduce it. Actual persons and their relationships are mere instantiations of the structure, and the ultimate goal of the anthropologist is to discover its governing principles, beneath the veneer of empirically existing situations. This formal model, with its units clearly defined and logically related, clearly demonstrates the master's 'scientific' intent.

Social structure can further be partitioned into discrete institutions or subsystems, such as systems for distribution and inheritance of land, for conflict resolution, for socialisation, for division of labour in the family, etc. – all of which contribute to the maintenance of the social structure as a whole. This, according to Radcliffe-Brown, is their function and the cause of their existence. At this point, we have a problem. Radcliffe-Brown seems to claim that institutions exist *because* they maintain the social whole; that is, that their function is also their cause. The relationship of cause to effect becomes vague and ambiguous, and such 'tautological' or 'backward' reasoning is generally frowned on in scientific explanations. This critique, however, applies equally to all forms of functionalism, including, but not limited to, Radcliffe-Brown's variation on the theme.

Such problems might have worried the structural-functionalists, anxious as they were to be regarded as proper scientists, but they did not. Radcliffe-Brown's linkage between Durkheimian social theory and ethnographic material, and his ambitions on behalf of the discipline, generated an attractive new research programme, to which talented researchers flocked, which in turn increased the theory's prestige. Since Morgan, anthropologists had been aware that kinship was a key to the understanding of social organisation in small-scale societies. It was still unclear just what this key unlocked. Radcliffe-Brown's Durkheimian use of Maine's old idea of kinship as a 'juridical' system of norms and rules, made it possible to exploit the analytical potential of kinship to the hilt. A kinship system was easily understood as an unwritten constitution for social interaction, a set of rules for the distribution of rights and duties. Kinship, in other words, was once again a key institution, this time as the engine (or heart, to use the biological analogies favoured by Durkheim) of a self-sustaining, organically integrated yet abstract entity called social structure (a term that was first used, incidentally, by Spencer).

With this key in hand, structural-functionalists went on to study other institutions in primitive societies: politics, economics, religion, ecological adaptation, etc. It was of particular importance to these researchers that kinship was seen to function as a framework for the creation of groups or *corporations* in such societies. The groups might have collective rights to, for example, land or animals. They might demand loyalty in the case of war. They might settle disputes or organise marriages. It was these groups and their dynamics that the structural-functionalists started out to study, not what Boas would have called 'culture'. Radcliffe-Brown himself was not particularly fond of the word 'culture'. To him, the central issue was not what the natives were thinking, what they believed in, how they made their living or how they had become what they were, but rather how their society was integrated, the 'forces' that bound it together as a whole.

Radcliffe-Brown's critique of the 'conjectural history' of the evolutionists was harsh. In his view, contemporary arrangements existed because they were functional today, certainly not as 'survivals' of a bygone era. They made sense in the present or not at all. He was also scornful of the frequently fanciful reconstructions engaged in by cultural historians and diffusionists. Where no evidence existed, there was no reason to speculate. Here, Malinowski and Radcliffe-Brown were in perfect agreement.

Malinowski and Radcliffe-Brown founded two 'lineages' in British anthropology, which in some respects were in direct competition, in others, complementary. With the consolidation of these schools just before the Second World War, British social anthropology was well on its way to become an established academic field (some would say a 'science'). The 'lineages' were not wholly endogamous. British social anthropology was a small tribe where everyone knew everyone else. The tribe was made up of two corporate groups; one centred at Oxford, where Evans-Pritchard was already established when Radcliffe-Brown returned from Chicago in 1937, and one at the London School of Economics, the stronghold of Malinowski, Seligman and, in the next generation, Raymond Firth. Nearly all social anthropologists who were educated in the interwar period were associated with one of these centres. (At Cambridge, the *ancien régime* was still in place) Since Radcliffe-Brown and Malinowski were rarely in the country at the same time, many students were acquainted with both and followed their lectures. Most had studied first with Malinowski, and some subsequently transferred to Radcliffe-Brown. The latter group included Evans-Pritchard, Fortes and Max Gluckman. Students who remained 'Malinowskian' in their orientation included Firth, Audrey Richards, Edmund Leach and Isaac Schapera. Both Malinowski and Radcliffe-Brown had a lasting impact on the discipline; Malinowski's field methods were eagerly adopted by members of the other camp, and everyone had to relate to Radcliffe-Brown's concepts of structure and function and the ensuing 'kinshipology' for at least a decade after his death. As late as 1954, Malinowski's student, Edmund Leach, felt that he had to declare himself a structural-functionalist (before going on to demolish that paradigm mercilessly).

In demographic terms, the expansion of social anthropology was sluggish; before the Second World War there were fewer than 40 devotees throughout Britain. Nevertheless, the institutional expansion, both at home and in the colonies, was impressive. Radcliffe-Brown had no small part in this. During his long 'nomadic' period, he had established viable anthropology departments in Cape Town, Sydney, Delhi and Chicago. During his stay in Cape Town (1920–25), he collaborated with an old student of Malinowski's, Isaac Schapera, who would later direct the department there for many years. While in Sydney, he stimulated the scientific study of Aboriginal languages, and established Sydney's role as base camp for fieldworkers active throughout the Pacific area. In Chicago from 1931 to 1937, he contributed to the 'Europeanisation' of part of American anthropology, inspiring, among other things, an innovative style of micro-sociological anthropology that later became highly influential. Finally, in India, Radcliffe-Brown's student M.N. Srinivas was instrumental in founding Indian social anthropology as a largely structural-functionalist discipline.

MAUSS AND THE SEARCH FOR TOTAL SOCIAL PHENOMENA

While Malinowski was still doing fieldwork among the Trobrianders, while Radcliffe-Brown was lecturing and doing fieldwork in South Africa, and while Boas was busy bringing up the first generation of American anthropologists at his base in New York City, Durkheim (who was born in the same year as Boas) died, a year before the conclusion of the First World War. His nephew, Marcel Mauss, who had already been working with Durkheim for two decades, now took his place as the leader of the *Année Sociologique* circle. It was not the easiest of times. Several of Mauss's brilliant contemporaries had recently died in the war, and he would later spend much of his professional energy completing and publishing their manuscripts. Mauss, who had been Professor of Primitive Religion at the École Pratique des Hautes Études in Paris since 1902, had his background in classical studies and comparative philology, and his knowledge of global cultural history and contemporary ethnography was immense. In his work, he cites the research of both Boas, Malinowski and Radcliffe-Brown along with a plethora of others, many of them learned Germans of the diffusionist tradition.

Mauss regarded his work as a continuation of Durkheim's, and the two men shared a *holistic* conception of society, the idea that society was an organically integrated whole, a 'social organism'. Mauss, on this background, divided the study of anthropology into three levels of inquiry: *ethnography*, which was the detailed study of customs, beliefs and social life; *ethnology*, which was the empirically based craft of regional comparison; and *anthropology*, which was the philosophically informed theoretical endeavour to generalise about humanity and society on the basis of the two former research efforts. Mauss never carried out fieldwork himself, but his graduate courses at the Institute of Ethnology, which he founded in 1925, were heavily focused on methodological issues. Students had to learn to become ethnographers before they learned to theorise.

Unlike Durkheim, Mauss's chief interest was in non-European and 'archaic' cultures. He sought to develop a comparative sociology based on detailed ethnographic descriptions of real societies and, thus far, his project was closely related to that of Malinowski, Radcliffe-Brown or Boas. His explicit aim, however, was to classify societies and discover structural features common to different societal types, in order to develop a general understanding of social life. In this, his work differed strongly from Boas's particularism. Also in contrast to his British colleagues, Mauss did not hesitate to draw on historical material whenever relevant. The 'general laws' Radcliffe-Brown spoke of are conspicuously absent from Mauss's work, which has a more humanistic than scientific bent.

Mauss spent much of his time teaching and editing the work of colleagues, and never published a book in his own name, although he co-wrote several. His most influential work, *Essai sur le don* (1923–4; *The Gift*, 1954) initially appeared as a long essay in Durkheim's journal, *L'Année Sociologique*, and was published between two covers only much later. But he wrote rich, dense essays on a variety of subjects, which still inspire scholars: essays on the body, nationalism, personhood, sacrifice, totemism, etc. Mauss's brand of anthropology is evident in all his work, but perhaps especially in *The Gift*, a book that has elicited a large and important commentary literature, engaging intellectual luminaries such as Jacques Derrida, Jean Baudrillard and Pierre Bourdieu during the latter half of the twentieth century.

The basic idea in *The Gift* is simple enough: there can be no prestation without a counter-prestation, and for that reason, gift exchange is a means of establishing social relations; it is morally binding and socially integrating. Gift exchange ties people together in mutual commitment and is instrumental in the formation of norms. It appears to be voluntary, but is actually regulated by firm, if implicit, rules. Gift-giving has a strategic and pragmatic aspect. It is manipulated by individuals seeking to promote their own interests, not least in politics. Finally, the gift has important symbolic aspects, since objects that are given and received become symbols of social relationships and even metaphysical phenomena. Discussing Polynesian material, Mauss talks about the *hau* or 'power/soul' of the gift. It possesses an inner quality that commits the receiver in particular ways, because of its history. (If this sounds obscure, think of the value accorded in our kind of society to antique furniture and ancient art!)

Although gift exchange occurs in every society, it has diminished in importance in European history. Mauss is particularly interested in a form of exchange, which he locates to traditional and ancient societies, and which he refers to as *prestations totales* ('total prestations'). Such gifts are the symbolic embodiments of a whole range of relationships, and may be said to express the very essence of society. In modern society, which is dominated by other forms of exchange (notably the decontextualised exchange of the market), Christmas presents are perhaps the closest approximation to *prestations totales*; they evoke a wide range of institutions – family, Christianity, capitalism, consumerism, holidays, childhood – as well as personal relationships.

In *The Gift*, Mauss asks how societies are integrated and how individuals are bound to each other through moral obligations. It is a synthetic work of economic anthropology, cultural history, symbolic analysis and very general social theory, which effectively bridges many of the gaps that have characterised later anthropology. Through his dual concern with individual strategies and social integration, Mauss even integrates structural and actor-centred analyses elegantly.

Although he was far from a prolific writer, Mauss's influence has been massive, both within and outside of France. He left a range of questions which were tackled with great sophistication by later French anthropologists, among the most famous of whom are Claude Lévi-Strauss and Louis Dumont. His work has also served as a stimulus to many Anglo-American anthropologists, from Evans-Pritchard onwards. Incidentally, Mauss and Radcliffe-Brown were never close, professionally or personally.

French anthropology in the early decades of the twentieth century included several strong personalities in addition to Durkheim and Mauss. Arnold van Gennep (1873–1957), who never became part of their inner circle, was a learned and innovative scholar, who developed rural community studies in France as part of anthropology (in other words, 'anthropology at home' is not a recent invention). Van Gennep is nevertheless particularly known for another of his works, *Les Rites de passage* (1909;

The Rites of Passage, 1960). The book is a comparative study of initiation rituals, in which persons move from one social status to another. The most widespread rites of passage are associated with birth, puberty, marriage and death. Anticipating Durkheim's sociology of religion, van Gennep argued that such rituals are dramatised expressions of the social order, which strengthen the integration of both initiates and spectators. Moreover, he argued that such rituals were universally divided into three stages: separation, liminality and reintegration, a perspective to which we will return later, in discussing Victor Turner's work (Chapter 6).

Another contemporary of Durkheim and Mauss, who introduced an alternative set of problems for anthropology, was the philosopher Lucien Lévy-Bruhl (1857–1939). Although his work is now largely known (by hearsay) as a laughable example of the incorrect views of bygone ages, there is no doubt that Lévy-Bruhl opened a new field for empirical research, which has stimulated generations of later anthropologists, including Evans-Pritchard and Lévi-Strauss. In *Mentalité primitive* (1922; *Primitive Mentality*, 1978) and subsequent books, Lévy-Bruhl argued that illiterate peoples think in a qualitatively different way from literate ones; they do not reason logically and coherently, but poetically and metaphorically. Although his contemporaries, from Lowie in the USA to Schmidt in Germany, were almost universally critical of his work, it framed an analytical field that has proven fertile later: the comparative study of thought styles, and the problems of intercultural translation associated with such differences. But Lévy-Bruhl's influence was stronger outside anthropology than within it. His philosophy was received with enthusiasm by the Surrealist movement, which equated 'primitive mentality' with freedom and creativity, and whose idealised views of 'primitive peoples' did not need to take empirical studies into account.

ANTHROPOLOGY IN 1930: PARALLELS AND DIVERGENCES

By 1930, communities of 'new anthropologists' had been established in Great Britain, France and the USA, with contacts among anthropologists working in Germany and Eastern Europe, South Africa, India and Australia. The groups were still small. All in all there were no more than a couple of hundred professional anthropologists in the world, and to speak of 'schools' in this context may thus seem slightly preposterous. Only eight years had passed since the two founders of the new anthropology in Britain had published their ground-breaking works – and it would be misleading to speak of a 'British School' at this early date. Radcliffe-Brown was still in Sydney, and would spend most of the 1930s in Chicago. Malinowski as yet had few students, and none of them had produced anything of importance so far. Diffusionism and more or less speculative 'armchair anthropology' were flourishing. Frazer still had eleven years left as professor at Cambridge. In 1930, it could by no means be taken for granted that the new anthropology would succeed in Britain, and the situation in France and the United States was not very different.

The founders of modern anthropology belonged to a small group and had much in common in spite of their many differences. Most importantly, perhaps, they all sought to ground anthropology in a 'detailed study of customs, in relation to the total culture of the tribe that practised them' (Boas 1940 [1896]: 272). The central point of this quote is the idea that cultural traits could no longer be studied in isolation. A ritual cannot be reduced to a detached 'survival' of an hypothetical past. It has to be seen in relation to the total society that it is part of here and now. It has to be studied in *context*. Anthropology is a *holistic* science – its aim is to describe societies or cultures as integrated wholes. So far, the four founders agreed, indeed, similar ideas were central to Marxist, Durkheimian and Weberian sociology as well, and had gained wide acceptance by the turn of the century. We might even claim that the concept that 'society is a system' is the most fundamental of all sociological insights, and it should come as no surprise, therefore, that when it entered anthropology, it produced a theoretical revolution, in which all four founders participated, in one capacity or another.

Despite the diminutive size of the discipline, the differences between the national traditions were already marked; in methods, theory and institutional organisation. Later, when all the founders were dead, certain images of each of them, and of their mutual relations, were formed in the discipline. These images or myths are widely dispersed today, and tend to allow certain of the more obvious qualities of each of the four men to overshadow all others. The reader should therefore bear in mind that academic relations among anthropologists are no less complex than human relations in general (see Leach 1984). Thus, Boas and Mauss both agreed that there was no deep conflict between cultural history and synchronic studies, and both therefore retained an interest in diffusionism, while Radcliffe-Brown and Malinowski regarded such interests as 'unscientific'. This division clearly mirrors the fact that the two British anthropologists were engaged in a 'revolution', while there was a far greater sense of continuity in France and the United States. But other divisions were equally important. Radcliffe-Brown and Mauss agreed that their studies were part of a large, comparative sociological project, while Boas, the least sociologically inclined of the four, was suspicious of the 'French science' that Radcliffe-Brown preached in Chicago, and distrusted the comparative method deeply. Malinowski, for his part, seems to have avoided comparison altogether. In this case, the Germanic heritage of Malinowski and Boas clearly unites them against the 'French school'. But this unity is also incomplete. While Radcliffe-Brown and Mauss were committed methodological collectivists who delved into the secrets of 'society as a whole', Boas and Malinowski were (German) particularists. But Malinowski's particularism focused on the bodily needs of the individual, while Boas believed in the primacy of culture.

The purely personal qualities of the four men also influenced the new science of society. Boas effortlessly assumed the role of the benevolent father figure of American anthropology. Indeed, his popularity was so great during his long career, that his obvious blindspot, his distrust of generalisation, became the blindspot of a generation. With very few exceptions (including, famously, Benedict 1934), wide-ranging generalisations were completely absent from twentieth-century American anthropology until after the death of 'Papa Franz'. In Britain, there was no such consensus. Well into their careers, Radcliffe-Brown and Malinowski were co-activists in the 'functionalist revolution', but as their common enemy receded, their mutual antagonisms came to the fore, and their students (and students' students) eagerly reproduced their conflict (Chapter 4); Radcliffe-Brownians would speak derisively of the 'Malinowskian' monograph – packed with boring details, but with no workable ideas; while the Malinowskians would chide their Oxford colleagues for producing models that were so coherent as to be incompatible with the facts.

Finally, there were systematic differences between the three national traditions that were neither academic nor personal. Due in part to the prestige of Boas, in part to the fact that research money was more accessible in the United States, American anthropology quickly became a larger and more established discipline than in Europe. When the American Anthropological Association (AAA) was formed in 1906, it already included 175 members. As late as in 1939, however, there were only some 20 professional anthropologists in the entire British Empire, and when the Association of Social Anthropologists (ASA) was established in Britain, in 1946, it had only 21 full members (Kuper 1996: 67; Stocking 1996: 427).

In France, we see an entirely different situation. The French academic system was more centralised than in the two other countries, and Paris attracted a large, talented and dynamic intellectual elite, which enjoyed considerable prestige. Membership in this elite was more important than disciplinary boundaries, and anthropologists were therefore involved in intensive cooperation and debate with sociologists, philosophers, historians, psychologists and linguists. Although anthropology is clearly being institutionalised here as elsewhere, there is not the same strong feeling of a new and revolutionary discipline taking form, defining itself as distinct from its predecessors, from other disciplines, and from other anthropological schools. Thus, French anthropology was in a sense both the most open-minded and the most elitist of the national traditions.

By the early 1930s, the four schools of early modern anthropology were firmly established. In the space of a short decade, the Victorian anthropology of Tylor and Frazer, the materialism of Morgan and the diffusionism of the Germans had collected a thick layer of dust. Some earlier theory still lay dormant, to be rediscovered by later generations, most notably the work of Marx and Weber; but as a whole, the enterprise of anthropology was perceived as fresh, new and exciting, as a newly discovered key to a true understanding of the human condition. The practitioners in each country were few and highly motivated, in some cases (we have Mauss's and Radcliffe-Brown's followers in mind) almost reminiscent of religious cults.

In Europe outside France and Britain, the spread of the new discipline had not yet started. In Germany, diffusionists held sway until well after the Second World War, and it was only in the 1950s that social anthropology was established in Scandinavia and the Netherlands (see Vermeulen and Roldán 1995 for partial histories of European anthropologies). Cultural history in the diffusionist or evolutionist vein, often sprinkled with ethnocentric prejudice (when speaking of others) and nationalist aspirations (when speaking of own 'folk culture'), would prevail in most of Europe for decades yet.

4   EXPANSION AND INSTITUTIONALISATION

Jazz and Stalinism, *Hitler-Jugend* and Al Capone, blood on the horizon and bread-lines in the street, the consolidation of colonial empires and the birth of mass media, the crash of stock markets and rise of the welfare state: the 1930s quiver like an arrow waiting for release. Then war rolls across Europe and the world – the most destructive war in history, leaving Auschwitz and the Bomb to feed the nightmares of the second half of the century.

The war obliterated the last vestiges of the world the Victorians had lived and believed in. The rational individual of the Enlightenment and the emotional community of the Romantics now seemed equally naive. Soon, the great colonial empires would also crumble, and with them their *raison d'être*, the White Man's Burden and *mission civilisatrice*, the assumed obligation to spread European civilisation to every corner of the world. Indeed, 'civilisation' itself was soon to be exposed as a hoax, a thin veneer of humanism concealing the vicious animal within.

Curiously, perhaps, it was in these years that anthropology blossomed into a mature discipine. The 1930s were a productive decade, when the founders' first students started making their mark on the field, and the founders themselves were still working. Neither did the 1939–45 war seriously disturb this upswing. In the USA, university life went on nearly as before, and in Britain, too, scholars continued to work. Even in occupied France the situation was not intolerable, and the countries most seriously affected by the war, Germany and the Soviet Union, were marginal to the new anthropology anyway. Nevertheless, some questions were clearly bottled up or postponed 'for the duration'. After 1945, at any rate, a new wave of radical reform swept through anthropology. Perhaps this was also because the war coincided with the retirements of Mauss and Radcliffe-Brown (in 1939 and 1946), and the deaths of Malinowski and Boas (in 1942). With the old world gone and the founders out of the picture, the time was ripe to state one's mind loud and clear. This story will be told in the next chapter. We now return to the early 1930s.

A MARGINAL DISCIPLINE?

Anthropology was now faced with immediate challenges generated by its own success. 'The Revolution', as Radcliffe-Brown and Malinowski called it, had been going on since the early 1920s. The methodological, theoretical and institutional foundation of the refurbished discipline had been laid. Research programmes were defined, funding was obtained, professional friendships, enmities and strategic alliances were built. The task now consisted in showing the long-term viability of the discipline. Students had to be educated, journals edited, publishers found for monographs, conferences organised, the media addressed, politicians and planners convinced, and – not least task – employment found for the growing number of scholars. In order to achieve this, the energy of the revolution had to be disciplined and channelled into predictable institutional routines. In Adam Kuper's important history of British social anthropology (1996), the chapter dealing with this period is called 'From charisma to routine', and, quite as Weber might have put it: after a charismatic awakening, routinisation is bound to occur, however reluctantly. In anthropology, this period of consolidation lasted from the 1930s to the end of the 1940s. In Britain, the lead was taken by Radcliffe-Brown and his students; in the USA, Benedict, Mead, Kroeber and others ensured the continuation of Boas' sprawling programme, while French anthropology was vigorous and creative in these otherwise grim decades.

As noted above, the new anthropology had a marginal identity from the outset. The founding fathers were themselves 'outsiders', and many of their successors ever since have been, like Radcliffe-Brown, nomadic, 'global scholars' who restlessly moved between universities and between homes and field sites. Surprisingly many were also personally marginal. Some were of foreign origin, like Malinowski and Boas – or Kroeber, Sapir and Lowie, who were also born in Germanic countries. Some came from the colonies, like Fortes, Gluckman and Schapera (from South Africa), Firth (from New Zealand) and Srinivas (from India). Many, like Mauss, Sapir or Alexander Goldenweiser, were Jewish. Several were women at a time when academic work was still a distinctly male domain – Mead and Benedict are well known, but Malinowski's students Audrey Richards (an important Africanist) and Hortense Powdermaker (author of a classic on field methods), belonged to the same generation.

Unlike nineteenth-century evolutionism, twentieth-century anthropology was also marginal in the sense that it placed 'dirty heathens' on an equal footing with middle-class Westerners. Malinowski's holistic field method, Boas's cultural relativism and Radcliffe-Brown's search for the universal laws of society suggested that all societies, or cultures, were of equal value. Studying 'from below' had already become the hallmark of anthropological fieldwork. As opposed to the other social sciences, which often worked with large groups and aggregate populations, anthropologists took the point of view of people on the ground, and were sceptical of decisions taken 'from above', by politicians and bureaucrats, who had no idea what life 'on the ground' actually was like. Nine out of ten anthropologists were, it seems, politically radical in one sense or the other. Even Mauss was an active socialist, though of a non-Marxist kind. Boas' sustained (and successful) attack on academic racism made him unpopular among politicians, and seems at one point to have led to the freezing of funds for new positions at Columbia (Silverman 1981: 161). His student Margaret Mead's books, comparing middle-class Americans to Pacific islanders, became bestsellers, and influenced American feminism and cultural radicalism deeply. And when Malinowski received standing ovations from packed auditoriums for his lectures about life in the Trobriand Islands during his 1926 tour through the USA, the message was clear: the potential of anthropology for cultural criticism and advocacy on behalf of native peoples was considerable.

It has been claimed that particularly British anthropologists submitted passively to the oppression of 'native peoples' in Africa, Asia and Oceania, and even that they actively cooperated with colonial administrations in return for research funds (see Asad 1973). In a scrupulously researched attempt to dig out the truth of this matter once and for all, Jack Goody (1995) concludes that the accusations are unfounded, and George Stocking (1995), a major historian of anthropology, supports his view, as does Kuper (1996). They point out that several leading social anthropologists were explicitly critical of colonialism. Goody further shows that the Colonial Office and the various colonial administrations neither funded nor in other ways encouraged anthropological research in particular areas or among particular groups. Goody points out that funding for fieldwork was as a rule obtained from American foundations. It is true that a handful of colonial administrators did get some training from Malinowski, Radcliffe-Brown and the Cambridge anthropologists, and a few scattered examples exist of research commissioned by the Colonial Office. On the whole, however, colonial administrators were indifferent towards anthropology, and vice versa (Stocking 1995: Ch. 8; Kuper 1996: Ch. 4).

Nevertheless, it may still be maintained that British anthropologists tended to pursue research interests that directly or indirectly legitimised the colonial project. The interest in political organisation in Africa, for example, seems a perfect match for the administrators of indirect rule (though again, there is little evidence of this research ever being taken seriously and put to use). The near-total absence of an interest in politics and economics among Boas' students may similarly reflect the fact that the original social organisation of the North American Indians had in most cases been lost; symbolic culture was all there was left for anthropologists to study. It has always been the case, and remains a fact that research agendas are constructed in particular historical contexts, and that they themselves bear the imprint of these contexts.

The marginal position of anthropology is perhaps quite easy to understand. The discipline recruited a particular kind of person, who could thrive on (or at least tolerate) long-term fieldwork under uncomfortable or unglamorous conditions. Ever since Malinowski's stay among the Trobrianders, this was the name of the game. Anthropology's subject matter was itself rather off the beaten track: kinship systems in Africa, exchange networks in Melanesia and North American ritual dances did not seem to belong within mainstream science.

With all these fragmenting and individualistic tendencies, it is in fact quite impressive that anthropology, in the course of the years we are now surveying, achieved an altogether respectable academic status. Charisma had been successfully routinised. In the following we shall turn to these processes as they unfolded in the main countries.

OXFORD AND THE LSE, COLUMBIA AND CHICAGO

In 1930, there was effectively only one academic centre of the new anthropology in Great Britain, at the London School of Economics, where Malinowski presided, under Seligman's benevolent gaze, from 1924 to 1938. At the LSE, Malinowski taught nearly the entire next generation of British anthropologists: Firth, Evans-Pritchard, Powdermaker, Richards, Schapera, Fortes, Leach and Nadel are some of the most famous names. The dependency on a single person naturally made the milieu vulnerable, but after Malinowski's departure for the USA, continuity was secured through Firth, a Malinowskian functionalist, who had been at the LSE since arriving there as a student in 1923. At Oxford, the old guard reigned until the mid-1930s, when Evans-Pritchard and later Radcliffe-Brown arrived to build up a haven of structural-functionalism here. At Cambridge, once a major powerhouse of anthropological scholarship in Britain, Haddon and Frazer presided until the Second World War, and anthropology was not revitalised until the appointments of Fortes and Leach in the 1950s.

In 1930, however, this was still in the future. Evans-Pritchard was on fieldwork in the Sudan, and would later take up a post in Sociology at the University of Cairo. Radcliffe-Brown was still in Sydney and would soon be on his way to Chicago, where he would spend six years. The most important institutional development in British anthropology in the early 1930s, was arguably the founding of the Rhodes-Livingstone Institute in Livingstone, Northern Rhodesia (now Zambia) by a group of young scholars under the leadership of Godfrey Wilson. Among the first research fellows was a South African, Max Gluckman (1911–75), who would in the coming decades direct a series of pioneering studies of social change in Southern Africa (Chapter 5).

Radcliffe-Brown's stay in Chicago in the 1930s was a fruitful one in the sense that it stimulated the formation of a group of non-Boasian anthropologists at an excellent American university. The department he worked in was a combined department of sociology and anthropology. Some of the sociologists there had used ethnographic methods in their studies of urban life, migration and ethnic relations. Radcliffe-Brown's sociologically inclined anthropology was met with great interest in this group, and he was a major source of inspiration for, among others, Robert Redfield, Sol Tax and Ralph Linton.

The undisputed centre of American anthropology was nevertheless still to be found in New York City, at Columbia University, where Boas reigned. In 1930, he had just finished training his second batch of students. Of the first group, who had taken their doctorates in 1901–11, the German Kroeber and the Austrian Lowie had left to establish the Department of Anthropology at Berkeley. Another, the Ukrainian Alexander Goldenweiser, had found employment at the New School of Social Research in New York. A fourth, the German-born Edward Sapir, had founded ethnolinguistics and become professor at Chicago – and a fifth, the Pole Paul Radin, moved from university to university and wrote innovative ethnographies (admired by Lévi-Strauss, among others) where the informants themselves were given space to express their views, thus anticipating the 'postmodern' movement in anthropology by half a century.

In contrast to this motley crew of European immigrants, Boas' second batch of students were born-and-bred Americans. The most influential of these were Ruth Benedict, Melville Herskovits and Margaret Mead.

In spite of this concentration of power in New York, the discipline was larger and more diverse in the USA than in Britain. The dominance of Columbia was far from complete, and, during the 1930s and 1940s, many influential anthropologists with no connection to Boas appeared in the country. Redfield (1897–1958) was one of them. His speciality was peasant studies, which he and his students pursued in Latin America, India and Eastern Europe. Another was Leslie A. White (1900–75), whose teachers included Sapir and Goldenweiser. White established himself at the University of Michigan in 1930, where he developed a materialist neo-evolutionist theory in direct opposition to Boas. Around the same time, the sociologist Talcott Parsons (1902–79) was employed at Harvard, where he would work for more than four decades on a grand synthesis drawing on both Weber and Durkheim, and which would eventually involve some prominent anthropologists as well. Linton (1893–1953), who had been educated at Harvard in the 1920s and who represented other refinements of the Boasian heritage than Benedict, came to Columbia as Professor in 1937. In the same year, George P. Murdock (1897–1985) began his *magnum opus* at Yale University: the *Human Relations Area Files* (HRAF), an enormous database of cultural traits worldwide, which has been both used and criticised by researchers for half a century.

As political conditions in Europe deteriorated and the Second World War approached, established European scholars appeared in the USA, and not just Jews from the German-speaking areas, although they were the most numerous group. One was Malinowski himself, who spent a few years at Yale before his death. Another was the British anthropologist Gregory Bateson (1904–80), who forged early links between structural-functionalism (which he criticised as early as in his first monograph in 1937), and the more psychologically oriented anthropology represented by Benedict and Mead (the latter, incidentally, became Bateson's first wife; he was her third husband). Yet another example was the Hungarian Karl Polanyi (1886–1964), who had been Professor of Economic History at Manchester before moving to New York in 1940. A few years later, Polanyi would be employed as an historian at Columbia, where he would inspire Julian Steward, a student of Kroeber and Lowie from Berkeley, who would later develop a materialist, historically oriented brand of neo-evolutionism at Boas' old department.

We shall eventually look at some of these developments in greater detail. First, however, it is necessary to take a look at twentieth-century French anthropology on the eve of its routinisation.

THE DAKAR–DJIBOUTI EXPEDITION

The intermediate generation of French anthropologists – younger than van Gennep and Mauss, but older than Lévi-Strauss and Dumont – are often neglected in Anglophone accounts of the history of anthropology. Indeed, one easily gets the impression that French anthropology passed through a time-warp between *The Gift* in 1923–4 to Lévi-Strauss's great book on kinship in 1949. In fact, French anthropology was thriving, and in many ways it was more playful and intellectually adventurous than its Anglo-Saxon counterparts. A major figure was Marcel Griaule (1898–1956), a student of Mauss and Professor of Anthropology at the Sorbonne from 1943. After a brief stint of fieldwork in Abyssinia (Ethiopia) in 1928, which resulted in a couple of books, Griaule was given the opportunity to lead a large, collective research project covering large areas of French Empire in Africa. In 1931, the French National Assembly had decided to fund an expedition from Dakar to Djibouti, with the aim of stimulating ethnographic research in the region as well as procuring objects for the ethnographic museum in Paris. The expedition, which lasted 22 months in 1931–3, involved several French anthropologists who would later make important contributions.

Early in the Dakar–Djibouti expedition, Griaule and his team visited the Dogon people in Mali, and this would be decisive for his later career. His later work consisted largely of detailed studies of this people, paying particular attention to their exceptionally complex cosmology (Griaule 1938, 1948). A number of other French anthropologists have also studied the Dogon, and as a result, they are one of the most intensively studied peoples in Africa. French field method, incidentally, differed from the ideals of participant observation that were promoted at the LSE and that were soon the accepted practice in both Britain and America. The French routinely employed native assistants and interpreters, and related to their informants in a more busi-nesslike way than the British and Americans, whose ideal was to participate as much as possible in daily life.

Anthropologists had started using film and photography in their analyses at a very early stage. Haddon and Boas were pioneers in the development of ethnographic film, and Mead and Bateson did a complex photographic study on Bali (Bateson and Mead 1942) in the 1930s. Griaule continued and expanded this tradition when he collaborated with the film-maker Jean Rouche during his work with the Dogon. Rouche became one of the founders of the *cinéma vérité* ('truth cinema') school in ethnographic film, a genre that integrates the anthropologist and the film crew into the film, in order to give a more objective depiction of the circumstances on the set.

Michel Leiris (1901–90) and Roger Caillois (1913–78) began their anthropological careers in the 1930s. Both had a marked influence on French intellectual life – though perhaps more so in the humanities than in the social sciences – but outside France their work is poorly known. Leiris and Caillois were familiar with Durkheim's and Mauss' sociology, but they also had close links with the philosopher Georges Bataille, and were considered part of the Surrealist movement in the arts. Caillois is famous for his studies of ritual, myth and the relationship between the sacred and the profane. He dealt with this Durkheimian topic through an analysis of taboos in societies divided into *moieties* (endogamous halves). After the Dakar–Djibouti expedition, Leiris, who was a novelist, poet and art critic as well as an anthropologist, published *L'Afrique fantôme* (1934; 'Invisible Africa'). This is a lively philosophical and ethnographic travelogue which offers a subjective description of a series of encounters with strange and marvellous realities. The author also reflects on the problems faced by ethnographers, when their work of cultural translation involves them in power-relations in the societies they study. *Invisible Africa*, like Radin's ethnographies, anticipates 'postmodernism' or 'the reflexive turn' in anthropology by half a century, and it places itself at one extreme of the discipline, with Radcliffe-Brown's 'natural science of society' at the other.

Somewhere between these two extremes, lies the work of the Protestant missionary Maurice Leenhardt (1878–1954). Leenhardt, a self-trained anthropologist, carried out one of the most thorough field studies in the history of the discipline, among the Kanak of New Caledonia, a French colony in Melanesia. Leenhardt stayed there from 1902 to 1926, and combined a successful career as a missionary with systematic field research and a passionate defence for Kanak culture in the context of imperialism. Back in France, Lévy-Bruhl and Mauss helped Leenhardt to find academic employment, and in 1941, he succeeded Mauss as Professor at the École Pratique des Hautes Études. Leenhardt's voluminous work on the Kanak, published in six volumes between 1932 and 1947 (Leenhardt 1937 was an early synthesis), is not only remarkable because of its ethnographic richness, but is also very sophisticated in its treatment of cultural translation in the context of imperialism, topics that reached mainstream Anglo-American anthropology only in the 1960s.

During the 1930s and 1940s, French anthropology developed in near complete isolation from the British and American traditions. But there were some cross-cutting ties, even then. Paul Rivet (1876–1958), a South

Americanist who pioneered Amazonian studies in French anthropology, spent the Second World War founding research institutes in Mexico and Colombia, where he cooperated with North American anthropologists. Alfred Métraux (1902–63), who had studied with Mauss, emigrated to the USA in the 1920s, where he made his name as one of the foremost specialists on South American Indians. He was a prominent contributor to the monumental *Handbook of South American Indians* (1946–50), that Julian Steward edited.

During the war there was also another young French anthropologist in South America, who served as Professor of Sociology at the University of São Paolo, and later spent most of the war familiarising himself with the major ethnographic works of the Boas school on North American Indians. Already in the first postwar years, Claude Lévi-Strauss would emerge as one of the most important figures in the history of anthropology (Chapter 6).

CULTURE AND PERSONALITY

While Boas had very wide-ranging interests, his students tended to specialise. Each followed up a part of the master's total project, and could therefore with equal legitimacy claim to be true Boasians. Yet it is often said that the direct line of succession goes from Boas to the *culture and personality* school of Ruth Benedict (1887–1948) and Margaret Mead (1901–78). Whatever the merits of such a view, it is at least the case that Benedict was associated with Boas institutionally, since she worked at Columbia all her life, and took over Boas's Chair there after his death. Mead also had her headquarters in New York. Like Boas, both women were highly visible public figures. The books they wrote were read by wider audiences than those of any previous anthropologist. Mead was also an avid lecturer to popular audiences, which increased her fame further. The reason for this wide appeal was in part that they were both good writers who wrote accessibly, in part that they had the ability to challenge the reader's cultural and personal identity through surprising contrasts and striking comparisons.

Like many of Boas' students, Benedict and Mead paid little attention to the political and economic aspects of the societies they studied, concentrating instead on the relationship between psychological factors (personality, emotions, 'character'), and cultural conditions, such as socialisation, gender roles and values. These questions were almost entirely absent from contemporary British anthropology. The fundamental problem addressed by Mead and Benedict was to what extent human mental characteristics are inborn, and to what extent acquired. Boas had argued that the sheer amount of cultural variation among humans is a strong indication that culture is not inborn, and Benedict and Mead were also consistently 'culturalist' in their orientation.

When Benedict argued that emotions and culture were connected, she was taking a fairly radical step. Culture was a shared, collective phenomenon, while emotions were assumed to be individual. It was commonly held, not least in British anthropology, that emotions had nothing to do with society at all (besides, they were vague, feminine and unscientific). Mead and Benedict nonetheless argued that patterns of emotion could also be shared, that they were also parts of culture. Although much of their work has later been subjected to severe criticism, there can be no doubt that they took the first effective steps towards establishing a psychological anthropology, which were later followed up by many (particularly American) anthropologists. So was their interest in child-rearing and socialisation, which was another non-subject for British anthropologists.

Benedict came from a solid middle-class background, and it was not until she had turned 30 that she took up anthropology, under the tutelage of Boas and Goldenweiser. She carried out some fieldwork among North American Indians (like most American anthropologists at the time), but her influence derives mainly from two books which are not ethnographic monographs, but large-scale comparisons: *Patterns of Culture* (1934), one of the most widely read books in anthropology, and *The Chrysanthemum and the Sword* (1946). In her comparative work, Benedict was in fact distancing herself from Boas, who distrusted broad comparisons. This does not mean, however, that she became any more acceptable for, say, Radcliffe-Brown, whose strict and systematic style of comparison was very different from the kind of broad, impressionistic comparisons that Benedict proposed.

In *Patterns of Culture*, Benedict developed the idea that culture may be analysed as a macropsychological pattern. Rather than cataloguing the substance of cultures, she sought to identify the configuration of its collective 'personality', the 'emotional style' or 'aesthetics' with which it permeated action, emotion and thought. Benedict referred to 'cultural personality' as *ethos*.

One of the main empirical contrasts in *Patterns of Culture* is between two Native North American tribes, the Zuni and the Kwakiutl. The Zuni had a strong sense of group solidarity, political leadership was non-authoritarian, rituals undramatic and child-rearing practices mild. The Kwakiutl, in contrast, were a people of excess and exaggeration – their famous *potlatch* institution, for example, to which both Boas and Mauss had devoted much attention, was an agressive, spectacular and boastful gift-giving competition. Benedict referred to the ethos of these ambitious, hedonistic individualists as *Dionysian*, while the peaceful Zuni were *Apollonian* (both concepts derived from Nietzsche, and ultimately from Greek mythology). Benedict also attempts to explain how an ethos relates to social practices and institutions, and in these passages she comes close to the holistic views of the structural-functionalists.

During the Second World War, Benedict was commissioned to write a report about Japanese national character. Unable to do fieldwork in Japan (and unable to read Japanese), she based her conclusions on existing literature, and wrote the bestseller *The Chrysanthemum and the Sword*, which is to this day quite well regarded among East Asianists. The book attempts to describe the ethos of Japanese culture, and posits a fundamental psychological tension in this culture, between brutal violence and tender aestheticism.

During the war, Mead pursued similar interests in a large-scale comparative project exploring the 'national character' of various countries. Mead held that nations developed 'personality types' – national ethoses, associated with particular attitudes, values and styles of behaviour. This notion was controversial in Mead's time, and is even more so today. Still, the idea of national character has never disappeared from anthropology, and it resurfaces in the new research on nationalism that commenced in the 1980s (see Chapter 8).

Mead's parents were both social scientists, and she grew up in a liberal, tolerant family of intellectuals, constantly moving from place to place. While Benedict was a shy and at times self-effacing personality, Mead was a self-assured young woman of 24 when she embarked on fieldwork to Samoa. Later, she did fieldwork in New Guinea and Bali. The photographic study from Bali, which Mead and Bateson conducted together (Bateson and Mead 1942), is an attempt to describe and analyse body-language. The authors assume that the 'collective emotions' of ethos would be expressed in this language, and that their study would add empirical substance to Benedict's (rather speculative) claims. In the late 1970s a similar idea was proposed (and backed up with far greater theoretical sophistication) by the French anthropologist Pierre Bourdieu, who referred to it as *habitus*.

Mead was an influential populariser and lecturer throughout her career. Her message to Western audiences was simple: if culture shapes personality, then it is possible to change personality by changing culture. In her first bestselling book, *Coming of Age in Samoa* (1928), she compared the 'free' style of socialisation in Samoa with the strict, authoritarian style of the American middle class, arguing that Samoan girls were freer and happier than their American counterparts. Along with *Growing up in New Guinea* (1930) and *Sex and Temperament in Three Primitive Societies* (1935), her Samoan book belongs, along with *The Golden Bough*, *Patterns of Culture* and Lévi-Strauss's *Tristes Tropiques* (1955), among the most influential and most widely read books ever produced by anthropologists.

As an anthropologist and a person, Mead was never uncontroversial. Like Marx, she was simultaneously a researcher and an activist, and these two strands of her life were inextricably intermeshed, which is one (but not the only) reason why her academic work has often been criticised. The comparison with Marx, far-fetched as it might seem, is not completely gratuitous. Mead was a guiding light of American feminism, and her ideas inspired American liberal opinion for several generations. Her influence on academic anthropology was less marked. Perhaps what she and Benedict will be remembered for, in the long run, is the effort they put in to establish psychological anthropology as a subdiscipline. Like Rivers before her, Benedict was too far ahead of her time to succeed in laying the theoretical groundwork for this venture. Unlike Rivers, however, Benedict and Mead did succeed in establishing a school of anthropological inquiry which eventually transmuted into several schools of symbolic and psychological anthropology.

Many of Mead's colleagues regarded her books as unscientific. She was criticised for making unwarranted inferences about mental states and generalising on the basis of inadequate data. Her British contemporaries were frankly shocked. Evans-Pritchard probably accurately echoed the Oxford pub-talk of the time when he described *Coming of Age in Samoa* as 'a discursive, or perhaps I should say chatty and feminine, book with a leaning towards the picturesque, what I call the rustling-of-the-wind-in-the-palm-trees kind of anthropological writing, for which Malinowski set the fashion' (Evans-Pritchard 1951b: 96). As the quote implies, Mead was in part criticised because she was an (extremely successful) woman. A more serious objection, with which we will deal more fully in Chapter 7, was that her fieldwork was superficial and her substantial conclusions misleading (cf. Freeman 1983; M.C. Bateson 1985).

Psychological anthropology was not only promoted by Benedict and Mead. Ralph Linton, one of the select group of American anthropologists who were not Boas's students, is best remembered today for his work in microsociology. Linton nevertheless also developed a form of psychological anthropology, in collaboration with psychoanalyst Abraham Kardiner. Linton and Kardiner rejected Benedict's idea that cultures are 'personalities writ large'. In *The Individual and His Society* (1949) they propose that specific socialisation and child-rearing practices generate personality problems that are expressed in the organisation of society, which, in turn, amplifies the original problems. Deeply critical of Radcliffe-Brown's teachings at Chicago, which he considered reductionist, Linton defended a wide definition of culture, in which psychology figured prominently.

CULTURAL HISTORY

Several of Boas's closest associates and students had other interests from those of Benedict and Mead. A prominent example was Kroeber, the son of an upper middle-class German Jewish family in New York, and Boas's first student. After founding one of the great American anthropology departments in 1901 and building up one of the world's leading ethnographic museums, Kroeber continued to work at the University of California at Berkeley until 1946. Like Boas, Kroeber was an anthropological jack of all trades, but his main interest was in cultural history, and he wrote several voluminous historical studies of European and non-European civilisations. Kroeber's long-time colleague at Berkeley, Lowie, shared this interest, but added a hint of materialist evolutionism to it, which would soon inspire their prominent student, Julian Steward, to more controversial conclusions.

In the course of his long academic career, Kroeber collected vast amounts of data about Native North Americans. His *Handbook of the Indians of California* (1925) is a 1,000-page ethnographic volume, and in his later work, *Cultural and Natural Areas of Native North America* (1939) he emphasises the importance of history to an understanding of the native cultures. Such concerns were naturally absent from British anthropology at the time. Kroeber had at an early stage declared his dissatisfaction with the trait-by-trait comparative method that the evolutionists had pioneered, and that was still in common use, particularly in German anthropology (but even Boas used it at times). Trait-by-trait comparison was a superficial approach. Cultures were organic wholes (in a nearly Durkheimian sense) that could not be disassembled into their component parts without losing their meaning. Kroeber referred to the cultural whole as the *superorganic*, an integrated system that was more than biological, yet seemed to have its own innate dynamics, almost to live its own life. Indeed, Kroeber is often considered an extreme methodological collectivist. Thus, in his article 'The superorganic' (1917, reprinted in Kroeber 1952), he points out that innovations are often made independently by different people in different locations. This, he argues, is evidence that cultures have their own, autonomous dynamics, independent of individuals.

Though Boas had argued along similar lines back in 1896, both he and several other close colleagues thought that Kroeber was going too far. Culture was not an object independent of human beings. It must not be *reified*. Kroeber must have taken this criticism seriously, since he suggested a compromise towards the end of his long career.

In the 1950s, Kroeber worked on several collaborative projects (with Parsons and others), and his last contribution to American anthropology was a large, interdisciplinary research programme, where anthropologists would study 'culture', while sociologists studied 'society'. This project included among its participants two young men, David Schneider and Clifford Geertz, who will be introduced more fully in Chapter 6.

ETHNOLINGUISTICS

Another branch on the Boasian trunk was the synthesis of linguistics and anthropology established by Edward Sapir. Sapir was yet another German-Jewish immigrant to the United States, though he arrived as a child. He studied several Native American languages, spent 15 years at the Canadian National Museum in Ottawa, and was in charge of the ethnographic collections at the University of Chicago. Then he moved to Yale University, where he founded and directed a new anthropological department until his premature death. Sapir is regarded as the father of modern ethnolinguistics, and his main work *Language* (1921) is still a standard work of anthropological linguistics.

With his student and later colleague, Benjamin Lee Whorf (1897–1941), Sapir developed the so-called Sapir–Whorf hypothesis about the relationship between language and culture. According to Sapir and Whorf, languages differed profoundly in their syntax, grammar and vocabulary, and these differences entailed profound differences in the language users' ways of perceiving and living in the world. Therefore, a Hopi speaker will perceive another world than an English-speaking European. Hopi language is poor in nouns and rich in verbs, and promotes a world-view rich in movement and process, but poor in things. European languages, in contrast, have more nouns and fewer verbs, which would bias them in favour of a world-view focusing on objects. The Sapir–Whorf hypothesis has received a lot of criticism up through the years, some of it reminiscent of the criticism of Lévy-Bruhl's 'primitive mentality'. Still, as Bateson has pointed out, the main problem may be that the hypothesis cannot – on some level or other – *not* be true. Obviously language influences thinking; the question is only to what extent and in what way that influence is expressed.

For many years, the study of language and culture remained a purely American specialisation, but since the war, and particularly since the 1980s, the field has expanded dramatically. The Sapir–Whorf hypothesis became an issue in British anthropology in the early 1960s, during the so-called Rationality Debate, when philosophers and anthropologists discussed the problems of intercultural translation (Chapter 6).

Sapir's view of culture differed from Kroeber's as well as Benedict and Mead's. Kroeber saw culture as a superorganism, almost with a life of its own. Mead and Benedict saw it as a shared pattern of values and practices, reproduced by socialisation. Sapir did not deny that culture leaves its imprint on values and world-views, but he regarded culture as less monolithic and integrated than did his contemporaries. Most ideas are contested, he noted, and culture may therefore be regarded as a basis for disagreement, rather than a consensus. What we call culture are underlying, taken-for-granted, rules that make disagreement possible. Years later, similar ideas played a prominent role in the great debates on culture theory that started in the 1970s and reached a (temporary) climax in the early 1990s. That Sapir was rarely cited in these discussions can only be understood as a serious case of collective memory loss.

THE CHICAGO SCHOOL

Even while Boas was still alive, a number of research projects had been established, which in one way or another continued his ideas. Some of these projects would in time diverge radically from Boas's own convictions – this was particularly true of the neo-evolutionist movement of the 1950s and 1960s. But even when the students disagreed with the master, his influence was still present, at least indirectly, in most of what they did. Boas's interest in cultural history, diffusion, langugage, symbols and psychology made American anthropology far more varied than the European traditions.

But as we have noted above, there were quite a few anthropologists in the USA whose intellectual lineage did not include Boas, and the group in Chicago, founded by Park and Thomas in the 1890s, was the prime example of this. The urgent challenge for the early Chicago sociologists was to understand ethnic relations (or 'race relations' as they were then called) in the seething cauldron of metropolitan Chicago, which received a great influx of immigrants – black people from the South, Jews, Irish, Scandinavians, Italians, Poles. Would the American *melting pot* dissolve the boundaries between these groups, or would they continue to exist as separate communities, even after they had been integrated in a common labour market? Retrospectively, this research seems to have been decades ahead of its time. It was urban anthropology at a time when anthropology was still synonymous with the study of small, preferably 'remote' communities; and it was ethnicity studies at a time when the term 'ethnicity' had not even been coined.

Apart from studies of local communities in the metropolis, the Chicago school is best known for its research on peasant societies in Latin America and Eastern Europe, and – somewhat later – in India. *Peasant studies* had its roots in previous studies of rural communities, by East European sociologists, historians and economists. One of the most famous of these was Alexander Chayanov (1888–*c*. 1938), who developed a theory of peasant economics around the time of the First World War. Chayanov, who died in one of Stalin's purges, was almost unknown in the West until the 1950s. In part of his theory he asks why it is so difficult to get peasants to produce for profit, and concludes that they have a marginal, subsistence economy, which makes them unwilling to take risks. Simple as it may seem, this formulation has had fundamental consequences for anthropological studies of underdevelopment. Another important East European, who directly influenced the Chicago school, was the Polish poet and rural sociologist Florian W. Znaniecki (1882–1958). Znaniecki and William Thomas, one of the founders of the department in Chicago, developed a close collaboration, and while Znaniecki was in Chicago, they finished their great cooperative effort, the monumental five-volume *The Polish Peasant in Europe and America* (1918–20) – arguably the mother of all peasant studies.

In 1934, the first of Thomas and Znaniecki's successors was already in place in Chicago, Robert Redfield (1897–1958). Redfield, who was virtually born and bred in the Chicago school, was first influenced by the Boas school during Sapir's stay in Chicago from 1925 to 1931, and later by Radcliffe-Brown. Redfield himself did fieldwork in Mexico, and directed several projects in Central America. Theoretically, his research concentrated on two questions: first, could peasant societies be said to have their own culture, or is their way of life simply a product of economic necessity? Redfield responded that peasants had cultures, just like anyone else, and he did not see their hybridised ways of life as any less authentic than other cultures.

Second, Redfield asked how data about local peasant life could be integrated with data about processes on the national, regional or global level. Since the term 'peasants', as used in anthropology, most often denotes communities of subsistence agriculturalists who are also marginal participants in non-local processes of politics and exchange, their communities cannot be studied as if they were isolated and self-sustaining. Redfield initially proposed to deal with this situation by means of a simple dichotomy between *folk culture* and *urban culture*, or 'little traditions' (local, orally transmitted) and 'great traditions' (non-local, literate). This classification was based on cultural criteria, and was hardly concerned with economic and political aspects of peasant life, a fact that was severely criticised by the more materialistically oriented students of peasant life who surfaced in the 1950s. In a famous controversy in American anthropology, Oscar Lewis undermined Redfield's conclusions, by performing a re-study of the Mexican village where he had conducted his fieldwork and arriving at very different conclusions (Redfield 1930; Lewis 1951).

Redfield would eventually modify his views, suggesting that folk and urban culture were not dichotomous opposites, but the extreme poles of a continuum that included middle-sized towns, and incorporating processes of migration and cultural modernisation (individualisation and secularisation) into his model. However, he was not willing to abandon his emphasis on symbolic culture, a view he shared with many other American anthropologists. In fact, Redfield's view of culture was not very different from Benedict's. He was concerned with showing how the peasant way of life created a particular 'cultural character' or ethos, not, for example, with unearthing the power structures that dominated peasant life.

The Chicago scholars defined a range of research issues that only entered mainstream anthropology many years later. During the interwar years, they were already studying ethnicity, urbanisation, peasant society and migration. Chicago was also the birthplace of a peculiar microsociological tradition that focused on detailed analyses of person-to-person interaction in limited, often short-term settings (for instance, within an institution). This approach, often referred to as *symbolic interactionism*, was developed by sociologists, two of whom would later exert considerable influence on anthropology. These were Erving Goffman (1922–82), known for his subtle studies of interaction ritual and his work on role play, which would soon become part of the anthropological mainstream; and Raymond Birdwhistell (1918–94), a pioneer in the study of cross-cultural communication and body language, who followed up Bateson and Mead's interest in these themes.

Why was the rest of the anthropological community so slow in taking up these new research interests? At one level, the answer is simple. Neither immigrants in Chicago, semi-urbanised Polish peasants nor the staff of a modern hospital could be said to have a 'true' culture, and they were therefore 'unsuitable' as objects of anthropological inquiry. Long after the majority of anthropologists had lost their interest in grand theories about the 'original state of man' (as in Rousseau or Morgan), the notion that some cultures were more 'authentic' than others lived on. African tribes and threatened American Indians were more attractive for anthropologists than the hybrid cultures created by modernisation. This preference was not explicit, and Radcliffe-Brown – for one – greatly admired the work of the Chicago school. But when all was said and done, the 'real primitives' carried greater professional prestige. And there were also good reasons for such priorities. 'Real primitives' were rapidly disappearing from the face of the earth, and it was a pressing task to document their way of life before it was too late. One may still sympathise with this motivation today, since all generalisations about the human condition are dependent on the widest possible range of comparative data.

'KINSHIPOLOGY'

Despite the breadth of American research, it is not primarily this that is most commonly associated with the anthropology of the 1930s and 1940s. Instead, we remember the great British structural-functionalists and their classical monographs, which not only stuck to 'real primitives', but described the structural principles underlying their lives in a manner that, in its formal elegance, was eminently 'civilised'. The authors of these studies were mostly former students of Malinowski, some of whom were closer to Radcliffe-Brown than others. Until the 1950s, a few of the most prominent men (none of the women) in this group were appointed to leading positions at prestigious British universities. Most, particularly Firth's and Malinowski's loyal students, had to wait until the next decade.

One of Malinowski's star students, who would later become the main advocate of Radcliffe-Brown's structural-functionalism, was Meyer Fortes (1906–83), a South African Jew, who was originally educated as a psychologist. Fortes' break with Malinowski in the 1930s was dramatic, and was not exclusively motivated by academic differences. For example, Malinowski apparently asked Fortes in 1934 to make a written statement where he confirmed that he had borrowed all his ideas from Malinowski himself (Goody 1995: 37). Whereas Firth, the mild-tempered New Zealander, reacted to Malinowski's outbursts with stoicism and a large pinch of salt, Fortes took them personally. At any rate, by the time of the publication of the seminal *African Political Systems* (Fortes and Evans-Pritchard 1940), it had become clear that Fortes' interests were far closer to Radcliffe-Brown's than to Malinowski's. His speciality was kinship, a topic Malinowski never wrote about in detail, although for years he had kept promising a book about kinship among the Trobriand islanders. In 1932, Fortes began his first major fieldwork in the Gold Coast (now Ghana), and in the 1940s and 1950s he would publish widely on two of the largest and socially most complex peoples in this country, the Ashanti and the Tallensi. His *The Dynamics of Clanship among the Tallensi* (1945) is considered one of the high points of structural-functionalism. It was largely due to Fortes' efforts that the British anthropology of the period was often spoken of disparagingly as 'kinshipology'. Many, not least among the Americans, felt that all the attention accorded to kinship betrayed the holistic ambitions of the discipline.

The high point of structural-functionalism may be located to the years 1947–9, when Radcliffe-Brown, Fortes, Gluckman and Evans-Pritchard were all gathered at Oxford. Radcliffe-Brown had seen kinship as the engine driving primitive society, the glue that held it together and the moral universe in which it lived. This view was confirmed and strengthened through Fortes' studies, which – while based on massive ethnography – focused on 'mechanisms' and structural principles. His close professional ally and friend, Evans-Pritchard, shared Fortes' commitment to structural-functionalist kinship studies in the first half of his career, but struck off in a different direction during the 1950s (Chapters 5–6). Like most British anthropologists of his generation, Evans-Pritchard had studied with Malinowski at the LSE, but his teachers also included Marett of the Torres expedition and, more importantly, the Sudan specialist Charles Seligman. It was under Seligman's supervision that Evans-Pritchard carried out his field studies in the Sudan during the 1930s, mainly among the Azande and the Nuer. Evans-Pritchard and Malinowski were never close. Malinowski revelled in poetic, detailed and evocative descriptions of Trobriand life, while Evans-Pritchard had a passion for social theory and preferred sharp, elegant and logically coherent intellectual analysis. Besides, Evans-Pritchard was an exception to the rule that the early anthropologists were 'outsiders'. This 'very English Englishman, despite his Welsh name', as Leach (1984) describes him, indeed seemed to personify the British upper classes, from which Malinowski, as a foreigner, was forever barred.

Back in 1931, Evans-Pritchard had been duly impressed by Radcliffe-Brown, who stopped briefly in Britain *en route* from Sydney to Chicago. However, he was never a mere student of the Durkheimian master. When Radcliffe-Brown returned to Oxford in 1937, Evans-Pritchard already held a post there, and had not only spent years on fieldwork in the Sudan, but had worked for three years as a Professor of Sociology in Cairo. His first book, *Witchcraft, Oracles and Magic among the Azande* (1937), was published in the year of Radcliffe-Brown's return, and was immediately recognised as a masterpiece. The monograph deals with the witchcraft beliefs of an agricultural people in southern Sudan, and the thrust of its analysis, one of the most celebrated and much-discussed in anthropology, is two-pronged: on the one hand, it understands witchcraft as a 'safety valve' that redirects social conflicts into harmless channels, an integrating device in the best Durkheimian tradition; on the other hand, it is a bold attempt to make sense of an alien world of thought, presented in its own terms. What is remarkable is the way it knits these two approaches together into a seamless whole. The belief system not only stabilises and harmonises the existing social order, but is rational and consistent, given the logical presuppositions of Zande thought. Evans-Pritchard emphasises the prosaic, self-evident and practical side of these beliefs. Thought and faith are not abstract processes, outside the concrete events of everyday life, but an inseparable part of these events. Some commentators (notably Winch 1958) have made much of the structural-functionalist dimension of Evans-Pritchard's work, arguing that he reduces witchcraft beliefs to their 'social functions'. Others (such as Douglas 1980, but also Feyerabend 1975) have emphasised the very opposite, that Evans-Pritchard demonstrates that knowledge or belief are social products *anywhere*.

Evans-Pritchard's second major work appeared in 1940, the same year as the publication of the volume on African political systems that he edited with Fortes. *The Nuer*, a study of the political organisation of a patrilineal pastoralist people living just north of the Azande, is written more in the spirit of Radcliffe-Brown. The book sets out to address a central problem in the anthropology of *acephalous* ('stateless') peoples, namely how large-scale political mobilisation can occur in the absence of centralised leadership. The book, which vividly evokes the life-world of the Nuer, is also a *tour de force* of 'kinshipology'. Conflicts are organised along kinship lines. The principle of *segmentary organisation* – 'it is me against my brother, me and my brother against our cousins, brothers and cousins against third cousins', and so on – loomed large in this analysis, which also demonstrated the conflict-damping influence of relationships (such as marriages) that cross-cut the patrilineal system – an aspect later developed more explicitly by Gluckman (1956). In the final chapter, Evans-Pritchard elaborates his view of social structure, which he defines roughly along the same lines as Radcliffe-Brown, as an abstract system of social relationships which continues to exist unchanged in spite of changes of personnel. The continuity from the Azande monograph is also noticeable. Evans-Pritchard thought of kinship and witchcraft as two examples of 'modes of thought', and in both cases he is concerned to show how thinking is related to what Pierre Bourdieu (1990) would later call 'the logic of practice'.

Fortes' and Evans-Pritchard's monographs on the Tallensi, the Ashanti, the Azande and the Nuer, were, after Seligman's pioneering work, crucial in transferring the regional focus of British social anthropology from the Pacific to Africa, but it should be kept in mind that other important anthropologists also worked in Africa at the time – Richards among the Bemba, Schapera among the Tswana, Gluckman among the Zulu, Forde among the Yakö. *African Political Systems*, which included contributions from about a dozen British anthropologists, was a powerful demonstration of this new regional emphasis. In their much-quoted introduction, the editors distinguished three types of African societies: egalitarian, small-scale societies (largely hunters and gatherers), state societies (such as the Buganda kingdom) and the interesting, intermediate type, the lineage-based segmentary society, of which the Nuer became the paragon, which is decentralised, but able to form large, cooperative groups for specific purposes (such as war). As we shall see, the segmentary society preoccupied anthropologists for decades, and not only in Britain (see, for example, Sahlins 1968). During the great debates on kinship the 1950s and 1960s, the model presented in *African Political Systems* was subjected to criticism from many quarters. Some felt that it was simply too neat to fit the complexities of real life. Others disparaged it as evolutionism in disguise. Yet others (most prominently Lévi-Strauss) rejected its exclusive focus on *descent* as a principle of kinship.

FUNCTIONALISM'S LAST STAND

In 1930, the undisputed centre of British anthropology had been at the LSE, with Malinowski and his many gifted students. In 1940, Oxford had become a Radcliffe-Brownian preserve, and was rapidly moving towards hegemony. By 1950, Radcliffe-Brownians had secured jobs at Cambridge, Manchester and University College London, and the Malinowskians seem to have lost the competition for academic control. In many ways, the changing roles of these two men reflected their intellectual profiles and personalities. Malinowski was a charismatic leader (to use Weber's term) who, despite his unpredictable temper, kept his students on a long leash (Firth 1957). Radcliffe-Brown was an institution builder, who seemed to be following a long-term master plan, as he doggedly built up structural-functionalist enclaves at universities on four continents before returning to Britain in the late 1930s.

It was above all Firth at the LSE who secured the direct continuity of the Malinowskian programme. After initial work on the Maori of his native New Zealand, he had arrived in London to study economics, but transferred to anthropology after attending Malinowski's very first seminar (Stocking 1995: 407). He did pioneering work in economic anthropology, which would later have considerable influence. But in spite of his theoretical contributions (Chapter 5), Firth was (and *is* – at the time of writing, he is 100 and still active) first of all an empirical researcher. Like his mentor, he regarded interaction and the ongoing flow of social life as more fascinating (and more 'real') than abstract structures. He has published eleven books about the Tikopians, the inhabitants of a Polynesian island where he carried out long-term fieldwork on three occasions. His most famous monograph, *We, The Tikopia* (1936) is a 600-page volume which typifies both the strengths and the weaknesses of Malinowskian anthropology. Structural-functionalists were full of disdain for Firth's allegedly wishy-washy, all-inclusive account, which made no attempt to develop elegant models or even to accord some institutions priority over others. However, the book's long, detailed ethnographic descriptions documented the staggering complexity of 'primitive' life far better than the stringent structural-functionalist accounts.

Firth's monographs are typical Malinowskian studies, along with Reo Fortune's *Sorcerers of Dobu* (1932), Isaac Schapera's books from Bechuana-land (Botswana) and Audrey Richards' work from Northern Rhodesia (Zambia). These works all assumed that society was an integrated, functional system, but rarely specified the mechanisms of its integration. Here, the emergent Oxford anthropology appeared more polished, more scientific, more coherent and in every way superior. However, the last word had not yet been said: Firth, like Malinowski, was a methodological individualist, who focused on the daily life of living people, rather than on the abstract, juridical (Radcliffe-Brown) or logical (Evans-Pritchard) principles that (presumably) governed it. It is the ever-changing, tactical play among individual actors that is Firth's main concern, and this made him popular as a kind of ancestor figure for the entire generation of methodological individualists that came to the fore in 1950s and 1960s.

SOME BRITISH OUTSIDERS

British anthropology was small, elitist, closed and full of conflicts. Yet, in the course of a few years, it produced some of anthropology's greatest classics. But the milieu was indeed closed, and tended to marginalise anyone who did not belong to either the structural-functionalist or the functionalist camp. A good example is A.M. Hocart (1884–1939), whose work on Pacific societies in the interwar years, influential at the time, was later forgotten, but has occasionally been rediscovered in more recent years. Hocart carried out research in the Pacific in 1909–14, primarily in Fiji, but also in Tonga and Samoa. Hocart's concerns were both historical and subtly structural, and he was far removed from both Malinowski's brisk pragmatism and Radcliffe-Brown's search for simple 'laws' and 'mechanisms'. His chief interest lay in ritual and social hierarchies, and he developed a comparative method that has more in common with French anthropology from Mauss to Lévi-Strauss than with his British contemporaries. Indeed, his innovative book on caste (Hocart 1938) was published in a French translation before it appeared in English, and is more often cited in French than in Anglophone literature. Hocart never found academic employment in Britain, but succeeded Evans-Pritchard as Professor of Sociology in Cairo in 1934, where he remained until his early death.

Other outsiders include the Austrian Siegfried Nadel (1903–56), a skilled musician and Africanist, and a pioneer of psychological anthropology in Britain, who ended as professor at the Australian National University in Canberra. Another was Daryll Forde (1902–73), who was even more marginal than Nadel, having studied archaeology in Britain and later cultural anthropology with Kroeber and Lowie at Berkeley. Returning to

Britain with an unfashionable penchant for ecological studies, he nevertheless found a powerful ally in Evans-Pritchard, and was appointed as Chair
at University College, London, in 1945.

The most interesting of the young British outsiders in the interwar years,
however, was Gregory Bateson (1904–80). Bateson came from an academic,
upper middle-class family. His father, the famous biologist William Bateson,
had named his son after Gregor Mendel, the founder of genetics. Bateson was
studying to become a biologist, when Haddon, during a conversation on a
train bound for Cambridge, converted him to anthropology (Lipset 1982:
114), and he soon embarked on fieldwork in New Guinea. After a rather
unsuccessful attempt at fieldwork among the Baining, Bateson studied the
Iatmul, a lowland people whose *naven* ritual formed the backbone of
Bateson's first (and only) ethnographic monograph, *Naven* (1936).

While in New Guinea, apparently in a canoe on the Sepik river, Bateson
met Reo Fortune and his wife, Margaret Mead, who were doing fieldwork in
the same area. The description of this meeting has become a classic in the
history of anthropology. The encounter was intense in every way. The three
discussed anthropology and life in general, argued about the differences
between the peoples they were studying, and fearlessly analysed their own
personal relationships. When the dust settled, Fortune and Mead were
divorced, while Bateson married Mead and subsequently moved to the United
States in 1939.

The meeting between Mead and Bateson highlights the relationship
between British and American anthropology in these years. Bateson's
admiration for Radcliffe-Brown's elegant intellectualism was challenged by
Benedict's insight into psychology and emotions. What was the proper role
of the anthropologist – to uncover general sociological principles, or to
describe the subtleties of human communication? Did the one exclude the
other? Or did there exist a common language that could encompass both?
Bateson's monograph is an expression of these dilemmas. In the *naven* ritual,
Iatmul men dress like women and mimic homosexual desire for their young
nephews. Bateson approached this ritual from three distinct analytical perspectives. The first was 'sociological and structural', inspired by
Radcliffe-Brown. The second he called 'eidos' (a culture's cognitive and intellectual style), and the third 'ethos' (from Benedict). He found it very difficult
to reconcile, not to say synthesise, these three approaches, and eventually
abandoned the effort. *Naven*, as it was originally published in 1936, thus
stands as an unsolved riddle. Only in 1958 did the book come in a second
edition, with a long appendix, where Bateson tried to tie the disparate
strands together.

Bateson's monograph was an ambiguous work that had little impact on
contemporary anthropology. His British contemporaries did not know what
to make of it (Kuper 1996), but its prestige has increased as it has become
clear that it anticipated several of the changes that have occurred in the
discipline since the 1950s. Thus, Bateson is critical of the idea of 'function',

which, in his view, is teleological (it implies that the effect precedes the cause). Functionalist explanations should always be examined closely, to see whether they in fact specify all the links by which the 'purposes' and 'needs' of the whole are communicated to the individual actor. This will lead us to focus on process and communication rather than function and structure.

Bateson was an exceptional intellectual who still elicits admiring commentaries, some of them book-length (such as Harries-Jones 1995). After the war, his concern with communication and process would bring him into contact with brilliant scholars in many fields: psychiatrists, psychologists, ethologists, mathematicians, ecologists, biologists, etc. He soon became an interdisciplinary figure, who made significant contributions to subjects such as psychology and communications theory (see Bateson 1972), and pioneered the use of cybernetic models in anthropological explanation. Even before the Second World War, his 'photographic fieldwork' with Mead on Bali indicated his willingness to explore the limits of anthropology. During the war, Bateson contributed to Mead's studies of 'national character' and worked on a theory of communication that has influenced many, both anthropologists and others (Chapter 6).

It seems appropriate to end this chapter with Gregory Bateson's early career. Seen as an iconoclast and an eccentric throughout his life, Bateson's first attempt at theoretical synthesis consisted in bridging the gap between interwar American and British anthropology. He himself regarded it as a failure. This should remind us that the gulf between the two traditions was very real. While Americans steeped in Boasian cultural anthropology studied symbolic meaning, 'cultural patterns' and the relationship between language and society, the Britons zoomed in on social life, status relationships, kinship systems and, increasingly, politics. Dominant tendencies in French anthropology followed a third path, to which we shall return in Chapter 6. Although every self-respecting historian of anthropology will claim that anthropology was, after all, one discipline, the Atlantic, and even the English Channel, were effective lines of demarcation in 1945. Moreover, although it would be simplistic to claim that these boundaries remained intact during the second half of the twentieth century, it would be naive to think that they had simply disappeared. The three national traditions continue to mark anthropology to this day.

In the next two chapters, the basic chronological structure of this book will be temporarily upset. Both chapters deal with the 20-odd years between the end of the Second World War and the new radical movements that caught on in the late 1960s. While Chapter 5 presents the mounting critique of structural-functionalism and some new alternatives, Chapter 6 shows how the power of symbols and rituals was understood by anthropologists on both sides of the Atlantic, often bridging old gaps and creating new ones in the process.

5 FORMS OF CHANGE

1946: the guns are silent, the bombers grounded. Millions of refugees pick their way through Germany's ruined cities, across the scorched earth of Russia, Poland and the Ukraine. France and Britain have been deeply shaken, and their great empires will soon be only a memory. As a contrast, the American economy is just settling down into superpower gear, wheeling out an ever-increasing plenitude of pink Cadillacs, TV sets, rock'n'roll stars and nuclear weaponry. Not far away – as an ABM flies – the Soviet Union will compete successfully with 'the free world' in the production of military hardware, while the production of Cadillacs (pink or otherwise) lags ever further behind. McCarthy looks for communist spies; Beria looks for capitalist spies. The atmosphere is tense, as people peer into an unprecedented future, which, against the background of the horrors of the recent past, seems to beckon towards progress and Formica kitchens, or threaten global annihilation.

Not only in the economy, but in most of the sciences as well – including anthropology – the USA was becoming the leading superpower, with more academics, larger research funds, more journals and conferences than anywhere else. In the 1950s, academics in countries like Norway or Denmark, who had hitherto published in German to reach an international audience, found it opportune to switch to English.

The racist views of Nazism had been politically discredited, and many felt that it was about time to abandon the concept of race in science as well. Many, but not all, geneticists and biologists agreed that racial differences were not deep enough to account for cultural variation. Virtually all social and cultural anthropologists held this view, and indeed, their discipline rested on the assumption of the 'psychic unity of mankind' that the evolutionists had first championed. When international anti-racist proclamations eventually came to be written and signed, it seemed natural to involve anthropologists in the paperwork. In this way, a British emigré to the USA, Ashley Montagu (1905–99), who held a Ph.D. from Boas's university, Columbia, became the secretary at a UNESCO conference about race in 1950. The resulting document, 'Statement on Race', in no uncertain terms proclaimed that biological factors were of negligible importance in shaping human personality. Thus, the cultural relativist perspective favouring nurture over nature was shared by most anthropologists on both sides of the

Atlantic, and became politically influential after the war, not least in the UN and its organisations.

The winds of change were emphatically universalist; they proclaimed the unity of mankind and equal human rights. To the extent that anthropologists related to this ideological tendency – and many did – they were ambivalent. On the one hand, the culturalist, anti-racist views promoted by Montagu in a series of popular and influential books were by and large seen as uncontroversial, even trivial. Most anthropologists were probably also in favour of decolonisation, which was clearly also a universalist project. On the other hand, anthropologists steeped in cultural relativism found it difficult to swallow the unwarranted missionary zeal seemingly inherent in the new, universalist human rights rhetoric, whether it emanated from anti-colonial movements, the US State Department or the United Nations. In 1947, the AAA (American Anthropological Association) made a lengthy statement, published in *American Anthropologist* and written mainly by Melville Herskovits, which amounted to a warning against the cultural imperialism ostensibly inherent in the incipient Universal Declaration of Human Rights (AAA 1947). This statement indicates the extremely strong position of the Boasian programme in American anthropology at the time (see R. Wilson 1997).

Not long after the war, however, a powerful alternative to Boasian cultural relativism and the accompanying view that culture was *sui generis* – its own creator – would be developed. Its obvious debt to Marx was rarely acknowledged openly, since being a Marxist in post-war USA was not an option for an academic who wanted tenure and research grants. Instead, its originators tended to look to Morgan as a founding father.

The year 1946 may be seen as a gateway to the lively, expansive period that anthropology now entered. It was the year when the British formed the Association of Social Anthropologists (ASA), the year when Evans-Pritchard succeeded Radcliffe-Brown at Oxford and Kroeber withdrew from Berkeley after having taught there for 45 years, and the year in which Julian Steward began to teach at Boas's old department at Columbia. Although 'the revolution' in the discipline was over, routinisation was perhaps also over, and change was again in the air. In the space of a few years, Steward's neo-evolutionist programme would challenge Boasianism on its home turf, Evans-Pritchard would repudiate structural-functionalism, Gluckman would become Professor at the newly formed Manchester department which later became known both for its political radicalism and its interest in the dynamics of change (a topic rarely addressed in structural-functionalism), and Lévi-Strauss's monumental book on kinship, published in 1949, would change the anthropological discourse on its favourite institution forever.

Although anthropology branched off in many directions in the decades following the war, it also became more tightly integrated than before, thanks to the continuation – and internationalisation – of core debates. Differences remained, but mutual knowledge across national boundaries also became more widespread. The annual meetings of the AAA gradually turned into global meetings, and familiarity with each others' journals was eventually taken for granted.

It would be futile to impose a simple linear narrative upon the complexities of the two decades following the war. It was a period when the New Guinean highlands replaced Africa as the most fashionable place to go for young fieldworkers, when the Caribbean and Latin America came into their own as ethnographic regions, when structuralism became a power to reckon with, interpretive anthropology made its breakthrough, and when new forms of symbolic, political and economic analysis were developed.

In this book, we have tried to resolve this mounting problem by splitting the 1950s and 1960s into two parts. The present, and longest, chapter deals with theories and perspectives that focus on the field of social life – the sphere of practical social organisation and interaction, of politics and economics. The next chapter will deal with theories of symbolic communication and meaning. While this distinction reproduces a debatable dichotomy between society and culture, it also highlights divergences and confluences among the evolving national traditions. American anthropology, which for a while was nearly synonymous with Benedict–Meadean studies of 'culture', sprang from an original holistic impulse, from a Tylor-esque definition of 'culture', in which social organisation naturally played a considerable role. Now, this aspect re-emerged with the new materialists. French anthropology, which Durkheim had defined in a wide, sociological sense, had, through Mauss, arrived at the fascinating problem of exchange. Exchange, usually thought of in economic terms, can – *pace* Mauss – be redefined as communication. Enter Lévi-Strauss, and the focus of the discipline moves from sociology to semiotics. Finally, the British, who clung to the sociological definition of their subject more stubbornly, once again imported a French theory, as they had done before with Durkheim. There is continuity and change in these movements. The distinctions between the national traditions begin to blur, but they are not erased.

NEO-EVOLUTIONISM AND CULTURAL ECOLOGY

Although the emergent materialist school in American anthropology was explicit in its anti-Boasianism, several of Boas's own collaborators and students were closer to the new thoughts than it might seem. At Berkeley, Kroeber was at least non-committal, and his colleague, Lowie, could even express sympathy for the evolutionist project, though his most famous book, *Primitive Society* (1920), contains a scathing critique of Morgan's *Ancient Society*. Like Boas himself, Lowie was primarily a cautious, empirically oriented scientist with an overwhelming respect for the facts. He was also a learned cultural historian, who rejected Benedict's ideas of 'national character' as vague and speculative, and regarded diffusionism as a more attractive explanation of cultural change than evolutionism, since its assumptions were simpler and easier to test against fact. But Lowie did not reject evolutionism completely. Although he declined to generalise on the subject, he appears to have accepted that cultures, in some cases, evolve along the same general lines, a view opposed to Boas's historical particularism. Lowie was also the first to use the term *multilinear evolution*, a concept commonly attributed to his student Julian Steward. Contrasting it with the *unilinear evolution* typical of nineteenth-century anthropology, Lowie held that evolution might proceed along different paths. Between these paths there were certain rough similarities, but also considerable variations. When Steward later embarked on his project of modernising evolutionism, he could thus draw on his teacher for inspiration and – at least tacit – support.

As Jerry Moore (1997: 166) points out, historical and evolutionist perspectives were more easily accepted in the USA than in Britain, where social anthropology by now had come to mean synchronous studies exclusively. Social change was not a concern either there or in France, where it would enter anthropology only in the 1960s through the work of Africanist Georges Balandier and his students. With the exception of Daryll Forde's work on the Yakö and a single, brilliant chapter in *The Nuer*, ecology was also practically absent from British anthropology – it would make a hesitant appearance only in the 1980s.

When neo-evolutionism came to the fore in the USA of the 1950s, this was largely due to the work of two men: Steward and Leslie White. Unlike most of his contemporaries, Leslie White (1900–75), who taught for 40 years at the University of Michigan (1930–70), rejected the cultural relativist idea that cultures should not be 'ranked' on a developmental scale, though he also emphatically rejected the moral connotations that the Victorian evolutionists had associated with such rankings. White was interested in discovering general laws of cultural evolution. Like Malinowski, he held a functionalist view of culture but, as he saw it, the function of culture was not to secure individual need satisfaction, but to ensure the survival of the group. His project thus had certain similarities to Radcliffe-Brown's programme, but White did not believe in the Durkheimian tenet that societies were autonomous entities with their own, self-sufficent dynamics. Societies were tightly integrated with their ecological surroundings. White distinguished between technological, social and ideological aspects of culture (he was later to add 'emotional or attitudinal aspects' – a nod in Benedict's direction). The technological dimension was crucial; in fact, he argued that it *determined* the social and ideological aspects of social life (White 1949).

The originality of White's theory was modest, although his single-minded technological determinism was often expressed in original ways, as when, in *The Science of Culture* (1949), he defined the level of cultural development as the amount of energy harnessed by each inhabitant, measured through production and consumption. Such quantitative ambitions had been absent in nineteenth-century evolutionism, but would soon become prominent among the new American materialists.

White's views met with considerable resistance. More than once, he was identified as a possible Communist in the paranoid McCarthy era of the 1950s. Among established cultural anthropologists, White's ambition to turn anthropology into an accurate science of cultural evolution and the socio-cultural effects of technology, was regarded as impertinent and irrelevant. Nevertheless, White developed an excellent department at Michigan, and his students include luminaries like Marshall Sahlins (who later studied at Columbia), one of the great figures of late twentieth-century American anthropology.

Lowie, the crypto-evolutionist, had strong reservations about White's technological determinism, but encouraged Steward to pursue a version of materialist evolutionism which, though less deterministic, had much in common with White's. Steward himself, after completing his Ph.D. at Berkeley – a standard Native American study in the culture-and-personality style – worked as an archaeologist for years, before transferring to Washington, DC, where he directed the Institute of Social Anthropology at the prestigious Smithsonian Institution and edited the seven-volume *Handbook of South American Indians*. Steward refined his theoretical approach during the 1930s and 1940s, and when he arrived at Columbia University in 1946, he brought along a mature theory, which provoked his colleagues and inspired his students. During his six-year stay at Columbia (which coincided nearly exactly with Karl Polanyi's years there, see p. 83), Steward supervised a truly impressive group of graduate students, who were soon to put the indelible mark of their new materialism on American anthropology. Elman R. Service, Stanley Diamond, Morton H. Fried, Eric R. Wolf, Sidney W. Mintz, Eleanor B. Leacock, Marvin Harris, Robert F. Murphy, Marshall Sahlins, Andrew P. Vayda, Roy A. Rappaport and others, all studied under Steward (or under his successor, Morton Fried) and several of them participated in his projects.

Steward was dissatisfied with the lack of theoretical ambition among Boas's supporters, and, like White, saw a key for generalisation in the study of technology and ecological conditions. Like Lowie, however, he was unenthusiastic about theories of unilinear cultural evolution. Furthermore, where White distinguished three cultural subsystems, Steward opposed the cultural 'core' to 'the rest of culture'. The core consisted of technology and the division of labour – which corresponds exactly to Marx's definition of infrastructure, an influence that Steward, like White, did not advertise. It would be his and White's students who finally made the link with Marxism explicit.

Steward's influence may have been even more powerful in archaeology than in anthropology, but at least three of his contributions have had a lasting impact, particularly on American anthropology. First, Steward founded modern *cultural ecology*. Though White, too, included environmental factors in his explanations, Steward regarded the totality of a society and its biological surroundings in roughly the same way as an ecologist regards an ecosystem. He saw society largely through the eyes of an ecologist. *Adaptation* was a core concept with Steward, who searched for institutions that concretely furthered a culture's survival in a given ecosystem. Some of these institutions were strongly determined by ecology, technology and population density; others were relatively unaffected by material conditions.

Second, Steward developed a theory of *multilinear evolution*, based on archaeological, historical and ethnographic evidence. Under particular conditions, such as irrigation agriculture in arid regions, he held that the cultural core would develop along roughly the same lines in different societies. By limiting his generalisations to a few important aspects of the cultures he studied and restricting the scope of his theory to societies with comparable natural preconditions, he succeeded in building up an evolutionism that did not lead to speculative generalisations that could easily be falsified. Neither Steward nor White regarded all aspects of the superstructure or symbolic realm as materially determined, unlike some of their predecessors as well as successors, Marxist and non-Marxist alike.

Third, Steward was, along with Redfield (whose orientation was definitely non-materialist) an important pioneer in *peasant studies*. Peasants (defined as subsistence farmers in complex societies who are partly integrated into a non-local economy) make up the largest population category in the world. The total lack of interest in them in pre-war anthropology confirms that the discipline was still hunting for the exotic, often at the expense of the typical. Steward's peasant research reached a high point during the large-scale Puerto Rico project he organised in the late 1940s. The project was one of the first area studies in anthropology, and was unique at the time for its integration of local and regional analysis. Here, for just about the first time in modern anthropology, the nation state and the world market figure actively in the analysis. Steward's students would continue and refine Steward's interest in peasant societies in the coming decades, and make decisive contributions in turning mainstream anthropological attention towards the Caribbean and Latin America in the 1960s and 1970s.

The most important result of White's and Steward's theoretical efforts was not their evolutionism, but their interest in the relationship between society and ecosystem. The emerging school of cultural ecology has often been described as just another form of functionalism, where the ecosystem replaces the social whole as the prime functional imperative. But this critique is only partly justified. The cultural ecologists were interested in cultural change, and, with the passage of time, developed a more sophisticated model of society than their British predecessors. In this, they were assisted by the great advances made in (biological) ecology during the 1950s, particularly as a result of the application of cybernetic models to problems of adaptation. In the 1960s, cultural ecology would prove a diverse source of inspiration among anthropologists. Gregory Bateson drew on models and ideas from cultural ecology in his contributions to general systems theory. Clifford Geertz – later known for his interpretive work on symbolism – published *Agricultural Involution* in 1963, a book on Javanese land tenure strongly influenced by Steward. Marshall Sahlins, who would also later move towards symbolic anthropology, began his career with several books which elaborated Steward's (and White's) interests, and, in a famous article about political leadership in the Pacific, he saw the contrast between Melanesian big-men and Polynesian chiefs in an evolutionist light, drawing on an analysis of household economy in accounting for political variations. The most consistent (and persistent) of Steward's and White's successors was Marvin Harris who, during the 1960s, developed his own brand of materialist evolutionism, which he referred to as cultural materialism (Harris 1979).

The high point of cultural ecology was, perhaps, Roy Rappaport's monograph *Pigs for the Ancestors* (1967), which quickly became a classic. Rappaport, a student of Fried's at Columbia and a friend and associate of Bateson's, carried out fieldwork among the Tsembaga Maring of the New Guinean highlands in the early 1960s. He was particularly concerned with understanding a complex ritual cycle, which involved both warfare and mass slaughter of domesticated pigs. Applying a cybernetically inspired ecological analysis to the ritual, he demonstrates the intimate connections between Tsembaga adaptation to their surroundings (nature, but also neighbouring human groups) and their world-view. Starting with the White-inspired premise that the availability of energy sources determines cultural adaptation, he ends with a subtle (and non-deterministic) analysis of the aesthetic language through which the Tsembaga conceptualise the world in which they live. Critics saw this analysis as a kind of ecological structural-functionalism which left little place for people's own motivations and independent cultural dynamics, and to which Rappaport responded in a long postscript to the 1984 edition of the book.

Another high point of cultural ecology, which was also a manifestation of its great breadth and scope, was the 'Man the Hunter' symposium organised at the University of Chicago in 1966 (Lee and DeVore 1968). Concentrating chiefly on contemporary hunters and gatherers, most of the contributors, largely American cultural anthropologists, saw culture chiefly in terms of ecological adaptation. They argued that since hunting was the original livelihood of humanity, any general theory of society and the nature of Man, would presuppose a close knowledge of the hunter's way of life. In addition to highlighting the familiar tension between culturalist and materialist accounts of culture and society, the symposium indicated how far from Boas and Benedict parts of American cultural anthropology had by now moved.

FORMALISM AND SUBSTANTIVISM

The emergent interest in material conditions was also expressed in other ways than through cultural ecology, and not only in the USA. From the 1940s onwards, economic anthropology was developed as a subdiscipline, in many cases in close tandem with anthropological peasant studies (see Wolf 1966).

Anthropological studies of economics had a venerable history. Malinowski's *Argonauts of the Western Pacific*, Mauss's *The Gift*, and a large number of lesser works focused directly on economic relations. Still, the pioneer in establishing economic anthropology as a subdiscipline was Raymond Firth (Chapter 4). Firth, who was first educated as an economist, had written detailed studies of the Maori and Tikopia economies (1929, 1939), which emphasised the pragmatic strategies of individuals. During the 1950s and 1960s, Firth continued this work, adding a theoretical emphasis to it that is often referred to as 'formalism' (LeClair and Schneider 1968). Formalism, which argues that classical economic theory may be applied cross-culturally, did not, however, crystallise into a distinct 'school' before it was challenged by what has been called 'the substantivist revolution'.

If Firth was the first important formalist in economic anthropology, the apical ancestor of substantivism was the Hungarian economic historian and political reformer Karl Polanyi (1886–1964). After some years at Manchester, he moved to the USA in 1940, where he spent six years as Professor of Economics at Columbia, at the same time as Steward's term in the anthropology department there. In *The Great Transformation* (1957 [1944]), Polanyi argues that what we call 'the economy', does not exist in pre-capitalist societies at all, and that classical economic theory can therefore legitimately be applied only to capitalist economies.

The bitter debate between formalists and substantivists involved anthropologists, historians and economists, and continued well into the 1970s, when it ended with the inconclusive and somewhat banal realisation that the two schools were complementary. The issues raised were nevertheless fundamental, and, in various guises, are still around today. Roughly speaking, the formalists assumed that an economy might be described as a particular kind of action that individuals have everywhere and always engaged in – action in which the individual strives to achieve the maximal benefit for himself and/or his household. As long as we are dealing with maximisation, in other words, we are dealing with the economy. Moreover, since maximisation is not limited to specific empirical contexts, but can occur in any kind of social interaction, the economy may be regarded as a universal aspect of human social life. This attitude, which (despite its universalist definition) is compatible with methodological individualism, was eagerly embraced by many of the critics of structural-functionalism in the 1950s and 1960s (see p. 89ff.). In contrast, substantivism argues that the economy is not a universal form of action, but (in Polanyi's words) an 'instituted process' (Polanyi 1957). The economy is contained by and limited to specific, historical institutions – of production, circulation (exchange) and consumption.

The strength of formalism was its emphasis on the pragmatic choices of individuals – which brings the variable and unpredictable aspects of economic action to the fore. The strength of substantivism, in contrast, lies in its ability to describe economic systems as being of fundamentally different kinds and characterised by different economic rationalities (formalism only accepts one economic rationality: maximisation). Substantivists would thus be more open to theories of historical watersheds, fundamental differences between cultures and irreversible change. Polanyi himself, in a typology that was later expanded by Sahlins (1972), distinguished three main types of economy: *reciprocity*, *redistribution* and *market exchange*. In reciprocity, which is typically found in small, non-hierarchical, kinship-based societies, there is no short-term calculation of profit or loss, and – as Mauss pointed out in *The Gift* – it is the giver rather than the receiver who wins prestige. In *redistribution*, typical of traditional chiefdoms, goods are collected at a centre, from which they are distributed to the population on the basis of the centre's priorities – often in conspicuous displays of 'generosity' – for here again, it is the giver that attains prestige. Only in market exchange, typical of capitalist societies, is this relationship reversed: the receiver wins, accumulates value and re-invests it in an endless cycle of profit maximisation, in which money plays a pivotal role. Each of these three 'ideal types' (to use Weber's term) is based on particular institutions (kinship, the state, money), and may be found together with the others in empirical societies. There are elements of market exchange in kin-based societies, just as there are elements of reciprocity (gift exchange) in our own economy. Polanyi, however, focused particularly on situations in which one or the other type of economy was dominant, and thus arrived at a vaguely evolutionist model of social development incorporating three stages (a fairly common model, as we saw in Chapter 2).

To the formalists, like Firth and Herskovits, this evolutionist tendency was anathema (see Frankenberg 1967), and they tried to show that maximisation regulated economic activities everywhere. The substantivists regarded this view as ethnocentric (Sahlins 1972), and their favourite classic was Mauss, who had emphasised the differences between dominant logics of action in different societal types.

The formalist-substantivist controversy fizzled out as Marxian economic thinking (which sought to incorporate both approaches) gained currency. But analogous controversies have continued to surface in other parts of anthropology, for example in discussions of ritual, where Leach (1968) defined ritual not (substantively) as confined to a particular kind of institution, but as the symbolic aspect of any action. Similarly, the debate on alliance versus descent theory (Chapter 6) opposed a view of kinship as a (formalist) 'alliance building activity' to an idea of kinship as a method of formation of (substantial) groups. Finally, it might be argued that postmodernism (Chapter 8) was a peculiar type of formalism, inasmuch as it sought to do away with essentialisation – the tendency to regard diffuse aggregates of processes as if they were distinct (substantive) 'things'.

MEANWHILE IN BRITAIN: THE MANCHESTER SCHOOL

By 1950, thanks to institutional expansion and retirements, the people who would be the leading figures in post-war British social anthropology were nearly all firmly in place at central academic institutions: Firth got his Chair at the LSE in 1944; Daryll Forde became Professor at University College London in 1945; Evans-Pritchard at Oxford in 1946, Gluckman at Manchester in 1949 (a couple of years after leaving the Rhodes-Livingstone Institute), Fortes at Cambridge in 1950, and Schapera at the University of London in 1950. Leach was appointed to a lectureship at Cambridge in 1953.

There were important nuances within this elite, which must nevertheless have seemed a tightly integrated clan seen from the outside, not least from the sprawling field of American anthropology. Fortes, Evans-Pritchard and Forde remained associated with structural-functionalism, although the latter two chose alternative paths – Evans-Pritchard repudiated the ideals of natural science, and Forde kept his interest in ecological anthropology from his student days at Berkeley. Firth, Richards and Leach developed different brands of Malinowskian functionalism. Finally, Gluckman and Schapera represented a kind of middle ground. They were self-declared structural-functionalists, but their thematic interests were closer to those of Leach and Firth, who, like them, were vitally concerned with studying social change. Of these leading figures, Leach and Evans-Pritchard would be most directly involved in changing the nature of British social anthropology. It was nevertheless perceived as a conservative sect well into the post-war years. In a debate with Firth in 1951, George P. Murdock accused the Britons of closing ranks and refusing to engage in the discourse of global (by which he perhaps meant American) anthropology. At the same time, however, Murdock confirmed that British social anthropology enjoyed a strong influence on younger American anthropologists (Stocking 1995: 432ff.), and he did not see it as being without merit.

The 1950s and 1960s saw major transformations in British anthropology. Some of the most important, notably the change in focus 'from structure to meaning', will be dealt with in the next chapter. By any standards, however, the research conducted at the Rhodes-Livingstone Institute (later at Manchester), which focused on urbanisation in southern Africa, was pioneering in its methods and subject matter, and was in no small measure responsible for the demolition of structural-functionalism – ironically, perhaps, since the main theorist of this school was Gluckman, a faithful follower of Radcliffe-Brown. However, there were inner tensions in structural-functionalism, which became increasingly difficult to resolve. As Malinowski, Firth and several American anthropologists had pointed out even before the war, a weakness of structural-functionalism was its explicit assumption that societies tend to reproduce themselves. This led to difficulties in accounting for change, but the notion was workable if – and only if – the societies studied by anthropologists did not change. The validity of this condition was, however, increasingly being questioned. In part, it was obvious that the colonised societies, in Africa and elsewhere, were changing rapidly. In part, there was a growing realisation of the fact that even 'untouched' primitive groups (for example in New Guinea) were in a state of constant flux. Change, in fact, seemed to be an essential part of the human condition.

It was therefore hardly surprising that the first British anthropologists to address this problem effectively were engaged in studies of people who were themselves undergoing rapid, unpredictable and irreversible change. The anthropologists associated with the Rhodes-Livingstone Institute, many of them later at the University of Manchester, carried out long-term fieldwork in regions characterised by urbanisation, labour migration and rapid population growth. Their studies, which often focused on the mining towns in Northern Rhodesia (Zambia), showed how traditional social forms, such as kinship, might be maintained and even strengthened in situations of rapid change – 'returning to life' in the modern world, pregnant with new meaning. A famous study in this genre was Peter Worsley's *The Trumpet Shall Sound* (Worsley 1968 [1957]), a study of messianistic *cargo cults* in Melanesia. These were religious movements that combined elements from a shattered traditional culture with elements of a poorly understood modernity (personified by the US troops stationed among them during the Second World War), into new and creative symbolic and organisational syntheses. Worsley, who was a member of the British Communist Party, was denied a research permit for political reasons, and had to base his study on existing literature.

Most of the studies emanating from this milieu, however, had Africa, and in most cases southern Africa, as their ethnographic base. Under the successive leadership of Godfrey Wilson and Gluckman, the Rhodes-Livingstone Institute initiated several new research fields associated with social change. The transformation of tribal life due to migration and wagework was investigated – many did fieldwork in the same tribal groups both in town and in their traditional settings. They studied ethnicity or 're-tribalisation' (Mitchell 1956; Epstein 1958). They investigated race relations in the mining towns, at a time when racial discrimination was still considered the domain of sociologists in much of mainstream anthropology. They also engaged in applied research, which was partly unknown, partly sneered at, at the metropolitan departments.

The methods they employed were equally innovative. Problems of studying social life in chaotic, turbulent mining towns had to be solved, and Malinowski's magisterial fieldwork on the tiny Trobriand Islands offered few clues. Some began to experiment with quantitative methods, which were otherwise uncommon in anthropology. Mitchell, Epstein and Elizabeth Colson all used statistics and regression analysis in attempts to give accurate data on social distance and network structure. Network analysis, pioneered by John Barnes (1990 [1954]) was designed to trace the changing relationships between people who were not firmly localised. Jaap van Velsen (1967) proposed the 'extended case method', a mode of inquiry where a single dramatic event or series of events was isolated and studied in successively wider and wider contexts, thus enabling a look 'from below' at vast social structures, such as nations, which would otherwise be impossible to cover with traditional participant observation.

The parallels to the Chicago school are striking, and the people in Rhodesia were familiar with their work. But they were still primarily British social anthropologists. The success of the Salisbury-Manchester school was premised on the fact of colonialism, and on the possibilities it opened up for alliances between metropolitan university departments and small research institutes in the periphery (a similar arrangement existed between the University of Cambridge and the the East African Institute of Social Research at Makerere in Uganda, led successively by Aidan Southall and Audrey Richards). The department in Manchester, where Gluckman was established by 1949, could offer many of its students three-year research fellowships at the institute in Salisbury. The relationship between the two institutions was broken off only at Ian Smith's unilateral declaration of independence in 1966.

What the Manchester anthropologists demonstrated, above all, was that change was not a simple object of study. One could not, as the structural-functionalists at times assumed, understand change simply by describing the social structure as it existed before and after the change, and postulating some simple transformational rules, which would 'explain' what had in the meantime occurred. Gluckman and his colleagues showed that when the local effects of global processes are investigated empirically, they dissolve into complex webs of social relations, which are in constant change and mutually influence each other. This was the idea behind Barnes' 'network theory', a more dynamic concept than Radcliffe-Brown's 'social structure'. The idea that change could be understood as simple, rule-governed transformations between given social conditions was thus slowly replaced by an idea of change as fundamentally unpredictable – because it was a result of countless individual relations, each of which was reflexive and variable. This thought in itself represented a fundamental challenge to structural-functionalism – irrespective of the fact that Gluckman himself always professed his allegiance to Radcliffe-Brown and never attempted to develop an alternative theory.

Gluckman had taken his Ph.D. at Oxford under Evans-Pritchard and Fortes, and came to the Institute in Rhodesia in 1939, serving as Director there from 1942 to 1947, when he left for England. Much of his research in southern Africa dealt with law, politics, conflicts and their resolution (see

Gluckman 1965). In spite of his moving to Manchester, Gluckman's indirect leadership continued throughout the 1950s, and the connection between Manchester and the Institute remained close. His background, as a left-leaning Jew from South Africa, did not give him much in the way of automatic support from the British academic establishment, and it was clearly thanks to Evans-Pritchard and Fortes that he got the Chair at Manchester. (His arch-rival Leach might have felt that the position ought to have been his.) In any case, Gluckman remained loyal to the broad framework of structural-functionalism, and he once said about Malinowski that 'his data are too complex for comparative work' (Goody 1995). In spite of this – typical – disdain for Malinowskian ethnography, there were (as we remarked above) marked similarities between Gluckman's research concerns and those of Malinowski's students. In his history of British social anthropology, Kuper (1996) notes that the two lineages practically converged in the late 1950s, through the remarkably similar work of Frederick Bailey and Fredrik Barth (see p. 91). Like Firth, Gluckman was strongly concerned with change early in his career. Already in his contribution to *African Political Systems*, he called attention to the tensions between the traditional political system of the Zulu and the colonial administration that had been imposed upon them.

Gluckman's interest in social conflict was inspired by his political radicalism and ultimately by Marx, but unlike Marx (and like Evans-Pritchard), he saw conflict as ultimately integrating. For Gluckman, social integration always implied striking a balance between group interests: conflicts might be undercommunicated through compromises between political leaders, or the underlying tensions of society might be channelled through a 'safety valve' to a harmless outlet such as witchcraft accusations (Gluckman 1956) – thus letting off steam without challenging the system. Unlike many of his contemporaries, Gluckman was acutely aware of the conflict-ridden nature of most societies, which were kept in one piece imperfectly and through hard work.

Another approach to the issue of social change was initiated by Godfrey Wilson, whose *Essay on the Economics of Detribalization in Northern Rhodesia* (1941–2) discussed the question of 'acculturation'. Wilson predicted that colonialism would ultimately result in massive cultural change and 'detribalisation'. This view was later taken up by Philip Mayer, who, in a study of urban politics in South Africa, argued that 'trade unions transcend tribes' (Mayer 1960). However, several of the leading anthropologists in Rhodesia argued against Wilson's view, claiming instead that the effect of urban life on identity was *re-tribalisation* (Mitchell 1956; Epstein 1958), since the migrants were, in the new complex setting, continuously reminded of their identity as members of one group as opposed to another. This perspective has later proved useful in studies of ethnicity and nationalism (Chapter 7).

Gluckman's interest in tensions and crises would also lead to important research in a field that is not usually associated with the Manchester School, namely ritual. The idea that ritual can mitigate conflict and strengthen social cohesion is prevalent as early as in Durkheim's sociology of religion. In Gluckman's work, and more pointedly in that of his student Victor Turner (1920–83), this basic idea serves as a loose framework for the study of ritual as dynamic social processes. But since Turner's work was important in shifting the emphasis of British social anthropology from social cohesion to symbolic meaning, it will be presented in the next chapter.

METHODOLOGICAL INDIVIDUALISM AT CAMBRIDGE

The contributions from the Manchester school were important in reorienting British anthropology – from integration to process, from continuity to change. Yet the people in question were cautious. Their intellectual lineage came from Durkheim via Radcliffe-Brown and Evans-Pritchard, and the metaphor of society as a functionally integrated organism was implicit in most of their work, however innovative it might have been, throughout the 1950s. For Malinowski's students, unhampered by axiomatic notions of social integration, it might seem easier to tackle social change. Since Malinowski himself had given the individual primacy over society, his view of social life gave more room for improvisation, variation and creativity than structural-functionalism, which was increasingly seen as a straitjacket as the 1950s went on.

Like his teacher, Firth was not primarily a theorist, but an ethnographer. Wherever he went on fieldwork – among Maoris or Tikopians in Polynesia, among Malay fishermen, among Englishmen in London – he saw dramatic social change taking place. Moreover, he saw the exceptional individual as a crucial agent of change. In his major theoretical work, *Elements of Social Organisation* (Firth 1951), he tried to nudge social anthropology towards a more flexible view of society. In 1950, the 'kinshipology' of Radcliffe-Brown and his students was at its height. Evans-Pritchard had not yet announced his defection, and all major departments except at the LSE were directed by structural-functionalists. It would have been impossible for Firth to ignore this fact. He therefore relates critically, but cautiously, to the core concepts of function and structure; he does not repudiate the notion of a stable, 'empty' social structure, but proposes a complementary concept, which captures the dynamic, shifting character of social action. That concept, borrowed from none other than Radcliffe-Brown, is *social organisation*. While social structure refers to the stable arrangements of society, social organisation is the actual flow of social life, in which individual interests meet, conflicts and compromises develop, and the pragmatics of everyday life may deviate considerably from the norm (social structure) without destroying it. In other words, and contrary to Radcliffe-Brown's belief, action does not follow directly from norms, but passes first through a filter of (tactical and strategic) choice.

The mild-mannered Firth was the most important conflict mediator in his generation. He bridged gaps within the British school, gently preparing the ground for the more aggressive assaults on structural-functionalism that were to come, while also maintaining an active dialogue with American anthropologists during a period when sustained contacts across the Atlantic were rare. Ironically, it was Cambridge that would become the hotbed for the radical Malinowskians, who would eventually not only question the idea that society is inherently cohesive, but, in some cases, try to shift the focus of the entire discipline away from social wholes and towards individual action. Cambridge, a backwater in British anthropology until Fortes accepted the Chair in 1950, would for the next two decades simultaneously be a stronghold of structural-functionalism – primarily through Fortes and his student Jack Goody – and a vital centre of innovation in the discipline. In 1949, Fortes published the article 'Time and social structure', a structural-functionalist *tour de force*, which showed that while the maintenance of the social structure of households unfolded over time, structure would *seem to change*, while in fact merely repeating a well-known movement. In 1958, this cue was taken up by Goody in his edited volume *The Developmental Cycle of Domestic Groups*. Goody (1919–) did long-term fieldwork in Ghana, but made his name not as a writer of monographs, but as a bold forger of grand, provocative – and increasingly unfashionable – comparative syntheses. Fortes, and Goody too, responded to the spirit of the times: even if the change they described was illusory, it was still (in the short term) change.

Edmund Leach (1910–89), perhaps the most formidable personality among the young Cambridge anthropologists, pursued very different interests. Leach, a former student of Malinowski and Firth, who was an engineer before he became an anthropologist, was appointed to his position at Cambridge in 1953. In 1956, another influential student of Malinowski's, Audrey Richards, also came to town, to direct the new Centre for African Studies. Richards, who had done extensive fieldwork among the Bemba of Northern Rhodesia (Zambia), had been an early critic of Evans-Pritchard's work on the Nuer, arguing that the facts on the ground did not fit his simple models – a very Malinowskian objection. Like Firth, Richards did pioneering work in economic anthropology before the war (Richards 1939); her early work on nutrition make her one of the founders of medical anthropology (Richards 1932); and in the year she came to Cambridge, she published an influential study of female initiation rituals, *Chisungu* (Richards 1956). It was through Richards' offices that the connection between Cambridge and the East African Institute at Makerere in Uganda was forged. Other anthropologists associated with Cambridge in the 1950s included John Barnes (mentioned above); Frederick Bailey (1924–), a South Asianist and political anthropologist; and Fredrik Barth (1928–), a Norwegian, who, while at Cambridge, would write the classic *Political Leadership among Swat Pathans* (1959) – a title that echoed Leach's own seminal *Political Systems of Highland Burma* (1954). There were, in other words, quite a few political anthropologists at Cambridge in the 1950s, who had a weak sense of loyalty towards the dominant orthodoxy.

This focus on politics (a subject that was rarely foregrounded in Fortes' and Goody's kinship-oriented work), was part of the legacy from structural-functionalism (after all, politics stood at the heart of *The Nuer*). It could well be argued, in retrospect, that in stressing the importance of political institutions, structural-functionalism was digging its own grave. Politics is a power game. It is 'the art of the possible', not 'the art of the legal'. It is about stretching rules (and breaking them, whenever opportune), not about stable allegiance to shared moral norms. Sooner or later, political anthropology would have to come to terms with the inherently manipulative dimensions of politics.

This happened in various ways with the Cambridge anthropologists. Bailey (1960) wrote about caste-climbing and local politics in Orissa, east India. Untypically in South Asian studies, he looked for individual strategies and conflicting interests, and found plenty of both.

Barth wrote about politics in Swat, north-east Pakistan, as a process fuelled by individuals' interests and their strategies. His approach drew on a then new model from economics and political science, the theory of games, which sees social life largely as a series of zero-sum games: one person's gain is another's loss. Trying to model social life formally, like Evans-Pritchard before him, Barth tried to grasp the dynamic flow of a social field fissured by conflicting interests, and was assisted in this by the fact that the science of formalised modelling had progressed very considerably since the 1930s. In Barth's work, social structure was relegated to the background, appearing, in his dry, economical prose, as 'incentives and constraints' (Barth 1959). A comparison of *Political Leadership* and *The Nuer* can be highly instructive, and indicates the shift that was taking place parts of British anthropology at the time. Both books deal with stateless societies and the problem of integration; both discuss political aspects of segmentary societies. However, the analyses differ in almost every other respect: Evans-Pritchard saw social structure as an overarching principle, while the principle of individual maximisation plays a similar part for Barth. Evans-Pritchard portrays his people with the aesthetics of a still life, Barth with that of a bustling tableau.

Leach, who wrote a monograph of the same general kind, represents yet another approach to this theme. *Political Systems of Highland Burma* was based on fieldwork among the Kachin and Shan of northern Burma before and during the Second World War. While Leach was doing military service in Burma, his fieldnotes were lost. The book, accordingly, contains few verbatim statements by informants and few accounts of actual people. Whatever the book had lost in empirical detail, however, it had won in analytical power, and it is perhaps the most influential of all the 1950s monographs.

Political Systems is a book about tensions and conflicts in politics. In this, Leach shares the interests of his main antagonist in British anthropology,

Max Gluckman, though their approaches differ radically. Leach was not the first anthropologist to study the relationship between myth and political process, but he was probably the first to argue that both are unstable and open to differing interpretations. The Kachin operate with two distinctive models of the political order; one egalitarian (*gumlao*) and one hierarchical (*gumsa*). Leach showed, in essence, that the political organisation of Kachin villages oscillated between these poles in the long term, and that there were ambivalent elements in their marriage system, their economic organisation and their myths, that could be invoked and exploited to justify both. Malinowski had been wrong in assuming that myths are 'social charters'. In Leach's version, they were charters for trouble.

In the first chapter of the book, Leach made an important distinction between models and reality that was highly pertinent at a time when the validity of Evans-Pritchard's models of Nuer society was still the object of heated debate. Models, Leach argued, are idealisations, which may be useful in analysis, as simplified points of reference for more realistic – and dynamic – descriptions of society. But even in wholly 'traditional' (and presumably stable) societies, norms are not simple blueprints for action (as Evans-Pritchard assumed), but points of ambiguity and stress produced by the meeting of opposed interests, and used by those interests to further their purposes. Leach is not entirely clear regarding the distinction between models devised by the anthropologist and native models, and this gives his conclusions a somewhat speculative flavour. The book nevertheless delves into the complexities of myth, revealing levels of significance that had previously been unseen. It demonstrated that social life is intrinsically volatile, that cultural categories are contested and open to different inter-pretations, and stressed the legitimating functions of myth in politics. It played a pivotal role in establishing a research programme that is still very much alive as we write.

Towards the end of 1960s, the atmosphere at Cambridge lost some of its edge, as the many talented students left to start their own careers. After Richards' departure, in 1967, only Leach, Goody and Fortes remained of the original group. Leach's interests had moved from politics to symbolism (Chapter 6), Goody pursued his comparative projects, and Fortes was approaching retirement. Of the students, Barth was the most influential. In 1961, he became Professor of Social Anthropology at the University of Bergen, Norway, where he built up a department devoted to methodological individualism. The contributions of this department included studies of development issues in the Sudan, entrepreneurship and economic marginality in northern Norway, and – increasingly – ethnic relations. In 1966, Barth published a pithy little booklet called *Models of Social Organiza-tion*, a spirited attempt to demolish the Durkheimian concept of society altogether. Barth here argues that social structure is a product of 'transac-tions', pragmatic-strategic exchanges between maximising individuals, which eventually generate a value consensus – as well as the statistical regularities in 'social form' that we refer to as society. This work, which was heavily inspired by the sophisticated formal modelling techniques that were gaining currency in economics and political science at the time, created considerable debate, and was probably the harshest attack on structural-functionalism to date. In 1967, Barth edited the book for which he is most widely known today (and to which we shall return in Chapter 7), namely *Ethnic Groups and Boundaries* (Barth 1969).

ROLE ANALYSIS AND SYSTEM THEORY

The study of social interaction, which had always been a mainstay of British anthropology, and which, with the new methodological individualists, had become even more prominent, had never attained the same position in the USA, where culture occupied centre stage. As noted earlier, however, there were important exceptions. The work of the Chicago school and the formalist economic anthropologists come to mind, as well as the psychologically oriented contributions of Ralph Linton (Chapter 4). It was Linton who introduced the later common distinction between *status* and *role* (Linton 1937), which (at the level of the individual) corresponds closely to Firth's later distinction between social structure and social organisation (on the level of society). Status, in Linton's terminology, is defined by moral norms, expectations from other individuals and a person's formal position in a system of relations. Role, in contrast, is the person's enactment of status in actual behaviour. While the status is static, a given, much like the script of a drama, the role is dynamic. It rests on status, as the actor's performance rests on the dramatist's manuscript, but it cannot be reduced to it. Role enactment demands and enables active interpretation and inventive departures from the script.

Linton was also the first to write systematically about the difference between acquired and ascribed statuses, and about role conflict. Nevertheless, the social theorist who is best known for his role theory is the Chicago microsociologist Erving Goffman, who carried out detailed studies of interaction and communication in very small-scale settings in modern society, and developed a subtle conceptual apparatus for describing the rituals and routines of everyday life. In contrast to Parsons – the dominant sociological theorist in the USA at the time – Goffman consistently focused on the actor, on his or her motivations, strategies and decisions. In *The Presentation of Self in Everyday Life* (1959), he introduced his *dramaturgical* perspective on social life, which took the metaphor of an actor on a stage very much further than Linton ever did. Adding terms like role distance, stigma, under- and overcommunication, frames and interaction ritual to the vocabulary of the social sciences, Goffman showed how each actor had ample room for manoeuvre within the constraints laid by status. His subtle observations of people interacting in everyday situations while observing, interpreting and communicating their (spontaneous, self-conscious or faked) intentions and reactions to themselves and each other – raised to new heights our understanding of the intense reflexivity that characterises human social life (see Goffman 1967).

Unlike much of the work undertaken by American anthropologists in the 1950s and 1960s, Goffman's fresh, lucid and often provocative writings crossed the Atlantic quickly, where they were happily deployed in the war against structural-functionalism, though Goffman himself was in fact heavily influenced by Durkheim. In the USA, in contrast, his influence was at first largely confined to sociology.

Another innovation of the early post-war years had a somewhat similar fate. *Cybernetics*, the theory of complex, self-regulating systems (computers are a prime example), was developed in the late 1940s by an interdisciplinary group under the leadership of mathematician Norbert Wiener (1948), and instantly attained practical importance in computer design. Ecologists, biologists, perceptual psychologists, economists and scholars in a number of other sciences also quickly put the theory to use. Cybernetics entered anthropology at an early stage, thanks to Gregory Bateson, who was associated with Wiener's group. Cybernetics, a very complex and technical discipline, focuses on relationships of circular causation or *feedback*, where 'cause' and 'effect' mutually influence each other. Moreover, cybernetics studies the flow of *information* in such circuits. By linking circuit to circuit by means of logical switches (which direct the flow along specific paths through the system), a vast, interconnected web conveying meaningful impulses is formed. The ecosystem and the body are examples of such webs, and, as Bateson realised, there is no reason why society cannot be described in the same way. The result is a kind of functionalism, and indeed, it may be claimed that cybernetics renders at least part of the criticism against tautology obsolete, absolving functionalism, at least potentially, of its most obvious sin. Cybernetically inspired anthropology differs from functionalism, however, in that all the internal connections of the system must be specified explicitly.

In a number of articles that were later collected in *Steps to an Ecology of Mind* (1972), Bateson devised a theory of human communication that he applied (inventively and, at times, whimsically) to such diverse subjects as aesthetics, ecological flexibility, animal communication, schizophrenia and the constitution of the Self. An important contribution was his concept of *metacommunication*, which denotes messages embedded in normal communication that inform the recipient that he is receiving information *of a specific kind*. By framing messages in this way, we are able to define for each other the context to which they belong (this is love; this is play; this is politics).

In this aspect of his thinking, Bateson resembles Goffman, and like Goffman, he was ignored by most American anthropologists in his day. However, again like Goffman, he would exert unsystematic, but pervasive influence on anthropologists in most countries during the rest of the twentieth century.

A world that is changing demands theories tailored to study change. This was the basic challenge faced by anthropologists, both in Britain and in the USA. In both cases too, this challenge emerged against a background of hegemonic social theories that described a heavily idealised image of society (social structure) or culture (ethos). Both groups of innovators therefore reacted with a focus on the practical side of life. However, if they shared an interest in the practical, material processes of change, they disagreed deeply as to how these processes ought to be studied. In the USA, the rediscovery of Marx and Morgan implied a focus on institutions, structural analyses of inequality, the conditions for development and underdevelopment, and other aspects of large-scale change. From Benedict's individualist, psychological anthropology, Steward and White, and their students moved from the individual towards large-scale historical processes. In Britain, the opposite was the case: attention moved from the collective towards the individual. The leading orthodoxy, structural-functionalism, was collectivist in its orientation, and it was attacked not only for offering a static, frozen image of the world, but also for not leaving the individual space for manoeuvre. While in the American analyses, change was a result of impersonal, historical processes, the typical agent of change in Britain was a calculating strategist or an innovative entrepreneur. Moreover, while the American evolutionists saw power (with Marx) as an outcome of global economic dynamics, the British interactionists (with Weber) saw it as a political resource subject to individual competition. Thus, the movement towards 'change' was diverse.

Other major changes also took place in anthropology during the 1950s and 1960s. If this chapter has shown how economics and politics were re-conceptualised, the next chapter will show how new theories of symbolic meaning transformed the subject. Here, too, developments in the USA and Britain differed, although the problems raised were similar. Yet the single most important theorist was French.

6 THE POWER OF SYMBOLS

In the 1950s, anthropologists were discovering change, either as an evolutionary movement (in the United States) or as an individual innovation (in Britain). But they were also discovering meaning. Speculation on the meaning of symbols was nothing new. Indeed, in the United States, the 'discovery' was not the least subversive. The most important young American symbolic anthropologists, Clifford Geertz and David Schneider, both saw themselves as direct inheritors of the Boasian tradition. In Britain, the situation was different. Here, the study of meaning was still associated with Frazer, who had speculated extensively on the functions of magic in *The Golden Bough*. Durkheim had studied religion, but in its ritual aspect, rather than as a universe of meaning. It was the organisational practice of religion, rather than its content with which he was concerned. Weber's interpretive sociology was not well known. Thus, the study of meaning, in the British context, was tainted with evolutionism and was best avoided. The great exception to the rule, here, was Evans-Pritchard, who had boldly followed Frazer's topic in his study of Azande witchcraft, before becoming a main promoter of structural-functionalism. Now he would turn apostate and lead British anthropology into this new realm. In France, an entirely different path was taken. Lévi-Strauss's structuralism was widely seen as the crowning achievement of the tradition from Durkheim and Mauss. But was it? Later French intellectuals would spend many years discussing this question.

FROM FUNCTION TO MEANING

We turn to the British situation first. Now, the interest in meaning was not entirely absent from the mainstream of British social anthropology. An example was the seminal article by Jack Goody and the literary theorist Ian Watt, 'The Consequences of Literacy' (Goody and Watt 1963), which argued that writing irreversibly changed both the social structure and the structure of reasoning (or cognitive style) of society. The article, which sparked a debate with complex ramifications – in part because it intersected with the elaborate conception of 'action as text' proposed by the French philosopher Paul Ricoeur (see Ricoeur 1971) – is definitely concerned with meaning, but with the social *functions* of meaning, not with meaning itself. Evans-Pritchard's interests were more radical than this.

He could afford to be radical. When he succeeded Radcliffe-Brown as Professor at Oxford in 1946, he had already authored two hugely influential monographs and co-edited a book – *African Political Systems* – that defined the mainstream research agenda of British anthropology for two decades. The companion volume, *African Systems of Kinship and Marriage*, edited by Radcliffe-Brown and Forde, had much less impact. Firth at the LSE and Fortes at Cambridge notwithstanding, Evans-Pritchard was beyond doubt the most powerful social anthropologist of the time. When, in his Marett lecture on 'Social Anthropology: Past and Present' in 1950, he repudiated structural-functionalism and distanced himself from his teacher, this was headline news and impossible to ignore for the anthropological community. In the lecture he claimed, on the one hand, that it would be nonsense to believe that synchronous studies could yield insights of the same depth as historical studies; on the other, that in terms of method, social anthropology had more in common with history than with the natural sciences. He was rejecting two of the mainstays of structural-functionalism. In his later work, Evans-Pritchard abandons the search for 'natural laws of society' and attempts, more realistically, to understand the meaning of particular social institutions. His second Nuer book, *Kinship and Marriage among the Nuer* (1951b), was much more descriptive and less theoretically ambitious than *The Nuer*. On the other hand, it contains fewer contestable ideas. It was in no small measure the elegant, but simple models of *The Nuer* that led to the 'revolution' described in the previous chapter.

In 1958, the philosopher Peter Winch published *The Idea of a Social Science and Its Relation to Philosophy*, a book that would subsequently exert considerable influence on anthropological discourse about intercultural translation. In the book, Winch argued that it was impossible to establish objective, 'testable' knowledge about cultural phenomena, since their meaning was defined by the cultural universe of which they were a part. He adopted a strongly relativist position, arguing that there exists no privileged, 'context-independent' position from which to compare and evaluate other cultures, except for our common experiences of universal bodily processes, such as 'birth, copulation and death' (Winch himself quotes Eliot at this point). Social anthropology was, in Winch's view, a Western cultural oddity on a par with the witchcraft institution among the Azande, and had no right to see its access to knowledge as privileged. Winch used the Azande monograph as the main example of a philosophically untenable position, since Evans-Pritchard presented a 'scientific' explanation of the 'obviously mistaken' belief in witches. What if the tables were turned? How can we judge whether a 'witchcraft' explanation of the 'obviously mistaken' belief in science would be less true? Winch's book was the starting-point of a long and important debate about rationality and cultural translation, to which both philosophers and anthropologists contributed (B. Wilson 1970; Hollis and Lukes 1982; Overing 1985).

It is worth noticing that Evans-Pritchard seems to have arrived at a similar position independently of Winch. The third volume of the Nuer trilogy, *Nuer Religion* (1956), is more interpretive than explanatory; at the outset, the author declares that his main ambition is to make sense of the Nuer world-view, not to explain it sociologically. In this, he is in accord with his Oxford colleague and close associate in his later period, Godfrey Lienhardt, whose later work on the Nuer's neighbours, the Dinka, was similarly interpretive (see Lienhardt 1961). Understanding and translation now had become a more pressing task than explanation and the search for general 'laws'. On the other hand, it is also true, as Evans-Pritchard's student, Mary Douglas (1980) says, that his entire output was marked by continuity – from the Azande book onwards. Even *The Nuer*, which is often described as the archetype of orthodoxy, is in fact an evocative, even a poetic, book.

While the renewed focus on change in British anthropology is often described as a transition from structure to process, the change in Evans-Pritchard's position was a movement from function to meaning. Especially two of his intellectual descendants would, in the decades following the Marett lecture, fulfil the promise of a combination of a micro-sociology concerned with integration, and an interpretive method concerned with symbolic significance.

The first was Gluckman's student Victor Turner (1920–83). During the 1950s and 1960s, he developed a perspective on symbols and social cohesion which has become increasingly influential ever since. Unlike Leach, Turner was mainly concerned with ritual, not myth; and while Leach saw the germ of social dissolution in myths, Turner ultimately saw rituals as cohesive (though not as unchanging). As Durkheim had implied, they offered splendid material for the ethnographer since they expressed the central values and tensions of a society in an intensely concentrated form. Turner's approach to rituals, which was increasingly oriented towards symbols rather than social integration, nevertheless sought to combine a concern with symbolic meaning with an underlying Durkheimian notion of cohesion. In one of the most influential British monographs of the 1950s, *Schism and Continuity in an African Society* (Turner 1957), he introduced the concept of the *social drama*. Like most of his writings on ritual, its ethnographic focus is on the Ndembu of Northern Rhodesia (Zambia), and the main problem is a classic one, namely how matrilineal societies (like the Ndembu) solve the problem of integration. While succession, inheritance and group membership are united in a single principle among patrilineal peoples, different rights and duties are based on different criteria among matrilineal groups. In the social drama, which tends to be a rite of passage, underlying norms are given a symbolic expression, and the ritual thereby contributes to the integration of society.

Although the monograph was structural-functionalist in its basic assumptions, it suggested that change was on its way. In a series of articles written in the late 1950s and early 1960s, and published as *The Ritual Process* in 1967, Turner developed his influential theory of ritual communication. In 'Betwixt and Between: The Liminal Period in Rites-de-Passage', he introduced the concept of *liminality*, later a staple in anthropological studies of ritual (and, it sometimes seems, almost anything else). Taking his cue from van Gennep's early work on rites of passage, Turner regards the ritual, and in particular the initiation ritual, as a process of transformation whereby a person moves from one defined state to another, with an intervening period of uncertainty and crisis. It is this state of crisis – the liminal stage – that is the focus of the ritual, which seeks to control it and to impose the values of society upon the wavering individual who is, for a short but critical period, 'betwixt and between'. In this 'gap' between social statuses, neither old nor new rules apply, and the individual is compelled to reflect on her situation, her place in society and indeed the existence of society as such. Thus, liminality is both a critical and a creative state of being, and change seems a potential of any ritual. And yet, in the end, the initiate is nearly always re-integrated into society.

In other words, there is continuity with both Durkheim and Gluckman in Turner's work, which nevertheless stands out through its emphasis on the individual, its preoccupation with the meaning of symbols, and its focus on critical phases in social process. Turner also emphasised the *multivocality* or multiple meanings of symbols, implying that symbols themselves might be a tension-filled source of change, and that identical symbols could mean different things to different people, thus creating a sense of community among people who were otherwise very different. In another couple of decades, the latter idea would be followed up by students of nationalism.

Another Africanist of structural-functionalist descent who would give social anthropology a determined thrust towards the study of symbols in their social context, was Mary Douglas (1921–). A student of Evans-Pritchard, Douglas studied the Lele of Kasai, Belgian Congo, in the late 1950s. This brought her into close contact with French and Belgian anthropology, and she would eventually be more influenced by Durkheim himself than by Radcliffe-Brown. Her most influential early work was not the monograph that came out of the fieldwork, but a theoretical and comparative study of symbolic boundaries and classification, *Purity and Danger* (1966). The book combines an almost orthodox structural-functionalism with a highly sophisticated symbolic analysis drawing on both structuralist and psychoanalytical impulses. Hugely successful both within and outside anthropology, *Purity and Danger* is, in a way, a British counterpart to *Patterns of Culture*. In both cases, the concern is with group identity and values; but whereas Benedict does not look beyond the symbolic aspects of culture, Douglas consistently links symbols to social institutions in the classic Durkheimian way. In her view, symbols are means of social classification, which distinguish between various categories of objects, persons or actions, and keep them separate. The order of the classificatory system reflects and symbolises the social order, and 'intermediate', 'unclassifiable' phenomena therefore represent a threat to social stability. Snakes (animals without legs) and substances that pass in and out of the body, are regarded as problematic. Foods are often ordered in hierarchies of 'pure' and 'polluted', which have nothing to do with their nutritional value. Bodily waste is universally polluting and potentially dangerous, since it symbolically challenges the existing order. Where Barth, for example, would see an unorthodox, unclassifiable person as a potential entrepreneur, as someone who might make change come about, Douglas would see the same person as a classificatory anomaly. This contrast indicates the differences between systemic and actor-centred perspectives, as they appeared in British anthropology in the 1960s.

Both Douglas and Turner would refine and expand their perspectives through the next decades. Douglas, who is still active today, would eventually do pioneering work on economic consumption (Douglas and Isherwood 1979), risk perception and modern technology, and institutional anthropology. Turner, who moved to the United States in 1961, would develop his ideas of liminality into a general theory of ritual *performance* (Turner 1969, 1974, 1987). Though Turner died in 1983, his influence continued to grow during the 1980s and 1990s, when his concern with performative play and reflexivity would be welcomed by the postmodernist movement in anthropology, and by anthropologists concerned with bodily experience, emotions and the symbolic dimensions of power (Chapter 8). Though his intellectual itinerary thus passes from a fairly orthodox structural-functionalism to a radical focus on aesthetics and performance, he remained at heart a Durkheimian – although his Durkheimianism differed radically from that of Radcliffe-Brown.

ETHNOSCIENCE AND SYMBOLIC ANTHROPOLOGY

While many anthropologists in the early postwar years, especially in Britain, rejected attempts to turn anthropology into an accurate science, others went in the opposite direction. This was not only the case with the American cultural ecologists and the British methodological individualists, but also – perhaps surprisingly – with people working within the broad framework of American linguistic anthropology.

Several of Sapir's successors explored semantics and language structures in traditional societies in an accurate way. Some of these devised quantitative methods tailored to measure frequencies and connections between native terms, and worked closely with psychologists, linguists and others engaged in the emerging interdisciplinary field of cognitive science (Chapter 9). Among the foremost of these were Harold Conklin, Charles Frake and Ward Goodenough, who all contributed to the development of *ethnoscience* in the 1950s. Ethnoscience was concerned with describing 'cultural grammars', through identifying the building-blocks of semantic universes or systems of knowledge. They drew on both the culture and personality school's interest in socialisation, on formal linguistics and on the comparative study of classification, where both Sapir and Whorf (and, before them, Durkheim and Mauss) had done ground-breaking work. In its most technical form, ethnoscience appeared as *componential analysis*, which combined linguistic anthropology and quantitative methods with the general 1950s concern with kinship.

In its original form, ethnoscience died out some time during the 1960s, but the general issues it raised have been pursued later in cognitive anthropology (see D'Andrade 1995; Shore 1996). Regardless of methodology, they largely concern the relationship between the universal and the culturally specific in human knowledge systems. Colour classification was an early, and relatively simple field, which was explored in this way. There were also interesting parallels between the concerns of ethnoscience and the emerging rationality debate in Britain on the one hand, and the concerns of Lévi-Straussian structuralism on the other hand. However, unlike both Winch and Lévi-Strauss, the ethnoscientists worked inductively, amassing huge amounts of data which were processed by the massive, sluggish computers of the day.

After Boas's death, the *pater familias* of American anthropology was Kroeber. In 1952, he published, with Clyde Kluckhohn (1905–60), *Culture: A Critical Review of Concepts and Definitions*, which discusses 162 definitions of culture, and ends by recommending the abandonment of Tylor's and Boas's all-embracing concept in favour of a definition limited to cognitive (symbolic, meaningful) culture.

In the 1950s, American anthropology was still largely dominated by Boas's students, who produced rather predictable work in the culture-and-personality tradition, often merged with Durkheimian and Weberian ideas, which were gradually gaining acceptance in the USA, largely through the work of Parsons, who collaborated with several of the leading American anthropologists of the day. One of the most interesting monographs of this period was Kluckhohn's *Navaho Witchcraft* (1944), which resembles Evans-Pritchard's Azande monograph, in that it attempts to combine a sociological, functionalist analysis with a psychological perspective.

The swing towards the study of meaning which took place in British anthropology had its parallel in the USA, not least thanks to Parsons's influence. Parsons, the leading social scientist in the USA in the 1950s, had monumental visions for the social sciences, and was well connected with funding agencies. He suggested a 'temporary division of labour' between sociology and anthropology, in which the sociologists would study power, labour and social organisation, while the anthropologists (in accordance with the new, cognitive definition of culture) would focus on the symbolic and meaningful aspects of social life. In an article jointly authored by Parsons and Kroeber in 1958, this 'truce' (as the authors themselves called it) was programmatically endorsed (see Kuper 1999: 69). Although twentieth-century American anthropology had always concentrated chiefly

on the symbolic, this development entailed a further narrowing of the subject
– or, at least, part of it.

GEERTZ AND SCHNEIDER

Two of the postgraduate students who received funds through a joint
Parsonian-Kroeberian programme at Harvard were Clifford Geertz (1926–)
and David M. Schneider (1918–95). Both took part in interdisciplinary
projects during their Ph.D. studies – Schneider doing fieldwork on Yap, in
Micronesia, Geertz on Java. Both at the time endorsed the cognitive definition
of culture, with Geertz, in his early work, carefully distinguishing between
two 'logics of integration': society, or social structure, was integrated 'causal-
functionally', while culture, or the symbolic realm, was integrated
'logico-meaningfully'. The two subsystems, he argued, true to the 1950s
'truce', could in principle be studied independently of each other.

In the 1960s, Geertz and Schneider emerged as the most important
American symbolic anthropologists (along with Turner, who was by now
in the USA), with research programmes that were sharply opposed to the
materialist views of Steward's students, such as Wolf and Sahlins (for a while
a colleague of Geertz at Chicago). Both Geertz and Schneider eventually saw
the 'division of labour' between sociology and anthropology as a limitation,
but instead of re-conquering the social, they expanded the field of culture as
a symbolic system. They began to promote an idea of culture as an
independent, self-sustaining system, which could perfectly well be studied
without taking societal conditions into account. This view was met with
hostility in Britain, where the idea that meaning could be studied without
taking social organisation into account seemed patently absurd.

Schneider's best known work is *American Kinship* (1968), a study of
American kinship terms based on interview data collected by his students.
The 'American Kinship Project' was the result of a cooperation between Firth
and Schneider. The two anthropologists, who had spent a year together at
Stanford University during the late 1950s, agreed that it would be of interest
to extend the anthropological tradition of kinship studies to modern societies,
and inaugurated a comparative project of middle-class kinship in London
(Firth) and Chicago (Schneider). Although the comparative aspect of the
project was never realised, and the two studies were published separately,
Schneider's book became a milestone in kinship research, in part because it
demonstrated that kinship studies in complex societies were possible and
interesting, and in part because it fundamentally challenged the way in
which anthropologists thought about kinship.

After Evans-Pritchard's defection, kinship studies remained the last
stronghold of structural-functionalism, which had not yet been affected by
the new methodological individualism. Then, in 1962, John Barnes
published the critical article 'African models in the New Guinea Highlands'

(reprinted in Barnes 1990), which demonstrated conclusively that the theory of segmentary lineages, which had so successfully been applied in Africa, could not be transferred to the New Guinea context without seriously distorting the data. The problem lay not with the kinship terms themselves. It was possible to interpret the New Guinea material in the orthodox way, but such an interpretation flew in the face of native understandings of kinship as well as their practices.

Schneider's book made a similar statement, but its conclusions were more radical. While Firth, in his London study, had catalogued a fairly standard range of kinship terms, Schneider's informants were asked to give information about *all* the relatives with whom they had any kind of kin relationship. A far broader view of kinship thus became possible, indeed, it emerged that kinship constituted an entire cultural universe, within which the informants moved at will. This implied that the idea of kinship as a biologically based model of human relations was faulty. This was not a new observation, but in Schneider's version, a culture could construct kinship entirely from scratch, without any reference to blood-ties whatsoever. Moreover, within 'the culture of kinship' each individual term derived its meaning from the integrated semantic network of which it was a part, and which was unique for the culture in question. This meant that even elementary kinship terms, such as 'father', would have different meanings in different kinship cultures – which undermined the entire project of comparative kinship studies that had survived since Morgan.

Schneider's redefinition of kinship from social structure to culture has parallels in the work of Geertz. Geertz's association with Parsons at Harvard has already been mentioned. However, influences from European sociology, from Boas, and even from Steward's cultural ecology, are also apparent. Geertz's early work dealt with a wide variety of themes, from ecology (1963a) and economy (1963b) to religion (1960). His oft-cited and eloquent article on 'thick description' (1964, reprinted in Geertz 1973) states his methodological *credo*, and argues, in line with Malinowski and Boas, that anthropologists should seek to describe the world from the native's point of view. Of the European sociologists, Geertz was familiar with both Durkheim and Weber, in addition to Alfred Schütz (1899–1959), a German social phenomenologist who insisted on an interpretive approach to action. The decisive intellectual impulse in Geertz's mature work, however, came from the French philosopher Paul Ricoeur (1913–), who had argued that society (or culture) can be interpreted as a text, using the interpretive methods of hermeneutics that were specifically evolved for this purpose. Hermeneutics is a method of approaching a text that has its roots in medieval exegesis of texts, notably the Bible, and which has since been used extensively by historians, literary theorists and philosophers. Very briefly, it states that a text is simultaneously an assemblage of individual parts and a seamless whole, and that interpreting the text involves a movement to and fro between these two poles. When Geertz introduced this notion into anthropology, it seemed to obviate the distinction between methodical individualism and collectivism, since a society cannot be understood without taking account of both perspectives.

On the other hand, it also seemed to imply that social phenomena must be 'read', not only by the anthropologist, but by the members of society themselves. As opposed to the British anthropologists, who focused on the individual as a (normative or strategic) *actor*, Geertz thus introduced the individual as a *reader*. Against their assumption that society was rationally constituted and that the individual might participate in it through rational activity, Geertz posited the idea that the world is often incomprehensible, and that the subject must actively *interpret* what she sees. Thus, in the article 'Religion as a cultural system' (1966, reprinted in Geertz 1973), he argued that religion is not primarily a functionally integrated subsystem of a social whole, but a means for individuals to make sense of the world. In 1973, Geertz's most important early articles were collected in *The Interpretation of Cultures*, and his reputation has been on the rise ever since. During the 1980s in particular, he was viewed as a kind of postmodernist *avant la lettre*, although it seems obvious to the present authors that this is at least a partial oversimplification.

LÉVI-STRAUSS AND STRUCTURALISM

The son of prosperous Jewish parents of the cultured middle class, Claude Lévi-Strauss (1908–) studied philosophy and law in Paris in the early 1930s, and associated with the intellectual circle around the existentialist philosopher Jean-Paul Sartre. In 1935–9, he taught at the University of São Paolo in Brazil, and carried out short-term field trips to several peoples of the Amazon region. Being a Jew, he again left France during the Second World War, and upon the intercession of Métraux and Lowie, he was offered a position at the New School of Social Research in New York City, where he stayed until 1945. While in New York, he was influenced by Boasian anthropology, and met the great Russian-American linguist, Roman Jakobson (1896–1982), whose structural linguistics would become a mainstay of Lévi-Strauss's later work. He received his doctorate in Paris in 1947, and published his dissertation in 1949 as *Les Structures élémentaires de la parenté* (*The Elementary Structures of Kinship*, 1969). It was a book that would revolutionise kinship studies. Six years later, Lévi-Strauss published the ultimate anthropological travelogue, *Tristes Tropiques* (1955), a wide-ranging, beautifully written and intricately composed narrative, so full of suggestive and haunting passages that it would be useless to summarise it here. Then, after three more years, came a collection of articles, *Anthropologie structurale* (1958; *Structural Anthropology*, 1963a). Together, these three books established Lévi-Strauss's reputation as a formidable thinker with enormous ethnographic and theoretical knowledge, and outlined the monumental life-work that would unfold over the next four decades.

By now, he had also established structuralism, the theoretical approach for which he is renowned. Structuralism is a theory that attempts to grasp the general qualities of meaningful systems, most famously, in Lévi-Strauss's own work, of kinship systems and myths. Such systems consist of elements, but the elements themselves are not delineated categories or objects, but *relationships*. A kinship system, for example, is a meaningful system and thus consists of relationships, rather than positions ('statuses'). A father is not in himself a father, but only in relationship to his children.

The idea that meaning was relational was not in itself new. It was an important component of Jakobson's structural linguistics, as well of the semiotic linguistics established by Ferdinand de Saussure before the First World War. In both, meaning derives from the relationship – the contrast or difference – between linguistic elements (phonemes, words, signs). Relational meaning was also central to cybernetics – as Bateson liked to say, meaning is a 'difference that makes a difference' (1972: 453). Finally, and most importantly, relational meaning is implicit in Mauss's discussion of the gift. Here, objects are charged with magical power by the relationships through which they move. It is the exchange that gives the gift its meaning (see Lévi-Strauss 1987a [1950]).

The advantage of reducing meaningful systems to structures of contrasts is that the flow of time within the system is frozen. Living language is reduced to a static grammar. The confusing enactment of kinship in practice is reduced to a lucid, formal structure. Roughly, structuralist analysis consists, first, in unearthing this structure; second, in deducing its underlying principles – its 'logic'; and finally, in arriving at a universal 'logic of logics' of human communication. The technicalities of this process need not concern us here, but we shall briefly outline how it was expressed in *The Elementary Structures of Kinship*.

Structural-functionalism's reputation rested to a great extent on its analyses of segmentary lineage systems, which seemed to prove beyond reasonable doubt the role of kinship as the prime organisational principle in tribal societies. Lineage theory, in turn, presupposed a primary emphasis on linear kin relationships (grandfather–father–son), while lateral relationships (husband–wife, sibling–sibling) were often downplayed. All of this was upset by *Elementary Structures*. In Lévi-Strauss's view, kinship was not primarily a mode of social organisation, but a meaningful system, a system of relationships, and the primary relationship was not the 'natural' bond of blood (parent–child), but the socially constructed bond between husband and wife. Marriage is the point of indeterminacy in biological kinship – you cannot choose your parents, but you must choose your spouse. For Lévi-Strauss, this choice is the fissure through which culture enters kinship, transforming tribal society from biology to culture.

Clearly, the integrity of this choice must be safeguarded. It must not appear to be determined by nature. You must not marry your siblings; they are 'too close', 'too natural', it would be too much like marrying yourself. It would do nothing to 'open up' your world, to give it meaning by relating it to *something else*.

In marriage, as practised in tribal societies, women are exchanged between groups of men, and a meaningful relationship is formed between these groups – a *lateral* kin relationship which Lévi-Strauss refers to as an *alliance*. From this, the logic of kinship is deduced – that is from *lateral*, rather than linear, kin relations. The result is a theory diametrically opposed to lineage theory, that places alliance above descent, contrast above continuity, arbitration above norms, meaning above organisation. In a rather brisk letter written near the end of his life, Radcliffe-Brown told the Frenchman that they would probably always talk past each other. Still, Lévi-Strauss expresses more respect for Radcliffe-Brown than for Malinowski, 'for whom culture is merely a gigantic metaphor for digestion' (Lévi-Strauss 1985). Radcliffe-Brown and Lévi-Strauss had a common interest in uncovering the hidden structures that governed thought and social life, and a common ancestor in Durkheim – and though they belonged to very different segments of his lineage, well, blood (to give Radcliffe-Brown the last word) is thicker than water.

Lévi-Strauss's further writings are hard to summarise. His books are long, erudite, packed with facts, and held together by some very sophisticated, and at times very technical, thinking. Thus, *Le Totémisme aujourd'hui* (1961; *Totemism*, 1963b) seems to be a discussion of the concept of totemism (which is debunked), but it is also (among other things) a highly ambiguous critique of the Western opposition of nature and culture. *La Pensée sauvage* (1962; *The Savage Mind*, 1966) discusses a fairly standard 'primitive' vs. 'modern' dichotomy, reminiscent of Durkheim, Weber or Tönnies, but starts with an inventory of the detailed knowledge that 'primitives' have of their natural surroundings, and ends with a critique of Sartre's theory of history. In the first chapter of this book, 'The science of the concrete', Lévi-Strauss establishes the basis of 'savage' or 'mythical' (in contrast to 'modern' or 'scientific') thought. Both are equally complex and equally rational, but their governing rationalities differ. The *bricoleur* starts with the world that is directly accessible to his senses. He relates the objects found in this world to each other, and builds structures of meaning out of them, that are narrated, for example, as myths. Thus he creates *structure out of events*. The engineer, in contrast, creates *events out of structure*. He starts with a blueprint, an abstraction that the senses cannot perceive, and by manipulating it he changes the real world.

The Savage Mind marks the transition from Lévi-Strauss's 'kinship period' to his 'mythology period'. The most remarkable work of this latter period is the *Mythologiques*, a vast, four-volume compilation and analysis of Native American myth, published between 1967 and 1974. The sheer complexity of this work has limited its influence, just as the (relative) simplicity of *The Savage Mind* has made it exceedingly popular.

EARLY IMPACT

Lévi-Strauss's impact on Anglo-Saxon anthropology was limited before the 1960s, and his early work was belatedly translated into English. *The Elementary Structures of Kinship* appeared in translation only in 1969, and for a long time, the book was largely known indirectly, through an introduction written by a Dutch anthropologist – the founder of another, older structuralist school – J.P.B. Josselin de Jong (1952). In spite of the dearth of translated texts, Lévi-Strauss was from the first a controversial and influential author. In France, structuralism became an alternative to Marxism and phenomenology in the 1950s, and the impact of structuralism on general intellectual life was at least as pronounced as in anthropology. Important non-anthropologists such as Roland Barthes, Michel Foucault and Pierre Bourdieu were brought up on structuralism and eventually rebelled against it – and their rebellion was in turn noted and debated by anthropologists, who brought these authors into the canon of anthropology.

In Britain, Leach was the first of the leading anthropologists to be attracted to Lévi-Strauss. Lévi-Strauss himself had commented quite extensively on kinship among the Kachin, and Leach immediately recognised the relevance of his conclusions for his own data. In structuralism, Leach discovered a sophisticated alternative to the often commonsensical and pedestrian British empiricism, and in 1970, he wrote an introduction to Lévi-Strauss, which substantially increased knowledge of his work in the English-speaking world. The Oxford anthropologist Rodney Needham, who had studied with Josselin de Jong in Leiden, was another early enthusiast for Lévi-Strauss, although he had certain reservations from the beginning (Needham 1962). These were further strengthened by an unfortunate exchange with Lévi-Strauss himself, who repudiated Needham's interpretation of his kinship theory in a strongly phrased preface to the English edition of his kinship book. Needham, for his part, continued to develop structuralist thought about classification and kinship in innovative directions, but without referring to Lévi-Strauss. Most Anglo-American anthropologists were nevertheless deeply suspicious of structuralism. They were provoked by Lévi-Strauss's abstract models and deductive thinking. Many regarded his work as useless because it could not be tested empirically (an assessment Lévi-Strauss emphatically disagreed with).

Lévi-Strauss's kinship theory (often referred to as alliance theory, as opposed to structural-functionalist descent theory) was already debated in Britain during the 1950s (although misunderstandings were inevitable because of the lack of translations). Within structural-functionalism, there had been growing dissatisfaction with descent theory, which seemed to be

unable to account for kinship systems that were non-unilinear. The structuralist focus on exchange and alliance seemed to have the potential to
resolve these problems, since it accorded greater weight to lateral than lineal
kin relationships; thus it was widely embraced by anthropologists working
in societies without clear-cut unilineal descent groups. In a famous debate in
the journal *Man*, in 1959, Leach thus defended Lévi-Strauss's views, while
Fortes defended the descent model. But even Leach may have misunderstood
Lévi-Strauss's intentions, which were less sociological and more concerned
with meaning than his British colleagues tended to believe. Like the
formalist-substantivist controversy in economic anthropology, the debate
on alliance versus descent in kinship studies slowly petered out towards the
end of the 1970s. By then, there was a tendency to see the two systems as
complementary (a tradition that may be followed all the way back to
Morgan), and Lévi-Strauss himself proposed a theory of kinship that seemed
to incorporate both perspectives (see Lévi-Strauss 1987b).

    In France, Louis Dumont (1911–98) developed his own brand of struc-
turalism, by combining impulses from Lévi-Strauss with classical European
sociology (Durkheim, Tönnies) into an influential theory of social integration
and symbolic meaning. Dumont, who is particularly well known for his
erudite study of the Indian caste system, *Homo Hierarchicus* (1968), posited
that caste was a cultural system of classification, rather than a functional
means of social organisation (a view not dissimilar to Needham's). He
emphasised the irreducibility of Indian (Hindu) categories, in explicit
opposition to political anthropologists like Barth, who had described caste
in purely sociological terms, and argued that strategic actors were driven by
the same kinds of motivations as Europeans. Still, Dumont was more sociologically oriented than Lévi-Strauss, and his analysis emphasises the
uniqueness of Indian culture, values and categories.

THE STATE OF THE ART IN 1968

By 1968, anthropology had become a very diverse discipline. The 'Man the
Hunter' symposium had just been held, demonstrating the power of an eco-
logically oriented anthropology. The interpretive anthropology of Geertz had
begun to exert its influence. Peasant studies in Latin America and the
Caribbean had become a mainstay at some American departments. Barth's
radical 'transactionalism' (his preferred term was 'generative process
analysis') rubbed shoulders with the creative revitalisation of structural-
functionalism carried out by Douglas and Turner. The rationality debate was
on, formalism confronted substantivism, alliance theory confronted descent
theory, while structuralism loomed on the horizon, and young radical
Marxists and feminists waited in the wings for their share of the academic
pie. New journals, conferences and workshops, monograph series and insti-

tutions devoted to anthropological research made important contributions to the growth and diversification of anthropology.

The demographic expansion had been formidable. In 1950, a mere 22 Ph.D.s were awarded in the USA. By 1974, the number had increased to 409, a level that remained stable at least until the mid-1990s (Givens and Jablonski 1995). However, the discipline had grown not only in complexity and size, but in its geographic dispersal. Dutch, Scandinavian, Italian and Spanish anthropology became part of the mainstream – in the two former cases, the Anglo-American influence was strongest; in the latter, the main impulses came from France. In several Latin American countries, notably Mexico, Brazil and Argentina, indigenous anthropologies influenced both by the Boas school, by Steward and his students, and by French anthropology, flourished and did research on both Indians and peasants. But in spite of strong non-metropolitan milieus such as Leiden and Bergen, the discipline remained centralised. In Britain, Oxford, Cambridge and London still held the reins, although Manchester was becoming a power to be reckoned with, and anthropology was taught in several other places as well. In the USA, the dispersal was greater, since the numbers were greater, but prominent universities such as Columbia, Yale, Harvard, Berkeley, Stanford, Michigan and Chicago still had the lead. In France, all roads led towards the prestigious institutions in Paris.

The 1950s and 1960s also saw considerable diversification of the core areas for ethnographic research. During the 1920s and 1930s British anthropologists had expanded from the Pacific to Africa, American anthropology saw a less pronounced move from Native North America to South and Central America. In France, both Africa and the Pacific had been important since the 1920s and, after the war, Georges Balandier further strengthened the African orientation (Balandier 1967), while Dumont and his students flocked to the Indian subcontinent and Oceania. By the 1960s, the mountaineous New Guinean highlands had become an extremely fertile area for ethnographic research, and with this change came new perspectives on gender relations, warfare, exchange and kinship. For although anthropological research may be carried out anywhere, each region tends to confront ethnographers with new questions.

In spite of occasional attempts at dialogue, there was still little contact between the three dominant national traditions. As we have repeatedly pointed out in the last two chapters, research interests were frequently similar, but the theoretical approaches were sufficiently different to make direct discussion difficult. Firth and Schneider had to abandon their comparison of kinship in London and Chicago. Lévi-Strauss debunked Needham's interpretation of his work. While Kroeber and Kluckhohn presented 162 definitions of culture, few British anthropologists had discussed the concept since Tylor. There was a lot of individual movement going on, though mostly in a westward direction: Bateson, Turner and Polanyi had settled in the USA, and Lévi-Strauss spent the war there. Many others were to make the move later, particularly from Britain. The national traditions were nevertheless still relatively bounded.

Language differences played their part in this. The belated translations of Lévi-Strauss delayed the acceptance of structuralism by at least a decade in most of the English-speaking world, and research published in less prestigious European vernaculars than French generally fared even worse. Throughout much of the 'Third World' (a term introduced into English by anthropologist Peter Worsley in 1964; in French *le tiers monde* had been used, with a slightly different meaning, since the 1950s), these problems were exacerbated by the lack of adequate economic resources in academia. Finally, political conflicts delayed the internationalisation of the discipline. In the former colonies, hostility was often directed at anthropology as such, thus inhibiting and sometimes even halting its spread. With decolonisation, the relationship between metropolitan institutions and their colonial counterparts was severed. In Europe two decades earlier, the Iron Curtain had effectively prevented most academic contacts between East and West. Anthropology was becoming a global discipline, as scholars increasingly started publishing in English, but even in the West, scholars in, say, Stockholm, could draw inspiration from metropolitan anthropologists, but they could also feel certain that their own work would never be read outside of Scandinavia unless they chose to publish in a foreign language.

With the next chapter, we rapidly approach the present, and we begin to recognise research interests that are still high on the agenda at the turn of the millennium. The radical Marxism of the 1970s lies at the root of various present-day research agendas. The radical feminism of that decade has been transformed into sophisticated gender studies. Research on ethnicity in complex societies has continued, and spawned later burgeoning interest in nationalism. The new discussions of fieldwork methods that saw the light of day in the early 1970s were soon to be drawn up into wider debates on reflexivity and field ethics, which are still eliciting professional interest. On the other hand, the political awareness that was so powerful in anthropology during these years eventually receded, along with the optimistic hope that anthropological insight could change the world. Nevertheless, while anthropologists in 1968 were still grappling with problems that would soon seem outdated, several of the concerns of 1978 remained important in 2001 as well.

7 QUESTIONING AUTHORITY

The Cuban missile crisis, the Berlin Wall, Martin Luther King, the Prague spring, hippies in Haight-Ashbury, student riots in Paris, the Beatles, the Moon landing, the Vietnam war – all this is emblematic of the 'Sixties', as the term is understood in the West. But the radical political climate to which these events contributed did not come to bloom before the end of the decade, and belongs, strictly speaking, to the ten years *following* 1968. Certainly this is true of academia, where students may shout their slogans but the tenured professors remain as the years pass by. Anthropologists, always a radical bunch, may have searched their souls more deeply than many other academics, but were no less subject to the academic routine than them. Enter the 1970s, the forgotten decade, sandwiched between Flower Power and the Iron Lady, between Richard Nixon's election victory and John Lennon's death, the decade when world population hit 4 billion, when we had the Middle East oil crisis, the coup in Chile, the founding of Microsoft, the deaths of Mao and Elvis, the first Polish pope and the Sandinista revolution in Nicaragua. It was a decade of revolutionary dreams that would soon enough be crushed under the wheels of history – in anthropology as elsewhere.

As we get closer to our own age we must warn the reader more strongly of the unavoidable bias of any book such this one. As time goes by, the sheer size of the discipline must necessarily force us to be either extremely selective, or too superficial to be informative at all. By the late 1990s, the American Anthropological Association alone had more than 10,000 paying members, and around the globe there would be countless regional centres of academic and applied anthropology, each with their own specific research traditions. No historian in the world could do justice to this growing multiplicity – which, by the end of the 1970s, was already well advanced.

In this chapter, we deal mainly with two of the most powerful intellectual currents to arise from the radicalisation of academia, namely Marxism and feminism. Both were insistently present everywhere in anthropology in the 1970s, until disillusionment set in, and new agendas were set. But gender and power had arrived in anthropology, and were destined to stay.

An account of the 1970s which concentrated exclusively on radicalisation would leave out some very important features of the anthropology of that period: after all, it was also the decade when ethnicity studies came into their own, when sociobiology became a household word (and something either to abhor or to emulate), and when economic anthropology had its golden age. French anthropology had re-entered the international scene with Lévi-Strauss, and now a whole company of Frenchmen appeared on the scene, with messages that were not only politically radical, but intellectually challenging as well. It was a decade of controversies, and it is the first decade in which anthropology had grown so vast and interconnected, that it is no longer possible to trace even the most important of its connections. What follows, however, should give an impression of some of the more fundamental events that belong to the 1970s.

THE RETURN OF MARXISM

In the previous generation of anthropologists, Steward, White and Gluckman were probably the authors most decisively influenced by Marx – Steward in his materialism, White in his technological determinism, Gluckman through his interest in crisis and conflict. However, references to Marx in their work were all but absent. There are scattered references to Marx and Marxist theory in the work of a few Anglophone anthropologists in the 1950s and early 1960s, including Eric Wolf and Stanley Diamond in the USA, and Peter Worsley in Britain. The ideological climate of the 1950s and 1960s was neither congenial nor receptive to Marxists; this was especially so in the USA, but the situation was not much easier in Britain. A card-carrying English Communist like Worsley had experienced serious difficulties in obtaining research permits and finding employment, before finally securing a job in sociology at Manchester University, supported by Gluckman.

In Britain, the USA and France, all this changed quickly in the 1960s, certainly among the students. Marxist theory of alienation and ideology as false consciousness, the infrastructure–superstructure distinction and the concept of contradiction entered the standard academic vocabulary in the late 1960s, and many young anthropologists began seriously to engage with the then 100-years-old theory of social classes and historical change. Now, grafting Marxist theory onto contemporary anthropology was not an easy task. As described in Chapter 2, Marxism was chiefly a theory about capitalist society. Its attempts to describe and compare different modes of production and engage in long-term cultural history, the latter task mainly undertaken by Engels after Marx' death, were deeply influenced by Victorian, unilineal evolutionist anthropology. The discipline had been moving in other directions for almost a century since then. If anything at all held the sprawling profession together in the mid-1960s, it would have to be a commitment to empirical variation, a distrust of simplistic, universalist models, and an ingrown cultural relativism. To state, as Marx and Engels had, that some societies were 'more advanced' than others, was simply not good anthropology.

Evolutionism aside, Marx had also presented a compelling vision of the modern world, which in a context of ever more visible global injustices seemed no less relevant to the 1970s than to the 1870s. On fieldwork, anthropologists were increasingly exposed to such injustices, and many were eager to contribute to their demolition. Marx was the sociologist who spoke most eloquently of these problems, and so it was to Marx that the young revolutionaries flocked. No matter that Marxism was more than a social theory; that it had become the official state ideology of a substantial portion of the world, and had thus obviously become a resource of political power. To a Marxist in particular, this should have been a fact of deep significance, but it rarely was. Instead, the power structures of the great Communist states paradoxically reproduced themselves in the organisations outside those states that fought for freedom from other power structures. Meanwhile, in Western academia, devastating battles took place between Maoists, Trotskyites, Stalinists, Anarcho-Syndicalists and so on, who nonetheless all united to face the common enemy, usually personified in the local anthropology professor. Out of all this commotion grew the academic Marxist anthropologies.

There were several distinctive strands of Marxist anthropology. One, which we could label cultural Marxism or superstructure studies, arrived so late on the scene that it was already post-Marxist by the time it was established in anthropology in the 1980s. This was the brand of Marxism inspired by Antonio Gramsci's critical studies of ideology and hegemony and the Frankfurt School's, particularly Adorno and Horkheimer's, critique of the commodification of culture. This form of Marxian thought entered anthropology via Edward Said's *Orientalism* (1978), a book that criticised European representations of Arab and other West Asian peoples for unduly exoticising 'the other' (Chapter 8). Take Said's critique, mix with Michel Foucault's post-structuralism and add a dash of deconstructionism à la Derrida, and the result is the heady cocktail that would hit anthropology in the 1980s.

The two main flavours of Marxian anthropology were structural Marxism and political economy. It is a testimony both to the breadth of Marx' work and to the scope of anthropology that there was little contact between these schools, and that the questions they raised were strikingly different.

Finally, there was also a fourth brand of Marxism, that followed up Marx's own emphasis on the person as a productive, creative material body in a material world. We will return to this 'sensual Marxism', with its roots in German Romanticism, towards the end of this chapter.

STRUCTURAL MARXISM

One of the first harbingers of the new era was a paper published in 1960 by the French anthropologist Claude Meillassoux, who presented an unmistakably Marxist analysis of subsistence production in agricultural societies. Originally an economist and a businessman, Meillassoux had studied anthropology with Balandier and did fieldwork among the Guro of the Ivory Coast in the late 1950s. His research was from the start of a Marxian orientation, in that it not only concentrated on economic life, but tried to map out the dynamics between the social relations of production and the technological and environmental means of production in Guro society. Meillassoux's article (1960) represented the first evidence of an emerging French Marxist anthropology. He would later develop a typology of 'pre-capitalist modes of production' in Africa, but, unlike his younger contemporaries, Meillassoux was mainly a committed empirical researcher, and he would be increasingly critical of the lofty theories that would come to dominate French Marxist anthropology. Indeed, among the French Marxists, Meillassoux was the one most sympathetic to the British school. In a preface to the English translation of his 1975 book *Femmes, greniers et capitaux* (*Maidens, Meal and Money*, Meillassoux 1981), he writes that Balandier had introduced him to 'the best of current anthropology – that is British anthropology' and goes on to praise the work of Schapera, Gluckman, Monica Wilson and others. However, he notes that functionalism 'was based more on a sort of legalistic empiricism than on a thorough analysis of the content of economic and social relationships' (1981: viii), and that it concealed economic exploitation by allowing kinship to permeate the entire field of inquiry. A main task for Meillassoux, then, was to extricate economics from kinship. This was not an easy thing to do when writing about societies organised on the basis of kinship, and he eventually proposed a mode of production not described by Marx or Engels, which he called 'the domestic mode of production', based on the family and the household. Interestingly, Sahlins, in his *Stone Age Economics* (1972), developed a nearly identical concept, but with a different aim: rather than reconciling African economies with Marxist theory, he sought to rescue economic anthropology from the perils of formalism, where the individualist maximiser was the universal actor. In Sahlins's view, the household taken as a unit was not a maximising actor, and drawing on both Chayanov's early peasant studies and Mauss's theory of reciprocity, he argued that household-based production is not a means of maximisation, but a way of procuring necessities.

An enduring obstacle in Marxist theory for the new French anthropologists was the notion that power ultimately rests with control over the means of production, that is ownership of tools, fields, machinery and so on. Since, in traditional African societies, such ownership is often not individual but accorded to kin groups, there was a problem in locating power in such societies. Meillassoux has to concede, seemingly contradicting Marx, that 'power in this mode of production rests on control over the means of human reproduction – subsistence goods and wives – and not over the means of production' (Meillassoux 1981: 49).

Structuralism was not a decisive impulse in Meillassoux's Marxism. Others were more ingenious in forging links between Marx, anthropology and current intellectual sensibilities, including not only Lévi-Strauss's work, but also the original interpretations of Marx proposed by the philosopher Louis Althusser. When Althusser's *Pour Marx* and his co-written (with Étienne Balibar) *Lire Le Capital* were published in 1965, the books had a major impact not only on French intellectual life in general, but also on the new generation of anthropologists. Althusser's Marxism seemed to suit anthropology well, since it introduced a measure of flexibility in the infrastructure–superstructure relationship. A conventional reading of Marx would state that the infrastructure (material + social features of the process of production) determines the superstructure (everything else in society). In non-capitalist (or 'pre-capitalist') societies, it was often very difficult to see how this came about. Most non-Marxist anthropologists simply would not believe it; it contradicted everything they had ever learned. In British anthropology, politics or kinship were assumed to be fundamental, in American anthropology, symbolic systems were seen as an autonomous world, and the work of Lévi-Strauss (who explicitly but confusingly had characterised himself as a Marxist) was concerned with the superstructure exclusively. This was also true of Dumont, who rose to fame with the publication of *Homo Hierarchicus* in 1968. His view, that the values of a society ultimately determined its power structure, was directly opposite to that of the Marxists – indeed, it marked a departure in the opposite direction from theirs.

Althusser, who wrote extensively on ideology, legitimated research on rituals and myths as devices of domination. He further held that in a given society, any social institution can be dominant in the sense that it *de facto* dominates, but whether it does so or not will always ultimately be determined by the infrastructure. In medieval Europe, for example, the Church was the dominant institution, but it was ultimately determined by the feudal mode of production that the Church should dominate – and ultimately serve the ends of that mode of production. (The word 'ultimately' here points to a vague spot in Althusser, which was reproduced in many of his followers. According to an oft-quoted phrase the economy exerts 'determination in the last instance', meaning that even if it may seem as if other institutions than the economy are the most important in a given society, they are *ultimately* determined by economic relationships. Although the phrase 'determination in the last instance' is often attributed to Marx, it was actually uttered by Engels at Marx's funeral.)

In the hands of the most famous of the French Marxist anthropologists, Maurice Godelier (1934–), the influences from Marx, Althusser and comparative ethnography merged with an equally strong admiration for the work of Lévi-Strauss. Unlike Meillassoux and several other French Marxist anthropologists, who regarded structuralism as a form of neo-Kantian, idealist mystification, Godelier – who had worked with Lévi-Strauss in the early 1960s – saw structuralism as a real scientific advance. In his view, the Marxist concept of contradiction could make structuralism more historical, while the conceptual apparatus of structuralism was indispensable in locating the hidden mechanisms of society and culture. At one stage,

Godelier even went so far as to suggest that Marx was a structuralist *avant la lettre* (1966, republished in Godelier 1977).

Godelier, who was originally educated as a philosopher, was converted to anthropology by Lévi-Strauss and has done extensive fieldwork among the Baruya of New Guinea. More theoretically inclined than Meillassoux, his project, apart from reconciling Marx and structuralism, is a comparative study of different economic systems. The Baruya, with their non-monetary economy based on subsistence and barter, indicated important differences between capitalist and non-capitalist societies.

Godelier was also – like Meillassoux – concerned with kinship. Since kinship seemed to be 'everywhere' in traditional societies, he reasoned that it had to be seen as part of both the superstructure and the infrastructure (Godelier 1975). Rather than looking for particular institutions that took care of economy, ideology and so on, he proposed a 'formalised Marxism' that instead looked for *functions*. Such formulations are further indications of the need felt by many of these researchers for a more flexible Marxian theory.

Much of the structural Marxist scholarship dealt with modes of production. Marx and Engels' own idea of an 'Asiatic mode of production' was eagerly discussed, and notions of one or several 'African modes of production' were widely debated following the research of Meillassoux and others on that continent. These debates have mostly died out since the 1970s, along with most anthropological attempts at grand typologies.

British Marxist anthropology was largely a subsidiary of the French structural variety. At the eve of the late 1960s radicalisation, Lévi-Strauss was acknowledged as the most worthy antagonist of and discussion partner for homegrown theories, and since American Marxist anthropology (see p. 119) was close kin to human ecology – a non-existent field in Britain – this may seem easy to understand. To this, it must also be added that the most important British Marxist anthropologist, Maurice Bloch, was French by origins.

The fundamental problem with Marxism in anthropology was, and is, that it is essentially a theory of capitalist society, and that its message about 'pre-capitalist societies' was couched in the language of unilineal evolutionism. To reconcile orthodox Marxism with ethnographic research required a strong will, and as Jonathan Spencer (1996: 353) points out, when competent ethnographic analysis was carried out by Marxist anthropologists, 'it did become more obviously cultural, but looked less and less convincingly Marxist'. Nevertheless, many French Marxist anthropologists, notably Godelier, continued to publish anthropological work with a distinctly Marxist flavour through the 1980s and 1990s. Others, like Bloch and Marc Augé (see Chapter 9), eventually changed their research priorities. Though Joel Kahn and Josip Llobera, in a review article from 1980, wrote that it was too early then to 'produce a definitive critique' of the movement (Kahn and Llobera 1980: 89), it had already fizzled out as a cohesive trend when the review article was eventually published.

THE NOT-QUITE-MARXISTS

While the French Marxist anthropologists were most often politically active, within or outside the French Communist Party, this was rarely the case with the American Marxist or Marxist-influenced anthropologists of the 1960s and 1970s. In spite of this, it is easy to see in retrospect that their contributions had a more direct bearing on global injustice and essential political issues than the more academic efforts of their French colleagues.

Marxist anthropology in the USA developed among Steward's, White's and Fried's students in the early postwar years, began to make its mark towards the end of the 1960s, flourished in the 1970s and reached its high point only in the early 1980s. The concerns of these scholars, perhaps less bound by contemporary intellectual fashions than the French structural Marxists, continue to play an important part in anthropological studies of power and underdevelopment today. Though this generation of materialist American anthropologists included some of the most important figures of the 1970s, some (like Marvin Harris) never really became Marxists, while others (like Marshall Sahlins) followed complex intellectual itineraries of their own, passing through a Marxist phase but eventually abandoning it. Sahlins, originally an evolutionist trained by White, engaged creatively and energetically with the Marxist debates about modes of production and forms of subsistence, arguing in a famous, almost Rousseauesque contribution to the 'Man the Hunter' symposium that hunter and gatherer societies represented 'the original affluent society' (1968, reprinted in Sahlins 1972), and that economies of scarcity were the result of the inequalities imposed by the agricultural revolution. In the centrepiece of his subsequent collection of essays, *Stone Age Economics* (1972), 'On the sociology of primitive exchange', Sahlins argued that the logic of generalised reciprocity, or sharing, was the norm in tribal societies, where the calculating, 'economising' actor of formalist economics was conspicuously absent. But already in this book, marked by Marxian concerns as it is, Sahlins was more convincing in his culturalist arguments than in his attempts to show causal connections between modes of production and symbolic culture. Then, in 1976, in his important theoretical treatise, *Culture and Practical Reason*, Sahlins angrily criticised Marxism for its reductionism and for not treating symbolic culture as it ought to be treated, as an autonomous realm.

The itinerary followed by Sahlins – from cultural ecology via Marxism to a concern with symbolism – was less idiosyncratic than it might seem. Several other American anthropologists followed similar (if not identical) routes. Columbia-trained Andrew P. Vayda, whose research priorities moved, between the 1960s and 1980s, from a strong version of cultural ecology to a cognitivist and almost postmodern attitude towards theorising, is one example (see Vayda 1994). A close collaborator of Vayda in the 1960s, Roy Rappaport also moved from a materialist position to a cybernetic vision.

In the long series of postscripts to the 1984 edition to *Pigs for the Ancestors*, Rappaport reveals a decreasing commitment to ecological determinism and increasing sophistication in his analyses of feedback loops in communication. The influence of Bateson was decisive in his case.

With Marvin Harris (1927–2001), the situation was very different. Though a student at Columbia under Steward, he was committed to mainstream Boasian anthropology in his student years, discovering White's and Steward's work only in the mid-1950s. Following fieldwork in Mozambique, when he was confronted with the miseries of Portuguese colonialism, Harris's politics were radicalised, and his analytical interests were also sharpened. Over the next decades, Harris would develop his own research programme, or 'paradigm' as he might have called it, based on the notion that the material facts of economy and ecology *determine* culture – not merely 'in the last instance' but directly. In a famous article from 1963, he discusses the sacred cow of Hinduism, and concludes that the cow's special status may seem to be an exotic feature of Hindu religion, but it is actually a perfect example of economic and ecological rationality. Accusations of functionalism, to which Harris paid no heed, were inevitable. Later in the 1960s and 1970s, Harris's materialism became more pronouncedly non-Marxist, and in his main theoretical work, *Cultural Materialism* (1979), he spends half the book repudiating what he regards as inferior alternative research programmes – from sociobiology and Marxism to 'eclecticism'. Harris was the strongest positivist materialist in American anthropology, and he saw the Marxist insistence on a 'dialectical relationship' between infrastructure and superstructure as a mystifying and non-scientific device. His opponents, and there were many, would class him variously as a crude materialist evolutionist or a vulgar Marxist with no understanding of the subtler aspects of society. Describing his own intellectual roots, he states that '[t]he basic materialism came from Marx and [behaviourist psychologist] B.F. Skinner; the importance of economic factors also from Marx; the overall evolutionism from White; and the environmental and demographic foci from Steward and [cultural historian Karl] Wittfogel' (Harris 1994: 76). Harris published a popular textbook and, in 1968, a history of anthropology (*The Rise of Anthropological Theory*), which describes the history of the discipline more or less as a unilinear evolutionist narrative (with minor branches and dead ends), ending not unsurprisingly with cultural materialism.

Even in Britain, the debate between Marxism and cultural ecology was activated. Having hovered on the outskirts of respectable university life for decades, cultural ecology finally found a few tenured adherents, and it soon became clear that although cultural ecology and Marxism pose many of the same questions, they answer them in profoundly different ways (Burnham and Ellen 1979). In a pyrotechnical demolition of Rappaport's work on the Tsembaga Maring, Jonathan Friedman (1979) – who had re-analysed Leach's Kachin work in a structural Marxist framework in his Ph.D. dissertation – argued that Rappaport's ecological analysis of Tsembaga ritual fell into the classic traps of functionalism, by positing, as it seemed to do, 'the great ecologist in the sky' as an omniscient subject regulating pig populations as needed. Rappaport's response would be a sophisticated Batesonian plea for the unity of 'mind', which argued that in the conceptual universe of the Tsembaga there was *no difference* between the material and the symbolic – hence no 'great ecologist' or 'functionalism' was necessary; the local symbolic vernacular was in effect a specialised discourse on ecology.

POLITICAL ECONOMY AND THE CAPITALIST WORLD SYSTEM

The leading proponent of Marxist or Marxist-influenced American anthropology (he did not describe his work as Marxist himself) was arguably Eric Wolf (1923–99). The 'high point' of American Marxist anthropology alluded to above was the publication of his major work, *Europe and the People Without History* in 1982, a magisterial inquiry into the complex economic, cultural and political effects of colonialism on the peoples studied by anthropologists. Here Wolf concentrates, as he did in much of his work, on features of the lives and histories of non-Europeans that had been neglected by generations of anthropologists. Wolf, originally an Austrian, was yet another of Steward's and Benedict's Columbia students, and he retrospectively pointed out that both his teachers had, 'each in their own way, intensified my own interest in how subgroups and regions came to be welded into overarching nations' (Wolf 1994: 228). A member of Steward's Puerto Rican project in the late 1940s, Wolf later worked on peasant issues in Mexico, and published an important synthetic work, *Peasants*, in 1964. Opposed to the single-society approach favoured by dominant schools of anthropology, Wolf explored, throughout his life, how the destinies of localities are intertwined with large-scale processes. More often than not, the engine of these processes is economic profit, and the result is capital accumulation in the centre and exploitation in the periphery. Peasants were, more than any other group, the victims of this exploitation. Deprived of land and producing for the global market at often ridiculous wages, they also tended to live in poor countries, whose national autonomy was undermined because of their unequal integration into the world economy.

Wolf was far from alone in pursuing these interests in world-system theory, imperialism and underdevelopment during the 1970s. Along with Marx, anthropology had discovered Lenin, whose theory of imperialism was a logical add-on to Marx' own theory, and an alternative to prevailing views (outside anthropology) about the civilising effects of colonialism. In a period when rural sociology was a rapidly expanding field of inquiry, not least in Latin America, Marxist political economy seemed a natural part of any Third World-oriented scholar's field kit, particularly since social scientists had begun to engage in development issues on a far larger scale than ever before (see Grillo and Rew 1985). The most ambitious attempt at a synthesis along these lines during the 1970s was Immanuel Wallerstein's neo-Trotskyist *The Modern World System* (Wallerstein 1974–9), a massive study of the development of a tripartite world of centres, semiperipheries and peripheries, with resources generally flowing from the outer reaches to the centres. On a less grand scale, it was also the decade of Johan Galtung's structural theory of imperialism (Galtung 1971), which showed how global inequality was maintained through alliances between the elites of the centres and the elites of the peripheries.

The 1970s also saw the rise of *dependency theory*, that close cousin of world-system theory. While theorists of development had formerly held that all societies would eventually 'catch up' with the West, a crypto-evolution-ist position that was anthropologically unpalatable (and besides, hardly empirically correct), sociologists and economists like Andre Gunder Frank and Samir Amin, writing about Latin America and Africa, respectively, sought to demonstrate that exchange between rich and poor parts of the world – whether *de facto* colonies or not – amounted to capital accumula-tion in the north and deprivation in the south. However, the dependency theorists tended to be non-anthropologists, and the main exception, Peter Worsley, seemed merely to prove this rule. Although Worsley was Gluckman's student, he worked at a sociology department, and most of his work was in a sociological vein. It was not that anthropologists were cynical accomplices of world imperialism, that their cultural relativism had led them to moral nihilism, or that they were oblivious to the suffering of the world. On the contrary, during the 1970s (and earlier) many anthropologists had gone to great lengths to help 'their' peoples improve their situation. These efforts, however, were largely concerned with indigenous populations, the holders of 'authentic cultures'. In the 1970s, the study of the millions of urban poor and semi-modern peasants had become a growth industry for anthropological research, but the prestige afforded by fieldwork in such groups could not be compared to that of fieldwork among 'authentic' cultures such as those represented in African foragers, Amazonian horti-culturalists or Arctic hunters.

The problem of anthropology's relation to the issues of neo-colonialism and Third World exploitation was at least fourfold. First, as suggested, the poor masses of the tropics were generally not considered worthy of sustained anthropological attention. They were 'too acculturated', and though ethno-graphic studies of modern people had existed throughout the twentieth century, it was only in the 1970s that they started to become common. But as yet, the theoretical framework to deal with such groups had not had time to develop. Second, the single-people approach favoured for both theoretical and methodological reasons by both the Boasians and the British, could not easily be reconciled with a concern with global political economy, though Steward's Puerto Rico project could be seen to indicate a middle way. Third, the historical relationship of anthropology to colonialism had been one of indifference – the only anthropologists of note to include the horizon of colonialism in their studies before the 1960s belonged to the Manchester school. One of the most debated books in British anthropology in the early 1970s was the Saudi-born anthropologist Talal Asad's *Anthropology and the Colonial Encounter* (Asad 1973), where most of the contributors argued that the development of anthropology and colonialism had been suspiciously parallel in several parts of the world. Fourth, and not least important, the notion of 'development' was – and is – a difficult one to swallow for anthropologists, who had for several generations been taught to be sceptical of ethnocentric notions of social evolution. Lévi-Strauss has said that he regards himself as a 'fourth-worldist' as opposed to a 'third-worldist', meaning that he defends the small, vulnerable and unique peoples against not just the onslaught of Westernisation, but also against the development schemes of Third World governments (Eribon and Lévi-Strauss 1988). In this, he probably speaks for a large part, possibly a majority, of the anthropological community of the 1970s.

These problems, difficult as they were, could be overcome, as Wolf's work revealed. Years earlier, Redfield had argued that peasants 'had their own culture', and although the quest for 'authentic culture' remained strong in anthropology, there were no strong academic arguments for not studying the hybridised, mixed cultures of, say, Latin America and the Caribbean. A combination of in-depth fieldwork with a wider systemic and historical analysis was also perfectly viable, although it did not quite legitimise the use of non-ethnographic material. The relationship to colonial authorities was irrelevant by the 1970s. What remained, then, was the problem of 'development', which seemed nearly as difficult to overcome as the French Marxists' problems with infrastructural determination in tribal societies. Many of the most creative anthropologists who worked with the issues of political economy in the 1970s had encountered this problem. In most cases they would argue, true to the principles of anthropology, that development had to be defined from within, that is as an 'emic' (native) category. At the same time, they regarded the fact of global capitalist expansion as an objective, homogenising and unifying force in the world, and, in this sense, Wolf and others anticipated a 1990s trend in anthropology, namely the study of globalisation.

There was a distinct regional focus on 'the backyard of the USA' in the 1970s anthropological research informed by Marxist political economy and world-system theory. Sidney Mintz (another of Steward's old students) at Johns Hopkins University, was, along with Wolf, the most important proponent of this school in the 1970s and later. Mintz is a Caribbeanist, whose finest works include a collection of essays on historical change in the Caribbean (Mintz 1974) and a cultural history of sugar, *Sweetness and Power* (Mintz 1985). This regional focus tended, like Steward's earlier efforts, to stimulate academic anthropology and rural sociology in the countries under study themselves. Unlike most places in the Third World, countries like Argentina, Mexico and Brazil offered thriving academic facilities, with a steady output of potential 'native' collaborators for Western anthropologists, with whom they could cooperate on an equal intellectual footing. This was good news for the many young, politically committed Western anthropologists, who carried out fieldwork among Latin American peasants within a Marxist theoretical framework (Melhuus 1993).

While French structural Marxism today appears as a dead end, it left a lasting imprint on the profession. It forcefully directed attention to the complex inter-weavings of local and global strands of inequality and power, resistance and survival; it grappled resolutely with historical change and with the difficult relationship between 'development' and culture. Most important of all, perhaps, it directed the attention of a blandly Durkheimian or Boasian mainstream to the imperative material conditions for life. This it had in common with the work of both the American materialists and the British interactionists. In the work of Godelier and Meillassoux, we may neverthe-less see the beginnings of a theory that addresses these issues in a wider perspective, trying to overcome the distinction usually drawn between the material and the ideational.

We have stated above that the boundary between structural Marxism and political economy was practially watertight. This was not always the case in practice, and there are some rare examples of 'crossover' anthropologists. The Argentinian anthropologist Eduardo Archetti is one such case. Archetti did undergraduate studies in sociology in Argentina before going on to study with Godelier in Paris in the late 1960s, when Mintz was also teaching in Paris. His main research interest was not in issues of infrastructural deter-mination or African modes of production, but in the underlying logic of peasant societies and their relationship to the outside world. He wrote an early, authoritative assessment of Chayanov's work. Under Godelier's supervision, he carried out fieldwork on peasants in Argentina, and wrote a doctoral thesis on which theories of underdevelopment and dependency made a deeper imprint than structural Marxism. When, in the mid-1970s, he began to teach at the University of Oslo, the professor who hired him reminisces that 'we took him on because we needed someone to teach the latest fads in French structural Marxism' (A.M. Klausen, personal commu-nication). One should always remind oneself that intellectual trajectories are rarely simple, and boundaries are rarely clear-cut.

FEMINISM – AND THE BIRTH OF REFLEXIVE FIELDWORK

In 1954, under the pseudonym of Elenor Smith Bowen, the American anthropologist Laura Bohannan published *Return to Laughter*, a remarkably candid and personal account of a (fictional) American woman anthropolo-gist on fieldwork among the Tiv of Nigeria. The pseudonym was deemed necessary, because it was not considered proper form to speak publicly about the personal aspect of fieldwork, the doubts and mistakes, fortuitous circumstances and general disjointedness that lurked behind the Malinowskian blanket term 'participant observation'. In 1966, Malinowski's old student Hortense Powdermaker published *Stranger and Friend: The Way of the Anthropologist*, where she describes a life of fieldwork expeditions to the most varied localities. Again, the impression is that fieldwork is perhaps not quite the orderly data collection that Radcliffe-Brown envisioned. Then, in 1967, Malinowski's own personal diaries from his Trobriand fieldwork, were found, edited and published – and created an immediate scandal. The master himself, it seemed, had been no more than mortal. He had been homesick, he had cursed the natives, masturbated and felt sorry for himself. How could anyone claim, after this, that they produced 'objective knowledge'?

Just a few years later, the philosophically inclined participants in the great Rationality Debate would grapple with these very questions, but in the meantime a group of young American women anthropologists responded more practically to the issue at hand. In 1970, the year Bryan Wilson's *Rationality* was published, an edited volume entitled *Women in the Field: Anthropological Experiences* (Golde 1970) appeared. Each of the many essays in this book recounts the concrete experiences under which the author's field research had occurred, and reflects on the effect of her experiences on the quality of her data. The essays are very different, reflecting a wide variety of practices and experiences in the field, but they all agree on one thing: the fact that they were women had a profound effect on the conclusions they brought home with them. In this way, the idea of 'positioned' fieldwork emerged, the idea that by reflecting on her personal role in the field, the anthropologist learns to understand exactly what kind of data she has received. Thus, *Women in the Field* put two debates on the agenda: how should we act, as reflexive fieldworkers? Moreover, what role does gender play in social systems?

The first question was responded to with a series of detailed, practical accounts of how concrete fieldwork situations had in fact been tackled. A further example of the genre is Rosalie Wax's *Doing Fieldwork: Warnings and Advice*, published in 1971, where the budding anthropologist is told, in no uncertain terms, What You Are Getting Into.

The second question – how can gender be studied anthropologically? – introduces the first male participant into this hitherto completely female account. The man was the British anthropologist Edwin Ardener (1927–87), who published 'Belief and the problem of women' in 1972 (in Ardener 1989). An Oxford anthropologist who had carried out extensive fieldwork in Cameroon and Nigeria, Ardener was an original and intellectually challenging anthropologist whose most important theoretical papers (collected in Ardener 1989) deal with the relationship between social anthropology and linguistics, problems of translation, generalisation and intelligibility. He was also, however, concerned with issues concerning power, not least regarding who controls the power of definition in a society.

Combined with his sustained interest in language – a rare specialisation in British social anthropology – it should not come as a surprise that Ardener should make such an important contribution to this field. His wife, Shirley Ardener, was a leading figure in British feminist anthropology at the same time, and edited two important collections in the 1970s (S. Ardener 1975, 1978).

Ardener began his essay with a memorable sentence: 'The problem of women has not been solved by social anthropologists.' He immediately went on to add that 'the problem' was not that of the position of women, although much later feminist scholarship would lament the absence of this topic from classic anthropology as well. Ardener's 'problem' was the conspicuous absence of women from the pages of most of the classics of anthropology, even in books that had been written by female anthropologists – though he mentions Audrey Richards' work *Chisungu* (1956) as an exception. The main cause for this absence was probably a general male bias in Western society, but this did not fully account for the problem in anthropology. Ardener went on to argue that ethnographers, male or female, more easily found a rapport with male informants than with women. In nearly all societies, men dominated the public sphere, and they were more used to talking to outsiders. The cultural models of society that the ethnographer brought back from the field were therefore chiefly those of the men. He spoke of women as *a muted group*, not in the sense that they were not permitted to speak, but in the sense that their statements were generally not framed in terms that were easily transferred to fieldnotes. On this point, Ardener's analysis was reminiscent of sociolinguistic studies of class, race and language in the USA, where it was shown that black and working-class children did badly in school partly because of their 'context-dependent' style of expression (see Giglioli 1976). At any rate, Ardener's paper and the debate it occasioned, raised similar questions in Britain as Golde's book had in the USA.

Two years later, the response came, again from a group of American women anthropologists, in the form of another edited volume, but now in a more theoretical vein: *Woman, Culture and Society* (1974), edited by Michelle Z. Rosaldo and Louise Lamphere. Ardener's two main questions were dealt with there.

First, Ardener had presupposed – as a premise for the mutedness of women – that societies generally distinguish between a private and a public sphere, where men control the latter and women are confined to the former. Rosaldo, one of the editors, discusses the domestic–public contrast comparatively in her contribution, showing that in general, women's efforts are confined to the immediate vicinity of the home, due to the physical constraints imposed by frequent childbirths. They constitute a domestic sphere around them on the basis of these (publicly muted) activities. Men, on the other hand, roam further afield, and constitute a public sphere around such (publicly visible) activities as ritual, politics and trade.

Second, towards the end of his paper Ardener had noted that women are often associated with 'wild' nature, while men are considered essentially 'human'. Sherry Ortner, who would later write about the Sherpas of Nepal, as well as producing several influential theoretical articles, asked, 'Is female to male as nature is to culture?' (Ortner 1974). She posits that 'each culture, in its own way and on its own terms', regards women as 'in some degree inferior to men' (p. 69), and describes the train of symbolic associations that connects the socially oppressed to the non-social world. Another article in the collection (once again) demolishes the myth of the original matriarchy (Bamberger), yet another discusses sexual imagery and the division of labour (O'Laughlin).

The lasting impact of *Woman, Culture and Society* – and there are probably few anthropologists trained after the mid-1970s who have not come across it – owes much to its distinctly un-revolutionary tone. It was a collection of anthropological essays about gender relations, not a political manifesto. The book, and numerous later edited collections about women and (increasingly) gender, contributed to permanent changes in the research priorities of anthropology, although – and this is in the nature of change – these changes themselves continued to change in the 1980s and 1990s.

It is difficult to assess the impact of feminism on anthropology. In the last two decades of the twentieth century, its theoretical impulses were often hard to distinguish from the growing current of postcolonial, multicultural and postmodernist studies. The new emphasis on 'women's worlds' led to a series of ethnographies which focused on women, from Jean Briggs' account of emotional life among Canadian Inuit (1970), to Annette Weiner's sophisti- cated re-study of the Trobriand Islands (1976), to Michelle Rosaldo's discussion of language and emotion among the headhunting Ilongot of the Philippines (1980), to Robert and Yolanda Murphy's gender-sensitive monograph on the Mundurúcu of Brazil (1985). These and other books challenged the orthodox view of what life was like in traditional societies. In 1967, it had still been unproblematic to speak of non-agricultural societies under the heading 'Man the Hunter'. In 1981, the collection *Woman the Gatherer* was published (Dahlberg 1981), and since the late 1970s, this kind of economy has been known as foraging, or hunting and gathering economy. In many cases, it was shown the gathering conducted by women and children contributed much more to subsistence than the men's hunting.

Feminist perspectives have also had more subtle effects on anthropologi- cal work, as the next chapters will show. The anthropology of the body, the study of kinship and gender, the interest in 'resistance' among oppressed groups, and numerous conceptual re-workings of the concept of power, would have been difficult to imagine without the growth of feminism as an intellectual movement within and outside anthropology. That decade was also, significantly, a period when female students in large numbers entered the discipline. Women in anthropology had hitherto been muted (though not completely, as Margaret Mead's or Audrey Richards' careers show). Now they were about to speak.

ETHNICITY

A third trend in 1970s anthropology, less immediately relevant to the world outside academia than either Marxism or feminism (but soon to be perceived as very relevant indeed!) was ethnicity studies. The growth in ethnicity studies was associated with at least four distinct centres. One was represented in the work of George DeVos and his associates at Berkeley (see, for example, DeVos and Romanucci-Ross 1975). Working with various ethnic minorities in Europe, the USA and elsewhere, DeVos and his group were committed to an anthropology aligned with the culture and personality school, but also inspired by social psychology and its interest in identity formation. To them, a crucial aspect of ethnicity was (and is) self-identification, but they were also concerned with the personality configurations of cultures in the tradition from Benedict.

Another body of research was concerned with 'plural societies'. Elaborated by British-trained Jamaican anthropologist Michael G. Smith (1965), the term referred to societies composed of multiple ethnic groups. Smith, originally a West Africanist who wrote increasingly from his native West Indies, saw the constituent groups of plural societies as culturally distinctive, often tight-knit corporations competing fiercely for power. A controversy related to the plural society addresses the question of whether the ethnic groups that make up such societies *are* in fact culturally discrete, since they have often been subjected to intensive cultural integration, not least in the Caribbean. The plural society debate recalls the Chicago school's discussion of the American melting-pot as well as the Manchester school's problems with de- and re-tribalisation in Africa, and led to no definite conclusion. Societies differ, and scholarly understandings of them differ as well. The plural society debate was particularly lively among Caribbeanists.

The two remaining trends in ethnicity studies were even more influential. They also converged on important issues. Both were British in origin, and both emphasised the instrumental, political dimension of ethnic relations rather than its cultural content. Both also had a major interest in identifying individual strategies.

Around 1970, several monographs by British Africanists on urbanisation and social change appeared. Abner Cohen, one of Gluckman's former students, published *Custom and Politics in Urban Africa* (1969), a study of trade and ethnicity in West Africa, which showed how Hausa merchants from northern Nigeria monopolised cattle trade through the use of networks based on kinship, ethnicity and, notably, religion. Writing from East Africa, David Parkin showed, in *Neighbours and Nationals in an African City Ward* (1969), how Luo tribal loyalties were transformed into modern ethnicity after migration into Nairobi. In these and other studies from the same period, the continuity with the Manchester school was strong. Indeed, Mitchell himself wrote one of the most important contributions to the edited collection *Urban Ethnicity* (Abner Cohen 1974b). In Cohen's introduction, and in his theoretical volume *Two-Dimensional Man* (1974a), this is abundantly clear. In this book, among the influences that may be discerned are Victor Turner's insistence on the multivocality of symbols, Mitchell's discussion of the transformation of tribal loyalty into modern ethnicity, and Gluckman's original fusion of structural-functionalism with an interest in social conflict. Cohen nevertheless went further than his mentors, with his explicit focus on the dual, emotional and political, character of ethnic symbols, and his observation that political entrepreneurs may manipulate such symbols to gain and guide the loyalty of their followers. Cohen also went far in divorcing ethnicity from culture, when he stated that 'City men' (London bankers) might well be seen as an ethnic group.

The most widely influential of the ethnicity studies from this period, however, was Barth's edited collection *Ethnic Groups and Boundaries* (1969). Based on a conference in 1967, and including contributions from leading Scandinavian anthropologists – including several of his former students – the book, and particularly the editor's introduction, was one of the most widely quoted works in academic anthropology during the last three decades of the twentieth century. Here Barth argued – not unlike Cohen, who worked on the same issues simultaneously – that ethnicity was chiefly a social and political, rather than a cultural, phenomenon. Barth, however, went on to say that it is 'the ethnic *boundary* that defines the group, not the cultural stuff that it encloses' (1969: 15). It is, in other words, the relationship *between* groups, not the culture *of* groups, that gives them meaning. The similarity with Lévi-Strauss's and Bateson's ideas of the nature of meaning is easily seen, and indicates the common interest of all these authors in cybernetics. Barth thus turned the focus of ethnicity studies away from the idea that ethnic identity is an aspect of shared culture, history and territory, to a more processual concept of boundary maintenance. The empirical studies that make up the body of the volume explore this idea, and analyse the economic, political and demographic communication that takes place across ethnic boundaries. The primacy of such communication was shown, for example, by the fact that major cultural differences could exist within a single ethnic group, or, on the contrary, that two distinct ethnic groups could have almost identical cultures. What mattered was not this, Barth stated, but the fact that the groups perceived themselves as different, and interacted on that assumption, proving their difference, to themselves and each other, through their interaction. Barth's formalist stance on ethnicity (all ethnic groups are defined by a universal *kind* of 'ethnic behaviour'), mirrors his preoccupation with formalist economics (e.g. 1967). The success of formalism in ethnicity studies has, however, been far greater.

Barth's contribution to ethnicity studies may in retrospect also be seen as a preamble to the later deconstructivist movement in anthropology, where the very notion of cultural wholes with a substantial content was questioned on epistemological, theoretical and methodological grounds (Chapter 9). For if the leaders of ethnic groups virtually fabricated differences vis-à-vis others for strategic reasons, what then remained of the Boasian conception of unique, cultural wholes?

Soon, furthermore, it would be discovered that the new models of ethnicity were compatible with the new trends in anthropology which emerged in the 1980s and 1990s, and focused on nationalism, globalisation and identity. In some of that work, several of the discrete tendencies discussed in this chapter came together: power inequality from Marxism and feminism, the global context from Marxism, 'muted' discourses and reflexivity from feminism, and cultural deconstruction from ethnicity studies. Though the leading European schools of ethnicity research described it mainly as a political and instrumental tool, more complex analyses were soon developed, which emphasised the dimensions of subjective identification and ontological security that are also inherent in ethnicity. Two influential books developing this aspect of ethnicity, rather than its sociological dimension, were Manchester anthropologist A.L. Epstein's *Ethos and Identity* (1978) and Anthony P. Cohen's *The Symbolic Construction of Community* (1985).

PRACTICE THEORY

In 1984, Sherry Ortner, who had contributed to Rosaldo and Lamphere's volume ten years earlier, published the article 'Theory in anthropology since the sixties'. Here she posits that a new, overarching theoretical paradigm had been emerging in anthropology during the previous two decades, which she refers to as 'practice theory'. Practice theory was, according to Ortner, an outgrowth of several dominant tendencies in the discipline, most prominently the old controversy between actor-oriented and structure-oriented approaches during the 1950s, and the Marxist and feminist work of the 1970s. This new, loosely defined tendency encompassed a variety of different research agendas, but there was a common meta-theoretical interest in unifying methodological individualism and collectivism, and exploring the role of the human body situated in a material world, as the main locus of social interaction. Though Ortner's references were mainly to American anthropologists, her conclusions were also descriptive of important trends in contemporary European social science.

The idea of a social theory that could unify actor-orientation and structure-orientation, as well as sociological and cultural-meaningful perspectives, was not new. Indeed, the very term practice (or *praxis*), the way it was used by the theorists referred to by Ortner, is derived from Marx, whose description of the human body as simultaneously exploited by and resistant to power derives from his value theory, and constitutes one of the most powerful statements in the social sciences. Moreover, the feminists, with their emphasis on power and gender, also forced the body to the forefront of analytical attention, as did the newly instituted sub-discipline, medical anthropology, which would become one of the most quickly growing specialisations in anthropology in the 1980s.

Some of these concerns would ultimately express themselves in a hesitant *rapprochement* of anthropology and biology during the 1990s (Chapter 9). During the 1970s, however, they attracted the attention of several of the leading lights of European social theory, two of whom will briefly be treated here, while we will concern ourselves with the third mainly in the next chapter.

In 1979, the sociologist Anthony Giddens (1938–), who has been described as 'Britain's best-known social scientist since Keynes', published *Central Problems in Social Theory*, a collection of essays that leaned heavily on Marx and Althusser, while also citing interaction theorists, such as Goffman and Barth. Giddens' explicit aim was to unify those two dimensions of social life which he referred to as *structure* and *agency*, respectively. In his *chef-d'œuvre*, *The Constitution of Society* (1984), Giddens covers much of the same ground as Bourdieu; instead of distinguishing between doxa and opinion (see below), he distinguishes between discursive and practical reason, adding the subconscious as a third level; and he reiterates the contrast between agency and structure as a fundamental tension in social life.

Accomplishing much of the same result as Bourdieu at a theoretical level, Giddens' work was poorer in empirical illustrations, and, partly for that reason, it was avidly read by anthropologists, but less used in actual research. His work, it may be said, engages more directly with the history of philosophy than with ethnographic or sociological data. It catalogues a range of perennial dichotomies in social science (materialist–idealist, power–resistance, individual–collective, conscious–unconscious, etc.), arranges them into a comprehensive, logically consistent system of thought, and lays down a number of important general principles of sociological research that were also relevant to anthropologists.

The concept of agency, which in Giddens' work evoked a conscious, strategic actor, acting within the structural constraints imposed by power on his body, is nearly identical to Ortner's concept of 'practice'. Practice is also the preferred term for the same phenomenon in the work of the French sociologist and anthropologist Pierre Bourdieu (1930–). Born into a lower middle-class family in a provincial town in France, Bourdieu studied in Paris (together with Michel Foucault and Jacques Derrida; see Chapter 8), and did fieldwork among the Kabyles, a Berber group in Algeria, during the War of Algerian Independence in the 1950s. He was deeply influenced by Marx and Lévi-Strauss, Mauss, Durkheim and Weber, and his project has been to unify all these influences into a simple but sensitive instrument for the study of human societies. Bourdieu has written on a wide range of subjects, including class, sports, art, taste, architecture, power, gender and exchange, and his influence on anthropology has been wide-ranging and profound. His most influential work to date, *Esquisse d'une théorie de la pratique* (1972; *Outline of a Theory of Practice*, 1977; cf. also Bourdieu 1990), uses Kabyle ethnography extensively, but is basically a sustained theoretical meditation on the relationship between collective norms, social power and individual agency, as these are expressed through and by the human body.

Two aspects of Bourdieu's theory will concern us here. First, the idea of *habitus*, which he borrows from Mauss and the German theorist Norbert Elias (1897–1990). Habitus is, roughly speaking, the permanent internalisation of the social order in the human body. The body inhabits a material world, a world of power, and a world of other people. The structural constraints inherent in this world are impressed on the body, forming permanent dispositions:

schemes of perception and thought, extremely general in their application, such as those which divide up the world in accordance with the oppositions between the male and the female, east and west, future and past, top and bottom, right and left, etc., and also, at a deeper level, in the form of bodily postures and stances, ways of standing, sitting, looking, speaking, or walking. (Bourdieu 1977: 15)

Habitus is thus a pervasive *aesthetical style* of action, which determines the actor in the manner of a dance – you cannot break out of it without loss of grace. At the same time, style, like dance, may be practised more or less skilfully, it may be utilised creatively, and opens infinite possibilities for variation and improvisation. Harking back to Bateson, and beyond him to Benedict, the concept of *habitus* seems to give tangible reality to the vague and general idea of *ethos*, by coupling it to power and the material world.

In the second part of his book, Bourdieu develops a model of symbolic culture, in which he distinguishes *doxa* and *opinion* as two basic forms of knowledge. Doxa refers to that which is taken for granted, which is beyond discussion and which, in many cases, cannot even be articulated by members of society. Opinion, in contrast, refers to those aspects of culture that are open to scrutiny, discussion and disagreement.

A third theorist with a profound impact on anthropological research on embodied practices, to whom we shall return in the next chapter, was the French philosopher and historian Michel Foucault (1926–84). In 1975, Foucault published an acclaimed study of the rise of the modern prison system in Europe, which rested heavily on the concept of *discipline*. Discipline, like habitus, is structure and power that have been impressed on the body, forming permanent dispositions. Foucault, however, stresses the violence of this 'impression' more strongly than Bourdieu, and gives a more vivid sense of the cost of modernisation for whoever is subjected to it. This aspect of Foucault's work had a fundamental influence on the anthropological studies of power and violence that came to the fore during the 1980s and 1990s (Chapters 8 and 9).

In sum, the practice theorists opened up a whole new field of inquiry for anthropology, by focusing on the human body as the central fact of all social existence. This interest connected them – directly or indirectly – to another group of researchers, who had been exploring the interface between biology and sociology. This group included Turner, whose late work on performance and ritual had a strong body-orientation. It included Bateson, who (with Mead) had worked on body language on Bali, and inspired such anthropologists as Ray Birdwhistell (1918–94), who did highly technical work on non-verbal communication. It also touched on the work of psychologists, linguists and cognitive anthropologists who had been exploring inborn or deeply imprinted linguistic and perceptual aptitudes (see Chapter 9). Finally, it connected to the work of a group of biologists and physical anthropologists who created a major stir in the discipline in the late 1970s through an attempt to redefine anthropology as a branch of the study of evolution (E.O. Wilson 1975). The strong resistance among mainstream anthropologists to this work is illustrated by the fact that when Victor Turner's posthumous 'Body, brain and culture' was published in 1987, his editor deemed it necessary to preface it with a long introduction, explaining that Turner had *not*, in his dotage, become a sociobiologist.

THE SOCIOBIOLOGY DEBATE AND SAMOA

In spite of its evolutionist overtones, Marxist anthropology was grudgingly acknowledged as a legitimate project by most of the senior figures in anthropology. Feminist anthropology was by and large welcomed as an elaboration of some of the perennial disciplinary concerns, and practice theory, particularly in Bourdieu's version, seemed to fit anthropology perfectly. With sociobiology, the reactions were different. It was met with extremely hostile reactions, and traditional antagonists – cultural materialists and hermeneuticians, British political anthropologists and French structural Marxists – temporarily joined forces in trying to exorcise the evil spirit of sociobiology. The centrepiece of the controversy was biologist Edward O. Wilson's book *Sociobiology* (1975). Most of it deals with non-human forms of 'social organisation', but in the final chapter, Wilson proposes to include the social sciences in the grand endeavour of evolutionary biology. He sees culture essentially as an adaptation in the biological sense; its main function consists in ensuring the production of offspring, and in order to understand what people are up to and how societies work, one has to see their activities in the light of the 'hardware' of their genetic apparatus. In Wilson's view, cultural phenomena such as religion, cooperation and morality have to be seen as biological adaptations. In the 'liberal' (which is an American euphemism for radical) intellectual milieux of the time, where feminism and Marxism loomed large, this biological determinism inevitably caused uproar. At a public meeting in 1978, a member of the audience poured a pitcher of ice-cold water over Wilson's head as he entered the podium to speak, and others chanted: 'Wilson, you're all wet now!' This event serves to illustrate the passion surrounding the project of sociobiology.

As the readers will be aware, the idea of biological determinism was not new to anthropology. However, it had not been a strong presence in the subject since Boas had argued against it at the beginning of the twentieth century. Scientific racism had been practically dead since the interwar years. Since the early 1960s, however, a few anthropologists, and quite a few biologists interested in human behaviour, had begun to think seriously about developing a Darwinist science of culture. A few popular books with tantalising titles such as *The Naked Ape*, *The Imperial Animal* and *The Territorial Imperative* appeared in the late 1960s, claiming for biology areas that had been monopolised by cultural relativists and other social scientists for most of the twentieth century. These books were academically lightweight, and caused less anxiety than irritation among professionals. With the publication of Wilson's book, and three years later, his *On Human Nature*, social and cultural anthropologists had a target worthy of sustained attack, and attack it they did. Even many evolutionary biologists, including Richard Lewontin and Stephen Jay Gould, went out of their way to discredit the simple view of humanity proposed by Wilson. In anthropology, Marvin Harris – who might have been thought of as a natural ally for the sociobiologists – wrote a chapter on the movement in *Cultural Materialism*, where he concluded that the cultural variation in the world had to be accounted for by reference to ecological, demographic and technological factors, and that the sociobiological proposals were either trivial or wrong. Sahlins, who had just completed his anti-reductionist *Culture and Practical Reason*, responded by writing a small book, *The Use and Abuse of Biology* (1977), which was published well before the debate in the journals had come to an end. In the book, or pamphlet, Sahlins pursues several arguments. One is that sociobiology is a kind of social Darwinism, an ideology of individualism and competition masquerading as 'real science'. Another, more technical argument concerns Wilson's and his followers' concept of 'kin selection'. This principle states that a person's loyalty and willingness to make personal sacrifices is contingent on genetic kinship, so that one would be more inclined to make sacrifices for close genetic relatives than for others. Obviously, a cultural anthropologist would have some misgivings about this kind of view, and Sahlins spends nearly half of the book showing that the ways of reckoning kin vary immensely worldwide, and that there is no necessary connection between genetic proximity and the social solidarity entailed by kinship. In a rejoinder to Sahlins, Richard Dawkins (in the second edition of *The Selfish Gene*, 1983) argues that cultural representations may well vary, but that this does not mean that practices vary accordingly.

The debate did not end there. Lévi-Strauss politely demolished sociobiology in his *Le Regard éloigné* (1983; *The View from Afar*, 1985), by pointing out that the idea of 'inclusive fitness' was an empty explanatory category since it was so flexible in practice that it could be used to account for anything at all. In his important book *Evolution and Social Life*, published a decade after *Sociobiology*, moreover, Tim Ingold (1986) devotes much attention to the book and the ensuing controversy. With an air of exasperation, he remarks that Wilson (in *On Human Nature*) unwittingly reinvents the nineteenth-century evolutionist comparative method in his attempt to create a biologically based social science from scratch (Ingold 1986: 71).

Just as the sociobiology debate was cooling down, at least in the anthropological mainstream, the publication of a monograph on Samoan social life led to its reawakening. In 1928, Margaret Mead had published her *Coming of Age in Samoa*, an intimate description of young girls growing up, which contributed substantially to the establishment of cultural relativism, not only in American anthropology but in mainstream American intellectual life. In the interwar years, it had been instrumental in discrediting the then-powerful eugenics movement, which favoured 'selective breeding' of humans, ostensibly in order to improve the culture. The book had also been an important inspiration for American feminism, and was often referred to by the new anthropological feminists of the 1970s.

In 1983, the Australian anthropologist Derek Freeman published a book-length assault on Mead's research, *Margaret Mead and Samoa: The Unmaking of an Anthropological Myth* (Freeman 1983). He had been doing research on Samoa on and off for decades, and at first, as he explains it, he had taken Mead's views on Samoan society for granted. Only gradually did he start wondering at the discrepancy between what he saw around him and the description given by Mead. Nothing seemed to fit: gender roles, socialisation and sexuality were not at all as Mead had depicted them. In his book, he attributes these discrepancies, in part, to wishful thinking, in part to Mead's having been cunningly misled by her informants. Freeman's own analysis appeared to show that Samoa was a dreadful place to grow up. Rape was common, suicide and mental disorder proliferated, and – in stark contrast to Mead's romantic portrayal of free sexuality among adolescent Samoans – there was an extreme cult of virginity.

Mead's academic work had been criticised before. It was generally agreed that her fieldwork in Samoa – as a young woman of 24, less than a decade after Malinowski's return from the Trobriands – had been methodologically questionable, and that the monograph was probably not a major scientific work. The virulence of Freeman's attack, and the fact that he chose to publish it after Mead's death in 1978 (he had been working on the book for decades), contributed to the almost unanimous pro-Mead reactions that the book provoked among American anthropologists. However, the 1970s had been full of re-analyses, from Talal Asad's demolition of Barth's work from Swat (1972), to Jonathan Friedman's accusations of functionalism in Rappaport's study (1979), to Annette Weiner's respectful, but thought-provoking follow-up and critique of Malinowski (1976). None of this caused such a stir as Freeman's critique of Mead. Not only, it seems, was he criticising Mead; he was being obnoxious to the memory of an icon of liberal humanism, and, worst of all, he was doing it as a biologically inclined anthropologist. Freeman was not treated politely by his fellow anthropologists, and he quickly became *persona non grata*; but he continued his crusade well into the 1990s.

Interestingly, other Samoan specialists do not, on the whole, take Freeman's side. One might have thought that they would: was not he the real scientist of the two, having worked doggedly for decades, collecting voluminous materials, taking time to learn the language – while Mead had never been more than a visitor with no time for more than fleeting engagements with her informants? Maybe so, but the specialists were cautiously equivocal in assessing the relative merits of Mead's and Freeman's research. One non-specialist pointed out, slightly tongue-in-cheek, that Mead's point that nurture was stronger than nature had been proven in the intervening years, since American society had moved from a very puritan view of sexuality to a more liberal view. Some regional experts praised Freeman for having provided them with a more complete picture of Samoan society, while Lowell Holmes, who had himself replicated Mead's work in the early 1950s, concluded by stating, in reference to his own work, that he would have loved to thrash Mead, but he was unable to do so: the resemblance between the real Samoa and the picture she had drawn of it was too strong (Holmes 1987).

Although the subject matter of this controversy is in itself bound to be fascinating and engaging to any anthropologist, what interests us most in the context of the history of the discipline, is the degree of passion, not to say aggression, it aroused. Even during the then-recent fierce debates about descent versus alliance in kinship, the assumed universality of male supremacy, the true Marxist meaning of infrastructural determination, or the autonomy of culture, the antagonists rarely moved beyond irony in castigating their opponents. With the sociobiology debate and related issues concerning nature versus nurture, the usual politeness of anthropological debate was discarded, and the pitcher of cold water was never far away.

Before we return to these (and other) issues, we must take the plunge into the turbulent and turgid waters of postmodernism. Regarded by some as a source of salvation, by others as a dead end, by still others as a tunnel with a light at the end, the diverse intellectual currents summarised as 'postmodernism' had few concerns in common, but were responses to a particular historical situation.

8   THE END OF MODERNISM?

If every age has its ambience, that of the 1980s is unmistakable. The decade seems to roll in on us in a heavy cloud of black leather, urban decay, AIDS and crack. The sound of The Cure issuing from a Walkman, drifting down the street, past the pale guy on the corner with his spikes and golden mohawk. Or go watch the girls in tight pastels swooning to Michael Jackson and dancing till dawn – while the first clunky personal computers hit the home market and the pale moon shines down on you from a sky that now contains ozone holes and greenhouse gases – weird phenomena, that an astute anthropologist will soon call *hybrids*. Another hybrid is buried in an unmentionable sarcophagus close to the small town of Chernobyl in the Ukraine. Reagan and Thatcher; Nicaragua and Afghanistan. Indira Gandhi assassinated; Saddam Hussein elected. Olof Palme assassinated. Mikhail Gorbachev elected. Right in the middle of the decade, deep-sea divers locate the sunken *Titanic* on the North Atlantic ocean floor, and plans are discussed for rescuing parts of the vast, luxurious wreck. But then the Soviet Union proclaims *glasnost* and *perestroika*, unilateral arms cuts, freedom of speech; and the world watches as the great Communist superpower falters and crumbles under its own weight. In 1989, the Berlin Wall goes down, and is sold piecemeal to individuals and corporations all over the world. Democracy and capitalism are triumphant. Nelson Mandela is freed.

The 1980s brought domestic political developments that few academics in the social sciences and humanities were happy with. The public sector was weakened, and universities restructured with a view to becoming more efficient. The future funding of 'useless' disciplines like anthropology became more uncertain than it had been for decades. Competition and individualism were proclaimed from the rostrums and enforced at the universities. After the outgoing, aggressive academic life of the 1970s, the 1980s seemed enclosed: claustrophobic or soul-searching. Disillusionment was widespread among a generation of anthropologists who had recently thought that they could change the world. By the end of the decade, some seemed to think that 'anthropology as we know it' was (or should be) dead and buried, while others continued to pursue their research, sending students off on fieldwork and keeping the institutions going – organising conferences, editing journals, reviewing monographs, working on applied projects, etc.

By 1980, anthropology had become a diverse and lively discipline with a number of clearly delineated research traditions. Despite the recent upheavals brought about by Marxists and other subversives, and despite the nearly constant self-criticism that anthropologists had practised for a decade or more, the leading theorists still commanded deference and respect. They were the generation who had cut their teeth in departments headed by people like Kroeber, Redfield and Herskovits, Firth, Evans-Pritchard and Gluckman, during the first postwar years. The rising star of American anthropology was Geertz, who had moved from Chicago to Princeton in 1970, two years after Turner *came* to Chicago and received his professorship there. Geertz was by then firmly established as the leading symbolic anthropologist, admired for his eloquent and subtle interpretations. His contemporary, Sahlins, arrived in Chicago in 1973. He had abandoned neo-evolutionism in favour of Boasian Marxism (if such a thing can be!), but would soon move on to develop his own brand of structuralism. All three phases of his work had their admirers. Schneider, also at Chicago, would soon proclaim (1984) that the concept of kinship was as good as meaningless; while Wolf, who would publish his *magnum opus* on the local impact of colonialism in 1982, had a sizeable following at the City University of New York. Harris would move from Columbia to the University of Florida in 1982, after publishing his theoretical manifesto on cultural materialism in 1979 – the same year as Bateson, pursuing his interdisciplinary interests in California, finished his first and only large, synthetic work, *Mind and Nature*.

Among British anthropologists, several left for the United States – Mary Douglas, Frederick Bailey, Victor Turner and others. Douglas continued to produce important work in the borderlands between structuralism and structural-functionalism – some consider the little-known *Cultural Bias* (1978) her best book ever. In the next decade, she would publish *How Institutions Think* (1987), a remarkable defence of structural-functionalism at a time when, in most people's eyes, it was safely relegated to the mists of history. In Britain itself, Needham and Ardener had their followings at Oxford; Needham with his more Dutch than French brand of structuralism and an ethnographic focus on South-East Asia; Ardener, the Africanist, with his 'post-structuralist' concern with language and cognition. At Cambridge, Leach and Goody presided, Leach continuing to attract attention for his theoretical views, influenced in about equal measure by Malinowski and Lévi-Strauss; Goody working persistently on his grand comparisons. Meanwhile, Ernest Gellner (1925–95), a Paris-born Czech philosopher, who had been attracted to Malinowskian functionalism while at the LSE, had converted to anthropology and published his first and only field study on Moroccan saints (Gellner 1969), would join the anthropology department at Cambridge in the early 1980s. Barth, a very active fieldworker, had completed studies in New Guinea and Oman, and was planning a new stint in Bali. In the mid-1970s, he had relocated from Bergen to the Ethnographic Museum in Oslo – and from his old interest in economy, ecology and politics to studies of knowledge. In 1987, he published *Cosmologies in the Making*, a regional study of knowledge traditions in Highland New Guinea, approached from a processual and generative perspective.

In France, all roads still seemed to lead to Paris, where Lévi-Strauss officiated. He had witnessed the phenomenal rise of structuralism during the 1950s, and then the relentless attack on it by the younger generation, headed by Foucault and Derrida. He continued to write new books, though he had few new students by now. Bourdieu had moved to Paris from Lille in the early 1960s, and became an international figure with the translation of *Outline of a Theory of Practice* into English, in 1977. Dumont, whose reputation as an anthropologist had been on the rise since *Homo Hierachicus* was published in English in 1970 (until then, he had been considered, outside France, as a 'mere' South Asianist), had gone on to write challenging works on hierarchy and values, individualism and collectivism, 'the West' vs. 'the East', and would acquire quite a substantial following during the 1980s.

By 1980, it could no longer be said that anthropological research was limited to certain 'core regions', or to studies of exotic, non-Western cultures. In the wake of the methodological revolution of the 1970s, fieldwork in Western countries had become commonplace, and the 1980s would see a considerable output of publications in this genre, including Marianne Gullestad's *Kitchen-Table Society* (1984) – a study of working-class urban Norwegian women; and Katherine Newman's *Falling From Grace* (1988) – a study of downward mobility among the American middle class under Reagan. Urban anthropology, pioneered by the Chicago and Manchester schools, had been established as an entirely respectable enterprise.

The older generation of anthropologists entered the 1980s with mixed emotions. For some, the retreat from political commitment seemed a betrayal of all that was sacred to anthropology. Others saw a chance to get back to work, after a decade of stormy political debates. For yet others, it was the long-awaited opportunity to get rid of the old idea of anthropology as a natural science, and institute a new humanism. An example of the latter was Victor Turner, who, in his posthumously published *The Anthropology of Performance*, writes of the 'systematic dehumanizing of the human subjects of study' in anthropological accounts, 'regarding them as the bearers of an impersonal "culture," or [as] wax to be imprinted with "cultural patterns," or as determined by social, cultural or social psychological "forces," "variables," or "pressures" of various kinds' (Turner 1987: 72). Turner had come a long way since his student years with Gluckman. In this book he calls for an experimental, playful anthropology, an anthropology that addresses the entire human being, as a living, breathing, emotional body. Turner welcomed postmodernism (though he disliked the label) because postmodernism, at least in some of its forms, offered a freedom from abstract systems and formal models, whether actor-oriented or structural, sociological or cultural. Formal models obscured the exuberance, creativity and humour of human life, and placed the scientific mind above real people.

There is a paradox in this, which we shall briefly indicate. For on the one hand, a theoretical hardliner like Bourdieu seems to be saying very much the same thing as Turner. His key concept of *habitus* is designed for the express purpose of bringing out the richness of human interaction – by focusing on the *body* – which is precisely what Turner recommends. On the other hand, Bourdieu's whole project, with its totalising ambitions and its involuted, formal argument, seems to contradict Turner's intentions completely.

Among the younger generation too, the views and interests were diverse. It is enough to take a look at some of the monographs they produced to be convinced of this. Take Gananath Obeyesekere's *Medusa's Hair* (1981), a psychoanalytically and medically inspired discussion of spirit possession in Sri Lanka; or Steven Feld's *Sound and Sentiment* (1982), which might be described as a jazzed-up structuralist essay on music, natural sound and emotion in Papua New Guinea; or Katherine Verdery's *Transylvanian Villagers* (1983), tracing three centuries of political, economic and ethnic change in a Romanian peasant community; or Henrietta Moore's *Space, Text and Gender* (1986), a study – inspired by Ricoeur and Marx – of gender, symbolism and power among the Kenyan Marakwet. Maurice Bloch's *From Blessing to Violence* (1986), the greatest and last structural Marxist thesis, treats history and power as expressed through an initiation ritual in Madagascar; while Bruce Kapferer's *Legends of People, Myths of State* (1988), delves into the cognitive underpinnings of Sri Lankan and Australian nationalisms, drawing heavily on Dumont's notions of hierarchy and Turner's theory of ritual performance.

We could continue in this vein indefinitely, but we have already seen enough to appreciate the very wide range of issues and places that were discussed in these ethnographies. But we should also note their pervasive theoretical eclecticism. The influence of Marxism and feminism is often seen; and there is a tendency to focus on the body, on power, on ritual – but the authors seem more willing than before to throw in a dash of Lévi-Strauss without swallowing his whole perspective, or to apply action-based network analysis in essentially Durkheimian studies of social integration. Steven Feld's study, moving at will through the theoretical landscape, is perhaps the best example of this in the bunch. Postmodernism proclaimed the 'death of the grand narrative', it 'deconstructed' the great synthetic projects, leaving the fragments spread out on the ground. So it is happy days for individualists, in anthropology as elsewhere, and every anthropologist with respect for him- or herself, seems to create a private analytical toolbox, never to be recycled by anyone else, except in fragments.

A glance at some of the more explicitly theoretical works of the decade seems to confirm this impression. Take Anthony P. Cohen's *The Symbolic Construction of Community* (1985), a slim book on local identity based on data from Shetland, and on Barth's model of ethnicity – as opposed to Marilyn Strathern's *The Gender of the Gift* (1988), a vast and intricate work on exchange and gender among the Hagen of New Guinea, engaging with a wide range of theorists, including Mauss and Lévi-Strauss; or take Roy Wagner's *Symbols that Stand for Themselves* (1986), a neo-Lévi-Straussian excursus on symbolic creativity in European philosophy and Papuan ethnography – as opposed to Arjun Appadurai's edited work, *The Social Life of Things* (1986), a discussion of consumption and value transformations in global economic systems, drawing on the value theories of Marx and Simmel.

All of these varied and incompatible projects took place against the background of a more general academic movement. Ideas often called 'post-structuralist' were spreading. Michel Foucault was becoming a household name among anthropologists. Heavy controversies turned around issues of representation, reflexivity and the very possibility of an anthropological science. If the 1970s were a decade of commitment, the 1980s were an age of doubt. And – partly as a result of the very individualism and eclecticism we have noted above – this doubt also affected the integrity of the various national traditions in the discipline. Their century-old boundaries were beginning to blur.

THE END OF MODERNISM?

By the mid-1980s, many younger, particularly American, anthropologists spoke about a crisis in anthropology, a crisis in how anthropologists described – or 'represented' – the people they studied (see, for example, Fabian 1983; Clifford and Marcus 1986). To various degrees, they accused the discipline of 'exotifying' the 'other', of maintaining a 'subject–object distinction' between the observer and the observed, which, it was argued, continued the 'othering' enterprise of colonialism by maintaining an inde-fensible, asymmetrical 'distinction' between 'Us' and 'Them'.

Jargon aside, the critics had much to offer in the setting of the 1980s. Many anthropologists and others had argued that the Western, and partic-ularly the Western scientific, intellectual tradition is heavily biased towards control, as embodied most visibly in the 'controlled circumstances' of physics laboratories (Latour 1991). As a science, it is clear that anthropology shares this 'disposition' (as Bourdieu might call it) to control its objects of study. The mere planning of a research project assumes this. And it is obvious that care must be taken at all stages of the research project, to keep the amount of – well – 'othering' at a minimum.

But the postmodernist movement was less straightforward than this. Indeed, one might well ask if it should be considered one movement at all, since its main proponents often held diverging views. There were in fact many different strains of 'postmodernism' (which was fully in keeping with the spirit of 'postmodernism' itself). Let us now trace the historical background of a few of these strains.

In the previous decade, Marxism and feminism had forcefully paved the way for the postmodern critique of anthropology. They had shown that knowledge and power were interconnected, and that world-views were never ideologically neutral. However, the Marxists and feminists themselves presumably inhabited some kind of meta-level from which they could safely and critically observe and analyse the world. Strip away that meta-level, and what you get is postmodernism. It is as if one were to take away the authority of scientific observation and description from the Boasians and Mali-nowskians. All that remained would be an indefinite number of versions of the world.

The term 'postmodern' was first defined in philosophy by the French philosopher Jean-François Lyotard, in his *La Condition postmoderne* (1979; *The Postmodern Condition*, 1984). Lyotard saw the postmodern condition as a situation where there were no longer any overarching 'grand narratives' that could be invoked to make sense of the world as a whole. Different voices would compete for attention, but would never merge. The book, an unlikely bestseller, was originally intended as a critique of the standardising and 'flattening' effect of computerised information retrieval systems on intellec-tual discourse. It described a particular historical situation in the West (which others have referred to variously as 'information society', 'consumer society' or even 'post-industrial society'), in which new technologies, new power relations and ideologies reigned. But postmodernism was also itself an ideology, an analytical perspective and an aesthetic that described the world (whether the world of the postmodern period itself, or any other world) as discontinuous and fragmented – a world of many, local, individual voices, rather than a world of hegemonic schools and ideologies. In architecture, film, literature and art, this attitude was eagerly embraced, resulting in a number of eclectic, collage-like productions, often playing ironically on nostalgic evocations of the styles and fashions of bygone days. In anthro-pology, the same attitude was quickly associated with an uncompromising cultural relativism, going far beyond that of, say, Boas. All worlds and world-views were equal – as long as they did not attempt to dominate each other. Each world was constituted by an independent 'language game' (a term Lyotard derived from the Austrian philosopher Ludwig Wittgenstein), and we are condemned to live in different worlds, without any overarching language that can bring us together. Visions of democracy or universal human rights were, as certain Marxists had also stated, part and parcel of a culture-specific, Western ideology, and could never be value neutral. We are reminded of Herder's critique of Voltaire (Chapter 1); the role of Voltaire in this context being played most notably by the German sociologist Jürgen Habermas (1929–), who developed a theory of *herrschafftfrei* (democratic, 'authority-free') communicative action in the 1970s.

The direct impact of Lyotard on anthropology was limited. Of greater importance to the new generation of anthropologists was Michel Foucault (1926–84), who, however, never regarded himself a postmodernist. A philosopher and critical social theorist, Foucault's main works deal in part with the conditions of knowledge (Foucault 1966), in part with the history of mentality (Foucault 1972), in part, as we have seen, with power and the body in the modern world (Foucault 1975). Foucault showed, through historical studies of the treatment of deviance (insanity, criminality and sexuality) in Europe, how the taken-for-granted frameworks for understanding and acting upon the world changed historically. He used the term *discourse* to delineate such frameworks. The term 'discourse' had been used by linguists for years, but in Foucault's usage it meant specifically a public exchange of ideas, in which certain questions, agendas and definitions – so-called 'discursive objects' – evolved as the result of power struggles between the participants in the discourse, and imposed themselves on the sensual human body. In his ruthless, intensely beautiful prose, often drawing on military analogies in its descriptions of discursive power and bodily discipline, Foucault spoke of the discourse as establishing a *regime of knowledge*.

At first sight, this theory might not seem to pose a challenge for mainstream, relativist anthropology, but rather to confirm its importance, in contrast to quantitative social science. However, anthropologists reading Foucault, notably Paul Rabinow (1989), stressed that anthropology was itself a regime of knowledge. Foucault's attack on power therefore not only struck at the cultures that anthropologists studied, but at anthropology itself. Courses in the history of anthropology could therefore no longer depict it as a value-neutral accumulation of knowledge and experience, but should see it instead as a *genealogy* of discursive objects ('culture' or 'actors') that were constituted, debated and challenged through the impersonal discursive flow, and imbued with authority by the power contained in discourse.

The anthropological work inspired by Foucault in the 1980s could be classified into two distinct categories: on the one hand, ethnographic studies of discursive power, such as Lila Abu-Lughod's work on gender and politics in the Middle East (Abu-Lughod 1986); and on the other hand, critiques of anthropological inquiry itself (such as Clifford 1988). The Foucauldian perspective was, either way, compatible with views that had previously been promoted by Marxists and feminists. Knowledge was always *situated*, and more often than not served to justify existing power structures. Moreover, as we have indicated above, and shall argue below, the perspective had a limited, but nevertheless striking affinity with a number of existing anthropological agendas, most notably with the cultural relativism of Boas and Benedict, but also with certain strands of British interactionist anthropology. Thus, both Geertz and Barth could claim that their analytical approaches were in effect precursors of postmodernism. American interpretive anthropologists and European students of ethnicity were thus (along with feminists and some of the erstwhile Marxists) among the first to display an interest in postmodern thinking.

When Foucault studied at the École Normale Supérieure in Paris during the 1950s, he was part of a group influenced by the structural Marxist philosopher Louis Althusser and the semiotician and literary critic Roland Barthes. In the 1960s, this group of 'post-structuralists' vehemently attacked Lévi-Strauss, in part for his lack of a conception of power, in part for the elegant sterility of his formal models. Derrida, a student of Foucault and eventually the leading figure of this movement, soon expanded his critique to Western philosophy as a whole. He developed a method of analysing texts that exposed the hierarchical assumptions inherent in them, which he referred to as *deconstruction*. To deconstruct a text is to locate the centre of power in it, and then look for unnoticed, marginal expressions, which escape power, and allow the reader to interpret the text in new ways. The paradoxical nature of this project – given that deconstruction itself had to be done in written texts – was evident to Derrida, and his deconstructions therefore always sought to deconstruct themselves. This made for an involuted, extremely self-reflexive style of writing, full of allusions, contradictions and irony, which in Derrida's own work is also meticulously exact – but which in many of his admirers seems obscure at best, and at worst imbues the text with a 'centralism' that is directly opposed to Derrida's aim. Derrida himself, who grew up in the periphery, as a Jew in French Algeria, had an intrinsic interest in the 'margins', and later in life would dedicate himself to such causes as the abolition of apartheid.

Transferred to anthropology, Derrida's method effectively entails the end of ethnographic authority. There is no privileged, fixed 'I-view' from which one can make neutral statements of any kind. Every concept is slippery, and every description can be contested and twisted. Again, these problems were hardly alien to anthropology. Ever since the Rationality Debate (Chapter 6) and the revolution in fieldwork (Chapter 7) similar problems had been at the forefront of anthropological debate, and before that as well they had been raised periodically. What was new about Derrida's proposal, was the suggestion that *any* text could be deconstructed. In other words, Winch's criticism of Evans-Pritchard's representation of Zande witchcraft was no more stable and valid than the text it criticised. In Derrida's philosophy, there is no fixed point of reference, no 'Archimedean point', to use a favourite term from postmodernism. The potential for self-criticism, already significant in anthropology, was thus raised to unheard of heights.

Though some anthropologists attempted (and usually failed) to follow Derrida straight through to the bitter end, there were also more moderate reactions. Thus, in 'The decline of modernism in social anthropology', Edwin Ardener (1985, in Ardener 1989) developed the idea that social anthropology was inextricably linked to *modernism*, loosely defined as an artistic and intellectual movement which makes a sharp distinction between modernity, on the one hand, and all other forms of human existence, on the other. Anthropological modernism, as epitomised, for instance, in Evans-Pritchard's work, built on several premises, including a clear subject–object distinction (the active fieldworker vs. the passive informant), a 'primitivist' notion (traditional societies are stable, integrated wholes), and an idea of timelessness (the society under study is presented as 'the Nuer', not 'the Nuer in 1936'). Ardener argued that these premises were now no longer tenable, and as a result, modernist social anthropology (functionalism, structural-functionalism, structuralism) lost its momentum and legitimacy around 1980. In Ardener's view, anthropological fieldwork would as a result be discredited, and texts would be produced that were nothing but commentaries on other texts.

THE POSTCOLONIAL WORLD

But other related concerns were also on the rise, and contributed to the post-modernist movement in anthropology. One of these was the postcolonial movement in the arts and humanities, which challenged the right of metro-politan intellectuals to define who 'the natives' were and what they were like, and, more generally, questioned the aesthetic and intellectual authority of metropolitan judgements. Derrida himself had been close to such concerns, but two other early writers would also influence anthropology profoundly. These were Frantz Fanon (1925–61) and, on a less theoretical note, Vine Deloria (1933–). Fanon, a Martiniquan medical doctor and writer, published two books with a lasting impact on thought about power and identity in inequal group relationships. In *Peau noire, masques blancs* (1956; *Black Skin, White Masks,* 1986), Fanon performs an Hegelian analysis of the relation-ship between black and white man in the colonies. The book is an acute psychological portrait of the sense of inferiority and humiliation that had been imposed on black people, who had been convinced by their white masters that their only hope was to become white – but whose skin *could never* become white. The only escape from this situation was to hide behind the mask of 'the native', seemingly obeying the master's wishes, while all the time, behind the mask, living an altogether different life. This book anticipated such concerns in anthropology by nearly three decades. It was subtle and terrible, and later led Fanon to declare, in *Les damnés de la terre* (1960; *The Wretched of the Earth,* 1967), the need for a black revolution.

Vine Deloria is a Lakota Sioux Professor in Native American Studies, a theologian, lawyer and activist, whose much discussed book, *Custer Died for Your Sins* (1970), was an impassioned attack on all kinds of liberal (and not so liberal) authorities, who spoke about and on behalf of Native North Americans, thereby effectively preventing them from speaking on their own terms. Deloria was particularly furious with the Boasian anthropologists, whose relativism condemned Native Americans to eternal exoticism, and prevented them from attaining equality with whites.

In spite of these and other important books written by non-anthropolo-gists (the Kenyan author Ngũgi wa Thiong'o is another example), the 1980s postcolonial movement was effectively launched by an American Professor of Literature of Palestinian origin, Edward Said. His *Orientalism* (1978) became a benchmark study, not only because of its intellectual originality, but because of its enormous influence. In the book, Said argued that representations of 'Orientals' in Western academia were permeated by an ambivalent fascination and disgust at the 'irrational', 'sensuous' and 'mystical' East – an ambivalence that went back to nineteenth-century colonialism, but could trace its roots much further back in the past (see Chapter 1). Said argued that to Europeans, 'The Orient' was a flexible location, consisting of very many and very different local societies, strung out across two continents from Morocco to Japan. Citing an infamous remark by Marx on 'Asians' to the effect that 'they cannot represent themselves, so they need to be represented', Said held that Western studies of Asians, including anthropological monographs, had created an 'essentialised' – or 'reified' – image of their way of life, based on a simplistic and misleading dichotomy between 'us' and 'them', where the West represented science and rationalism, the East its negation.

Said's critique, which focused largely on work dealing with his home area (West Asia and North Africa), was dismissed by many regional specialists who felt that he unjustly discredited serious scholarly work and glossed over the diversity in West Asian studies. Nevertheless, the argument stung the increasingly self-critical anthropological community, and its concerns overlapped with those of postmodernist anthropology. Said questioned the simple, unequivocal representations of 'whole cultures' that were common in anthropological research (though he seemed to approve of Geertz), and stressed the notion that knowledge was always 'positioned' (dependent on the social position of both known and knower). As in postmodernism, there appeared to be no privileged position from which neutral assessments of other peoples could be made.

'Postcolonial studies', which emerged as an academic discipline in its own right during the late 1980s, addressed the issues brought up by Said, Fanon and others, among them two influential theorists of Indian origin, literary critic Gayatri Chakravorty Spivak and cultural theorist Homi K. Bhabha. Both were (and are) more explicitly postmodernist in their approach than Said, but they share his concern with suppressed voices – the illiterate, women, low castes, blacks – and with giving them a place in the sun, by deconstructing the hegemony of male, Western knowledge.

The postcolonial perspective was given an ambivalent reception in anthropology. On the one hand, anthropologists might with some justification feel that their discipline could serve as an antidote to Orientalism, since it was the only major approach in academia to have its chief focus outside Europe. Had not a major objective of anthropology since Malinowski and Boas been to offer sympathetic interpretations of non-European world-views, and had not many important anthropologists – from Morgan and Boas onwards – defended small and powerless peoples against the forces of destruction? The answer was obviously yes, and yet many – within and outside the profession – would agree that anthropology often had an uncomfortably patronising tendency to represent others 'who were unable to represent themselves', and that the holism of many classical analyses served to create an image of 'the other' as uniformly passive and changeless – as an essentialised object of scientific inquiry. Thus, though Said goes unmentioned by Ardener, the latter's article on the decline of modernism in anthropology has important parallels with *Orientalism*.

In coming years, the debate would continue. In 1983, the Dutch anthropologist Johannes Fabian published his *Time and the Other*, which argued that anthropology has tended to 'freeze' the peoples it describes in time. In 1990, Ronald Inden, in his influential book *Imagining India*, demonstrated the relevance of the Orientalist critique for South Asian studies. Finally, in *Occidentalism* (Carrier 1995), several anthropologists and sociologists showed that not only do Westerners have stereotyped images of 'the East', but stereotypical images of the West are also widespread in the rest of the world.

In many parts of the Third World, in part as a result of the critique of orientalism, anthropologists have become increasingly unpopular with national authorities as well as local intellectuals. They are seen as hunters for exotica and intellectual adventurers – part of the problem rather than part of the solution for people who struggle to survive from day to day and to be allowed to represent themselves on their own terms, as respected members of the global community.

Anthropologists responded in a variety of ways to these critiques. A lasting effect on the discipline as a whole has probably been that traditional cultural relativism, as highlighted by the Boasians, has become a difficult position to maintain in the discipline. It is no longer possible for anthropologists to state publicly that they are, for example, opposed to the Universal Declaration on Human Rights for relativist reasons (as the AAA had done in 1947). Furthermore, as a result of the sustained self-criticism and the often bitter confrontations with vocal representatives of studied peoples that took place in the 1980s, the attention of anthropologists was increasingly drawn towards the large-scale processes of global history. The systemic and historical approaches favoured by anthropologists like Wolf and Mintz seemed more and more relevant for many young anthropologists, while synchronic, single-society studies increasingly seemed outdated and politically incorrect (Chapter 9). Finally, the orientalism debate stimulated attempts to conceptualise the specificity of anthropological writing about specific regions. Thus, in 1990, British anthropologist Richard Fardon edited a volume with many prominent contributors, which described the growth and transformation of 'regional traditions in ethnographic writing'. In his introduction, Fardon (1990) points out that such traditions, which typically associate an ethnographic region with specific analytical interests (exchange in Melanesia, lineage studies in Africa, etc.), are expressions of scholarly priorities which often have less to do with empirical conditions in the regions being described, than with established hierarchies within anthropology itself. However, he also stresses that such traditions have typically grown out of long-term exposure to the regions themselves through fieldwork, and that they are therefore not arbitrary, but contain important insights into actual conditions in the regions.

Although its main objectives were arguably political rather than episte-mological, the postcolonial critique of anthropology 'from the outside' to a great extent overlapped with the 'reflexive turn' that came from within the discipline itself in the 1980s, particularly in the USA. A handful of books published in the latter half of the decade may be seen as representative of this movement, and we now move on to a brief consideration of their message and impact.

A NEW DEPARTURE OR A RETURN TO BOAS?

What we might retrospectively speak of as the postmodernist movement in American anthropology was associated with the work of a fairly small group of scholars. The core included non-anthropologist James Clifford, a historian of anthropology with leanings towards literary studies; and anthropologists Stephen Tyler (a convert to postmodernism from ethnoscience), George Marcus, Michael Fischer, Renato Rosaldo and Paul Rabinow. Others associated with the movement included Fabian, Richard Handler (a student of Schneider's studying discourses of nationalism), Lila Abu-Lughod (a specialist on the Arab world), and Akhil Gupta and James Ferguson, who co-wrote and edited an important work on the discursive construction of space and narrative in the 1990s. In spite of differences (regarding, for example, the possibilities and limitations of ethnography), these and other scholars both in and outside the USA shared a number of concerns. They were uncom-fortable with the reified 'othering' typical of classical modernist anthropology, and sought to redress this in varous ways, often advocating 'experimental ethnographies', where the informants participated as equal partners in the production of knowledge (Clifford and Marcus 1986; Marcus and Fischer 1986). They were, moreover, critical of the Boasian (and, more recently, Geertzian) idea of cultures as integrated wholes with deep historical roots. Inspired by Foucault and cultural Marxists like Antonio Gramsci (1891–1937), they were also concerned with modes of representation and the power implied by particular styles of writing.

The year 1986, in many ways an *annus mirabilis* for this movement, saw the publication of two important books and the launching of a new journal edited by Marcus, and called – surprisingly timidly – simply *Cultural Anthro-pology*. The first book was Marcus and Fischer's *Anthropology as Cultural Critique*, subtitled *An Experimental Moment in the Human Sciences*. Arguing that the discipline suffered from 'a crisis of representation', they went on to present several of the problems outlined above, and to affirm the importance of reflexivity (positioning the anthropologist's knowledge) and wider systemic concerns (incorporating an understanding of world history and economics in ethnographic analyses). They argued that a main objective of the discipline should be to engage in cultural criticism 'at home', and that an appropriate way of achieving this was by *defamiliarisation* – creating a sense of 'strangeness' by pointing out the similarity of the readers' own culture to distant and 'exotic' cultures. In their view, the 1980s were a period of unique potential for the fulfilment of anthropology's promise as an instrument of cultural critique. The discipline was in disarray; the broad postwar consensus had broken down on both sides of the Atlantic; the post-colonial movement had generated uncertainty; grand theories had lost their appeal. In this situation, 'experimental ethnographies' could contribute substantially to critical self-reflection on Western society.

Anthropology as Cultural Critique, which emphasised continuity with the concerns of anthropologists like Mead, Sahlins and Douglas, was less radical than the edited volume *Writing Culture* (Clifford and Marcus 1986). Although this book contained about a dozen chapters written by different scholars, who represented various positions in the postmodernist debate, it was received as a single-minded assault on the dominant concept of culture. The contributors unanimously distanced themselves from the idea of culture as an 'integrated whole', questioned the rhetorical devices of 'scientific' anthropology, and argued the merits of both 'dialogic' methods (the main inspiration here being the Russian literary critic Mikhail Bakhtin), and historical contextualisation in the increasingly problematic art of anthropological representation.

The hugely influential *Writing Culture* was followed two years later by Clifford's *The Predicament of Culture*, which could be summarised as a long, historically based argument against essentialism. In the same year, Geertz published a small, elegant book called *Works and Lives: The Anthropologist as Author*. This was a collection of essays about famous anthropologists that focused on the rhetorical and literary aspects of their writings, and was based on a lecture series which antedated *Writing Culture*. Ardener's predictions now seemed to be confirmed from the other side of the Atlantic: the anthropological quest had been brought to a close, since it no longer dealt with living people, but with texts. Of course, this view had serious limitations. Never had so much fieldwork been done, in so many different places, as in the 1980s. Yet it remains a fact that some of the most hotly debated writings of that decade were reflexive texts, which deconstructed ethnographic authority, questioned the ethical legitimacy of turning 'natives' into data, and ultimately challenged the validity of ethnographic representation as such.

The connection between American postmodernist anthropology and literary studies was strong. Both looked to recent French philosophy for inspiration, and the young anthropologists, steeped in Geertzian hermeneutics, were predisposed to see cultures as texts. Their break with Geertz consisted largely in problematising the subject–object relationship between anthropologist and informant, and in not seeing cultures ('cultural texts') as integrated wholes. However, these problems were not foreign to Geertz himself. He once compared an integrated culture to an octopus, a loosely coordinated animal with a weak brain that does not always know what each of the arms is doing; and in *Works and Lives*, he effectively deconstructs the classical anthropological texts, describing them as imaginative, historically situated works. Indeed, seen from a distance, postmodern American anthropology might be said to represent an extreme form of Boasianism, rather than something entirely new. Geertz is the key figure here. Though the younger anthropologists, who congregated around *Cultural Anthropology*, had an ambivalent relationship to Geertz's hermeneutics, he was their favourite discussion partner. There was considerable continuity between his view of anthropology and the project of radical deconstruction advocated in *Writing Culture*. Geertz himself felt that the younger generation had gone too far, and coined the term 'epistemological hypochondria' to describe the excessive self-criticism that prevented people from doing good ethnographic work.

Many anthropologists would agree with Geertz, and even go further in their criticism than he. Some of the more explicit critics were Steven Sangren (1988), who saw the 'reflexive turn' as a retreat from anthropology's proper mission, and Jonathan Spencer (1989), who argued that anthropology might be better viewed as a style of working than as a form of writing. Marvin Harris, in one of his many position papers, thoroughly thrashed (some would say parodied) the likes of George Marcus, who seemed to favour an increase in 'the number of experimental, personalistic, and idiosyncratic field studies carried out by untrained would-be novelists and ego-tripping narcissists afflicted with congenital logo-diarrhea' (Harris 1994: 64).

Ernest Gellner, in a little book devoted to the defence of rational science in the face of the two-pronged threat of closed-world fundamentalism and limitless postmodern relativism, sternly berated the American postmodernists, singling out Clifford and Rabinow as his main targets, for sloppy thinking and poorly defined concepts, and ultimately for being more interested in their own interpretations than in understanding the world (Gellner 1992). While Gellner saw Geertz as an important precursor of the postmodernist movement, he noted that Geertz, at least, was still trying to 'say something about something', as Geertz himself once put it. Against the critique of Great Divide (or 'Big Ditch') theories (that contrast 'us' with 'them', 'modern' with 'primitive', and so on), Gellner confirmed his position as a modernist in Ardener's terms. Elsewhere, Gellner (1993) also voiced misgivings about postcolonialism, for undermining scientific truth claims, confusing ideology and analysis, and not understanding that the 'problem of power and culture ... is too important to be left to lit[erary] crit[icism]' (Gellner 1993: 4). Finally, Gellner hinted that there was an element of careerism in the postmodern movement, remarking that '*Sturm und Drang and Tenure* might well be their slogan' (Gellner 1992: 27). While there is undoubtedly something to this, the same might of course be said of all innovative movements in anthropological history, from the Malinowskian–Radcliffe-Brownian 'functionalist revolution', via Steward's evolutionist and Barth's interactionist 'revolutions', to the 'revolution' in nationalism studies that Gellner himself would sponsor.

It was also often noted that many of the ideas inspiring American postmodern anthropology had originated in France, and that the Americans tailored the French masters to fit their anthropology, often trivialising their views in the process. Foucault, in the American reading, became a theorist of discourse; Derrida a philosopher of relativism. Again, this may be true, but it is important to situate American anthropology itself as well. Boas, a German, had in his day understood very well the potential for ethnic and racial conflict in the sprawling, multinational United States, and events since his death have not proven him wrong. Clifford and Marcus may seem as crude as McDonald's to highbrow intellectuals from Paris, but relativism, even extreme relativism, was an understandable stance in a country split apart by a history of Afro-American slavery, Native American genocide and immigration from every part of the world.

Some critics also doubted that postmodernism was as radical a departure from anthropological tradition as it claimed to be. However, this argument was double-edged, and was also used by some of the postmodernists themselves to legitimise their project. Thus, Kirsten Hastrup, a Danish student of Ardener, whose work has been relentlessly anti-positivist, and who has in some ways represented a European counterpart to American postmodernism, argued that anthropology *had always been* a postmodern science, ever since it started to confront the West with images of other lifeworlds (see Hastrup 1995). Though Hastrup may have overstated her case here, there are definite affinities between the deconstructive efforts of the postmodernists and several previous trends in anthropological history. Thus, there are clear precedents to postmodernism in the Rationality Debate of the 1960s (Chapter 6) and in the 1970s revolution in fieldwork (Chapter 7), and debunking the objectivity of ethnographic method had been an anthropological parlour game on both sides of the Atlantic at least since the Second World War. But above all, of course, there is continuity with the historical particularism of Boas and the German Romantic tradition. In general, American anthropologists, who were steeped in this tradition, were therefore more favourably disposed to postmodernism than their European colleagues, who were the heirs of confirmed positivists such as Radcliffe-Brown (see Kuper 1996: 189). Schneider's deconstruction of kinship studies had nothing to do with postmodernism, but was the work of a devoted Boasian and a lifelong supporter of Parsons' sociology. Later, his work would be cited with approval in Great Britain too, by the Czech-British anthropologist Ladislav Holy in his textbook on kinship (Holy 1996). However, Holy's point of reference is not Boas, but the methodological individualism of the British anti-structural-functionalist movement of the 1950s and 1960s (Chapter 5). This movement is also often regarded as a precursor of postmodernism. When Barth, in the mid-1960s, demolished the concept of social structure and posited that stable social forms were a result of individual choice, this was (in a sense) a deconstructive argument which closely paralleled the postmodernists' deconstruction of Boasian and Geertzian concepts of integrated cultural wholes.

Nevertheless, the postmodern critique of anthropology, with occasional support from feminist and postcolonial scholars, did represent something new, though its originality was often exaggerated at the time. The newness, as far as anthropology was concerned, lay mainly in the reflexive emphasis on styles of writing, in the rejection of a neutral, non-positioned authorial voice, and (most fundamentally) in the application of reflexivity to anthropology itself. After postmodernism, anthropology could no longer be seen as privileged discourse with access to the objective truth about the peoples it studied.

OTHER VOICES

Postmodernism and 'the reflexive turn' were not the only show in town during the 1980s. For most anthropologists, it was largely business as usual, as the discipline continued to grow and diversify into increasingly specialised subfields. Postmodernism – a new and untested departure in the discipline – often had a noncommittal reception. Thus, in two recent introductory texts to anthropological theory, by Robert Layton (1997) and Alan Barnard (2000), postmodernism is afforded a prominent place, with about as many pages of text as structural-functionalism or structuralism. However, both authors are careful not to pass definite judgement on its merits and lasting effects on the discipline. In the massive *Companion Encyclopedia of Anthropology* (Ingold 1994), there is scarcely a mention of the movement at all.

However, during the 1980s, on both sides of the Atlantic, there were very many anthropologists who might be said to belong to the fringes of post-modernism, sympathising with some of its views, but incorporating them in established anthropological theory. These were largely scholars who, unlike Gellner and Harris, felt that their discipline was an interpretive activity whose claims to enduring truth were debatable. The most obvious example is Victor Turner, whose theory of performance would inspire many anthropologists studying ritual and related phenomena (see Turner and Bruner 1986). Another example was the Melanesianist Roger Keesing, who, in his last academic papers before his premature death in 1993 (Keesing 1989, 1994), contended that the classical conception of culture had been mistaken. He now argued that 'his' people, the Kwaio, had no homogeneous, more or less static culture, and that their ideas of their own culture were both politicised and influenced by ethnographic writings about themselves. Judith Okely and Helen Calloway's edited volume, *Anthropology and Autobiography* (1992), also paralleled some of the concerns of the *Writing Culture* group, but focused less on texts and more on ethnographic fieldwork. The latter scholars were the heirs of the anti-positivist, hermeneutic trend in British anthropology which began with Evans-Pritchard's late work. They turned the tools of hermeneutics inward, towards anthropology itself, to look critically at the juncture of knowledge production and personal experience. As in Keesing's case, the concerns of these authors were developed independently of the American postmodernists; Okely, for one, had produced a trenchant criticism of 'scientism' in anthropology back in the mid-1970s (Okely 1975). Another, probably unjustly neglected work of this general type, was the American anthropologist Robert Ulin's magisterial, but little read volume on cultural translation and rationality, *Understanding Cultures* (Ulin 1984). The book parallels the concerns of the *Cultural Anthropology* group, but instead of embracing postmodernism, it applied an historicising hermeneutic method (as opposed to Geertz's more ahistorical hermeneutics) inspired by the German philosopher Hans-Georg Gadamer (1900–).

One of the most important anthropologists to be inspired by the deconstructive method was Marilyn Strathern, a Melanesianist at Manchester, who succeeded Gellner at Cambridge in the 1990s. Strathern published several influential books in the late 1980s and early 1990s. In her magnum opus, *The Gender of the Gift* (1988), she explored concepts of personhood and exchange in Melanesia, and argued that Melanesian culture had been seriously misread by Europeans imposing their own concepts and prejudices on it. On a more general level, Strathern contended that classical theories of exchange and identity were defective in that they did not take gender into account. Is it meaningful, she asked, to say that objects are exchanged between two 'persons', or that a 'person' has a certain identity, if these 'persons' are *always* gendered? This is a fundamental critique, which has brought feminist perspectives close to the heart of several basic theoretical debates in anthropology, and thus increased its legitimacy in the discipline greatly. Later, in *After Nature* (1992), Strathern performs a comparison of concepts defining personhood, society and kinship in Melanesia and England, making an argument that at once deals with a substantial issue (new reproductive technologies) and with the (reflexive) relationship between anthropological and native concepts.

Strathern represents a 'postmodern' approach that is perhaps more significant in the long run than the rather programmatic work of the American postmodernists. The same might be said of the somewhat similar project of the American Melanesianist Roy Wagner, who published *The Invention of Culture* in 1975, an influential theoretical essay that anticipated some of the central issues of postmodernism. Wagner here argued that cultures were purely symbolic constructions, with an inherent capacity for change, innovation and reflexivity. In 1986, he further elaborated these themes in *Symbols That Stand for Themselves*, a complex, highly technical account of symbolic transformation and continuity, which combines the stringent analysis of Lévi-Strauss with a reflexive and processual perspective reminiscent of postmodernism.

Wagner was one of a number of authors during the 1980s who started to explore the repercussions of applying *phenomenology* (a school of thought founded by the German philosopher Edmund Husserl) to anthropological analysis. An early proponent of such an approach was the British anthropologist Tim Ingold, who had previously done work on ecological adaptation. In 1986, Ingold published a major theoretical and historical work, *Evolution and Social Life* (Ingold 1986), where he developed a framework for the study of humanity in its social, cultural, biological and environmental dimensions, without reducing one to the other. In at least two ways, this book is similar to the project of the American postmodernists. First, Ingold announces the need to 'clear out some of the accumulated conceptual debris of a century of social and evolutionary theorizing'; and, second, he emphasises that we 'cannot afford to maintain the illusion that we stand, like gods, aloof from the world' (p. 376). The latter attitude clearly recalls the ideas proposed by major phenomenologists such as Martin Heidegger (1889–1976) and Maurice Merleau-Ponty (1908–61). Like these philosophers (who rejected the subject–object dichotomy on completely different grounds than the postmodernists), Ingold emphasises that people are intimately connected to the non-human world they inhabit. His solution to the subject–object paradox is therefore almost the opposite of the Americans'. Discarding postmodernism as intellectual aloofness, he instead proposes to bring anthropology closer to other 'life sciences' (such as biology) – quite the opposite of comparing cultures to literary texts.

Ingold's movement towards biology parallels that of quite a number of anthropologists who, from very different perspectives, have sought to establish links between anthropology and the natural sciences during the 1990s. We shall return to this trend in Chapter 9; here, however, it is necessary to point out two related movements, that were already entering their boom years during the 1980s.

During the 1970s, Western countries increased their budgets for developmental aid to the Third World dramatically. The aid lobby became a power to be reckoned with in global politics, and anthropologists were increasingly drawn into the planning, implementation and evaluation of aid projects. Through UNESCO, the WHO, the World Bank, the EU and other international organisations, through the rich flora of NGOs that started engaging in aid-related work, and through the various national ministries of developmental aid that were formed at this time, the practical expertise of anthropologists was becoming increasingly in demand. From the start, the problem was to find niches where anthropological knowledge could be meaningfully deployed. The organisations were often dominated by representatives of 'hard' professions such as economy, law and engineering, who regarded concepts such as 'culture' and 'identity' with scepticism. Nevertheless, anthropologists quickly started making their mark in a number of areas. The increasing interest in peasant studies and economic anthropology during the 1970s clearly bears witness to this, and, as the years passed, and the practical problems of developmental aid became more apparent, anthropological viewpoints were increasing taken into account. Although the successes should not be exaggerated (technocratic and economic interests still dominate aid work), it should be noted that several key anthropological standpoints have today gained wide acceptance. Anthropologists were among the first to argue the need to orient aid work towards smaller-scale projects, towards women (as the stable nucleus of households in many poverty-stricken areas) and towards ecological awareness – viewpoints which today are widely accepted – in theory, if not always in practice.

One of the areas where anthropologists have most successfully forged alliances with dominant aid professions is in the field of health and nutrition, and, in the 1980s, when many other anthropologists were disillusioned with aid work, *medical anthropology* grew to become the fastest expanding subfield in the discipline. The roots of medical anthropology go back to the pioneering work of Audrey Richards in the 1930s, and to the efforts of a number of dedicated professionals who followed up and expanded her interests in the next few decades. An example is Ronald Frankenberg, who studied under Gluckman. Frankenberg, who is today something of a grand old man of medical anthropology, has done fieldwork in Central Africa and England (where he has written about football, among other things), and has written widely on questions of health and methods of healing (see Frankenberg 1980). He has acted as a consultant on a number of aid projects, and has done pioneering theoretical work on such issues as the conception of time in medical practice and the psychiatric understanding of children. During the 1980s he was drawn towards phenomenology and parts of the postmodernist movement, particularly the work of his old colleague and friend, Victor Turner, on performance, which inspired Frankenberg's interest in the the uses of ritual in (traditional and modern) healing. Frankenberg is an example of how 'deconstructionism' can be put to 'constructive' use. His criticism of the essentialisation of concepts of disease and mental health in the medical sciences, has inspired many to consider the social processes that generate such concepts.

In general, it might be said that medical anthropologists contribute an understanding of social context to standard medical work. The effect of a programme of regular health checks for pregnant women may for example be significantly enhanced by knowledge of the women's conceptions of propriety, their work schedules, the authority structures within their households, their kinship obligations, their conceptions of how disease expresses itself and what it means. Many prominent medical anthropologists are themselves medical doctors or psychiatrists, which gives them a high level of professionality and increases their legitimacy among the medical profession itself.

In the United States, where medical anthropology has seen the greatest growth during the 1980s and 1990s, one of the most influential figures has been Nancy Scheper-Hughes (at the University of California at Berkeley).

Scheper-Hughes, a student of Hortense Powdermaker's (Chapter 7) and a former civil rights activist, has done work on psychological anthropology and gender-related health issues in Ireland and Brazil (Scheper-Hughes 1979, 1992), and is at present working on a study of violence and democracy in South Africa. In 1987, she and Margaret Lock wrote the programmatic article 'The mindful body: a prolegomenon to future work in medical anthropology', which charted out an agenda for future applied and theoretical research in the field. In a recent interview, she describes her fieldwork in Brazil in the following terms:

... I started out with the question of the high incidence of infant mortality. What did that mean for women who had to face four or five, six, in some cases eleven deaths in a row? What did it mean for their understanding of motherhood? What did it mean in terms of their sense of optimism and hope? And what did it mean for the children who lived? How were they raised, given the spaces that they were made to fill [after] all the children who had died before? ... I decided I would track these deaths. ... I did interviews with ... close to a hundred women, getting them to tell me the context around each of the deaths of their children and what they thought were the causes of death. But also interviewing children, because children in northeast Brazil are the ones who bury the dead and they're the ones who form the procession. What do they think about death? (Scheper-Hughes 2000)

A third example from this subfield is Arthur Kleinman, Professor of Psychology and Senior Medical Anthropologist at the prestigious Department of Social Medicine at Harvard University, who has done extensive work on cross-cultural psychiatry, particularly in China (see Kleinman 1980; Kleinman and Good 1985). Kleinman, who has engaged in a wide variety of consultant work, has in recent years been Director of the World Mental Health Project, a very large-scale consultant project, sponsored by the Carnegie and Rockefeller Foundations, and organised under the auspices of the United Nations. Kleinman has also been one of the pioneers in the study of 'social suffering', which addresses the 'consequences of war, famine, depression, disease, torture – the whole assemblage of human problems that result from what political, economic, and institutional power does to people' (Kleinman et al. 1997).

As several of the above studies indicate, medical anthropologists are by no means limited to applied research, indeed, with the recent *rapprochement* between anthropology and the natural sciences, the establishment of body-oriented theories of practice, and the growing interest in phenomenology, medical anthropologists have made very significant contributions during the 1990s to fundamental research in a wide variety of fields. As we remarked in our discussion of Marilyn Strathern above (p. 151), such engagement with anthropology's basic theoretical discourse, tends to indicate that a subfield (feminist or medical anthropology) has reached a mature stage, and is no longer a marginal 'special interest' in the discipline.

Finally, we shall briefly discuss a third important research field that came to the fore in the 1980s, namely the study of *nationalism*. Like medical anthropology, though for very different reasons, nationalism studies were less vulnerable to the postmodern epistemological critique than many other parts of anthropology. This research did not posit the existence of 'discrete, homogeneous cultures' existing in a timeless 'ethnographic present'. Rather, it explored a particular feature of modernity, in whose name the existence of such cultures was claimed, at least partly for strategic reasons, by political and cultural elites. As we have seen, the concept of culture had the same historical roots (in Herderian Romanticism) as political nationalism, and anthropologists who sought to deconstruct nationalist ideologies, thus had many interests in common with postmodernist deconstructors of the culture concept. Though both empiricist and comparative in orientation, and thus potentially open to postmodernist attack, nationalism studies generally went unchallenged: they were neither essentialist (they deconstructed indigenous essentialisms), ahistorical (they located their object of study firmly in history) nor neo-colonial (many of the major studies of nationalism focused on Western societies). Furthermore, as nationalistically motivated political conflicts spread worldwide during the 1990s, anthropological studies of nationalism seemed increasingly relevant. And due to the excessive violence of many nationalist movements, it seemed natural for some nationalism scholars to contribute to studies of the effects of violence (as in medical anthropology; see Malkki 1995), and to studies of power (as in political anthropology; see Kapferer 1988).

The interdisciplinary flourishing of nationalism studies which took place during the 1980s was deeply inspired by three books which were published in the same year. The first was Gellner's *Nations and Nationalism* (Gellner 1983), where a main argument was that nationalism was a functional, cohesive ideology in an otherwise fragmented and alienating industrial society. The second was historian Benedict Anderson's *Imagined Communities* (Anderson 1983), which concentrated on the symbolic features of nationalism, comparing it to phenomena like kinship and religion. The third was historians Eric Hobsbawm and Terence Ranger's co-edited *The Invention of Tradition* (Hobsbawm and Ranger 1983), which demonstrated that many presumedly 'ancient traditions' were in fact invented by colonial authorities or other elites to create cohesion where it would otherwise be absent. Often inspired by these books, anthropological research on nationalism seemed to confirm Ardener's view that modernism occupied 'an almost precisely datable span from 1920 to 1975' in social anthropology (Ardener 1989 [1985]: 197). Research on nationalism and, more generally, the politics of identity was seen as a form of postmodern anthropology. Powerful monographs on nationalism, like Bruce Kapferer's *Legends of People, Myths of State* (Kapferer 1988), combined classical concerns of anthropology – the meaning of myth, the problem of social cohesion, the power of symbols – with an attempt to come to terms with contemporary identity politics, its violent imagery and frequently violent practice, its creation of enemy images and its relationship to the State. Here again we see the movement of a subfield from a relatively marginal position in the discipline, into its mainstream.

Although the debates on postmodernism stole many of the headlines during the 1980s, it is perhaps (as Derrida might say) in the margins of the postmodern movement, rather than among its most prominent spokesmen, that its most lasting contributions must be sought. Studies of exchange and identity, studies inspired by phenomenology, studies of health and nationalism, were all brought to the fore during this decade, and would deeply influence the anthropology of the 1990s.

9   RECONSTRUCTIONS

Lack of historical distance precludes a proper review of the 1990s, whether of the general cultural ambience of the decade or of the specific enterprise of anthropology. In both regards, it is nevertheless obvious that some of the trends of the 1980s were consolidated. Uncertainty, or ambivalence, became a standard feature (some would say an affectation) of intellectual life. Characteristically, Henrietta Moore, one of the most influential British anthropologists of the present generation, introduces her ambitiously entitled *Anthropological Theory Today* with the sentence: 'It is very tempting to begin a book of this kind with the statement that there is no such thing as anthropological theory' (Moore 1999: 1). She then goes on to note briefly that the critical projects of the 1970s and 1980s led, in the 1990s, to a widespread retreat from theory to ethnography and, in some cases, 'even from the project of anthropology itself' (1999: 1). Elaborating this, she goes on to state that there is no longer (if there ever was) anything like a single anthropology and, moreover, that the status of theory as such is increasingly questionable. 'Theory is now a diverse set of critical strategies which incorporates within itself a critique of its own locations, positions and interests: that is, it is highly reflexive' (Moore 1999: 9).

The impression one gets from this and other attempts to provide broad overviews of 1990s anthropology, is that the discipline is hopelessly fragmented and in profound disarray. At the same time, anthropology was phenomenally successful during that decade. The increase in the total number of publications and conferences was formidable, anthropological engagement in applied research had never been more widespread, and in many countries, anthropology was an extremely popular undergraduate subject. At the University of Oslo, about 75 first-year undergraduates were expected in the spring semester of 1990. As the teachers entered the auditorium to greet the new students, we were met by a crowd of 330, many of whom went on later in the decade to take postgraduate degrees. There are some obvious reasons for this increased popularity. Just as Marxian sociology offered a key to understanding the hidden agendas of class- and gender-related oppression in the politicised 1970s, anthropology supplied an understanding of cultural variation in a decade when young people in the rich countries travelled far more extensively than their parents or grandparents, and when multiculturalism, identity politics, ethnic discrimination and nationalist war were high on the agenda of politicians, grassroots movements, NGOs and the media almost everywhere. Ironically, the traditional anthropological concept of culture finally seemed to have made its breakthrough into the public sphere at about the same time that most anthropologists were having second thoughts about it.

The demographics of the discipline were increasingly complex, but anthropology remained larger and more diverse in the USA than anywhere else. In the late 1990s, the American Anthropological Association had about 10,000 members, while the British Association of Social Anthropologists had less than a tenth of that number, and the newly started European Association of Social Anthropologists had perhaps 2,000. The domination of the English language in academic discourse, which had been on the rise ever since the interwar years, was further strengthened in the 1990s. In a country like Brazil, there are many more practising anthropologists than in Britain, but with few exceptions, such as the work of Roberto DaMatta (1991), their publications are unknown to people who do not read Portuguese. Similarly, there are major bodies of anthropological and/or ethnographic literature in Spanish, Russian, Polish and other Central European languages, in Japanese and – increasingly – in Chinese. There is also a major English-language anthropological literature in India which is scarcely known outside specialist circles.

Finally, during the 1990s, non-metropolitan European anthropologies received increased attention, thanks to the foundation of the European Association of Social Anthropologists in 1988. Formed at the initiative of Adam Kuper at Brunel University, a main purpose of the EASA was to bring anthropologists from (Protestant/Germanic) northern Europe and (Catholic/Romance) southern Europe together. Then, in late 1989, while the anthropologists were busy planning the first EASA conference (to be held in Coimbra, Portugal in 1990), the world was struck by what would become the defining event of the 1990s: the fall of the Iron Curtain (soon to be followed by the dissolution of the Soviet Union) and the attendant cultural and intellectual liberalisation in most of Central and Eastern Europe. The political and economic changes that followed in the wake of these upheavals would be many and paradoxical – and would from the very start open up a completely new ethnographic region of continental dimensions for anthropological research (see pp. 170ff.). But for the EASA planners, the immediate concern was the opportunity for intensified academic contacts with co-anthropologists in these countries. Relationships could now be developed with anthropological traditions that had been practically unknown in Western academia for years. In the former Soviet Union, an ethnography was discovered that combined the historical approach of the German diffusionist tradition with Marxian evolutionism (see Dunn and Dunn 1974). In Poland, the Chicago-inspired methodology of Znaniecki (Chapter 4) had been further developed into a sophisticated urban micro-sociology (see Wedel 1986). Hence, the EASA from the first faced not only the challenge of forging bonds between northern and southern Europe, but also of integrating the anthropologies of eastern and western Europe.

Through the participation of anthropologists from all over the continent in EASA's conferences, and through recurrent panels on the history of European anthropology (see Vermeulen and Roldán 1995), a picture of the discipline's past has emerged which is far more complex than the one we have depicted in this book. Swedish ethnology, Polish surrealism, Slovene *Volkskunde*, 1930s Slovak structuralism, and the continued importance of Bastian in Germany and elsewhere are only a few examples of the possible new genealogies for European anthropology.

The fate of one of these traditions may be outlined briefly. As we have seen (Chapter 2), pre-revolutionary Russian anthropology was closely allied with the German tradition. This theoretical focus was retained during the 1920s and early 1930s, but most Soviet ethnographers were simultaneously practical workers, engaged in such tasks as literacy work, education and health care. Anthropologists were instrumental in developing the first written languages for many non-literate minorities of the Soviet Union. Under Stalin, both applied and theoretical ethnography was ruthlessly repressed, many practitioners were killed, and the profession was effectively reduced to mere empirical documentation (e.g. of material culture). The 1960s and 1970s saw a resurgence of analytical research. A sophisticated theory of ethnicity was developed by Yuliy Bromley at the Moscow Academy of Sciences (see Banks 1996); innovative work was done on statistical modelling of cultural cohesion by V.V. Pimenov (Leningrad); and large-scale ethno-sociological surveys were carried out by Yuliy V. Arutyunyan (Moscow). In the West there was very little knowledge of any of this work, in spite of the dedicated efforts of a few individuals, such as Stephen P. Dunn, a former student of Morton Fried's at Columbia, who founded and for 25 years edited *Soviet Anthropology and Archaeology*, a journal of translations, which brought a wide variety of Soviet publications into English. During the 1990s, Russian anthropology has been in a state of insurgence and disarray (see Tishkov 1992). While anthropologists of the older generation, many of whom occupy prestigious Chairs at the dominating institutions in Moscow, St Petersburg and Novosibirsk, tend to continue the traditions from Soviet ethnography, many younger anthropologists (some of whom were never educated as anthropologists at all), look to the West for inspiration (see Condee 1995 for examples). In St Petersburg, the foundation of the new European University, funded by the Hungarian-American billionaire George Soros, had to some extent crystallised this opposition, with more Western-oriented anthropologists clustering around Nikolai B. Vakhtin at the Soros University.

This brief outline gives a hint of the range of variation among the various national anthropologies that have increasingly made themselves felt during the 1990s. It also indicates perhaps the greatest limitation of the present book. Our narrative has concentrated heavily on anthropology as it emerged during the twentieth century in three language areas: German (until the interwar years), French and English (British and American). We have made this choice, because these traditions have effectively defined the mainstream of methodological and theoretical development in the discipline. In part, this is a matter of definitional power, and if, say, the best of Brazilian anthropology had regularly been translated into French and English, the history of the discipline as a whole might well have been different (though as we saw above, translation may be insufficient, in the absence of sustained personal contacts).

Like it or not, however, the current situation is that English is increasingly assuming the role of an anthropological *lingua franca* throughout the world; and that lack of English language proficiency is becoming a severe handicap. At the biannual EASA conferences, both English and French are official languages, but English is by far the most used; even many French anthropologists present their work in English on these occasions. During the 1980s and 1990s young scholars in countries with strong indigenous anthropological traditions were increasingly encouraged to publish their work in English. While there are perfectly sound academic reasons for this, the situation also creates a peculiar power asymmetry, since the English of non-natives is often a much poorer instrument of communication than their native language. Another, related question – for which there ought to be a qualified, anthropologically informed answer – is whether the current linguistic convergence of the discipline will ultimately lead to homogenisation or heterogenisation. On the one hand, a wider variety of scholars, writing from different national traditions, are exposed to each others' work through the medium of a shared language. On the other hand, the very transformation of that work into a foreign language inevitably removes some of its qualities (see Wierzbicka 1989). Any anthropologist who works in two languages – and the present authors both belong to that group – knows that the richness and nuance of expression that one cultivates in one's native tongue is difficult to transplant to a foreign language, which often even lacks concepts for what one wants to say. Few are endowed with the linguistic talents of a Malinowski, and even he was never 'at home' among the Trobriands.

Taking into account these caveats – the increasingly complex history of the subject (as accounts from non-metropolitan language communities are increasingly published in English) and the current lack of theoretical coherence in the discipline – we shall now turn to a tentative outline of some of the main trends in 1990s anthropology. In certain ways, the continuities with the past are reassuring – or disquieting, depending on one's point of view. Intensive participant observation was still unchallenged as the method of choice for procuring reliable and detailed knowledge about other peoples, although it was increasingly supplemented by a wide range of other methods, and it was now taken for granted that fieldwork in complex societies raised different methodological issues from village fieldwork. The idea that the world we inhabit is socially and culturally constructed was also still shared by most anthropologists – albeit with a variable admixture of postmodern relativism. In general, the 1990s also saw a backing off from extreme postmodern positions (as the postmodern revolution, like so many others before it, was assimilated into the discipline's mainstream), and a return to a more balanced ethnographic 'realism', which asserted that anthropological knowledge may well be relative, but it is no less relevant for that. In a similar vein, the extreme particularism and cultural relativism of the 1980s seem to have been supplanted by a more balanced interest in empirical studies of the *relationship* between the universally human and the culturally particular. As a result, some of the old controversies of the discipline reappeared in new guises; and some new research fields involved the rediscovery of older work – during the 1980s and 1990s, for example, Mauss was rediscovered in at least three contexts: as a theorist of the morality of exchange (Thomas 1991; Weiner 1992), as a theorist of personhood (Carrithers et al. 1985), and as a theorist of the body (see Mauss 1979 [1934]). All three fields were major concerns during the 1990s.

However, there were also some new features to the anthropology of the 1990s which cannot go unmentioned. Let us note some of the more obvious examples. First, as seen in the previous chapter, any simple distinction between us and them, or observer and observed, has become difficult to defend. 'Natives' are perfectly capable of identifying themselves, and are increasingly hostile to anthropological attempts to dictate who they 'really' are. This realisation has contributed to a sharpened awareness of ethical issues in anthropology, that has been growing ever since the American Anthropological Association – at the height of the revolution in fieldwork – published its 'Statement on ethics' in 1971. Today, ethical considerations form a routine part even of student work. Another reason for this is that 'anthropology at home' is no longer a curiosity, but a perfectly normal part of the enterprise – and ethical dilemmas are naturally more understandable and more pressing when we encounter them close to home.

Second, any simple 'modern–traditional' dichotomy has also become nearly indefensible, whether for epistemological or purely empirical reasons. Indeed, it seems to the present authors that this aversion to anything that even smacks of evolutionism was so strong in 1990s anthropology that it might have amounted to a blind spot. Thus, as the neo-evolutionists demonstrated in the 1950s and 1960s, it is easy to document striking empirical differences between (for example) small-scale hunter-gatherer societies and modern post-industrial societies, in terms of quantitative measures such as energy-flow per capita. The reason why such questions should concern us, is that *homo sapiens sapiens* inhabited the Earth as hunter-gatherers for some 150,000 years, while modern society is extremely recent (just how recent is a matter of theoretical taste and empirical focus). Since less than one-tenth of a percent of human history has been spent in 'modern' societies, it stands to reason that general theories of human sociality would benefit from insights into the difference between 'primitive' and 'modern' social systems.

Third, the world has seen a phenomenal growth in transnational connections of every kind – from migration to tourism, from international stock markets to the Internet. This powerful acceleration of social mobility across vast geographical distances has led many anthropologists to question the often taken-for-granted link between groups of people and bounded geographical localities to which they 'belong'. The whole concept of space suddenly needs rethinking, as anthropologists increasingly study globally dispersed groups, such as refugees and migrants, workers in a multinational firm or Internet communities. The classical synchronic, single-sited, single-society studies that used to be the hallmark of anthropology are becoming increasingly rare, and anthropologists are expected as a matter of routine to contextualise their work both historically and regionally. We shall shortly return to some of the theoretical thinking that has emerged from this. In discussions of methods, a new term has recently started to appear – *multi-sited fieldwork* – which seems to refer to a number of different kinds of non-localised studies, from studies of dispersed networks in cities or institutions, to studies of intercontinental migrant communities.

Fourth, and as part of the 'rethinking of space' that we have referred to above, we have seen a new interest in the physical territories occupied by people, whether they be traditional ecosystems, urban cityscapes, or virtual cyberscapes – all of which had seemed irrelevant to the extreme social constructionists of postmodernism. We sense an affinity between this interest in the physical environment, and the orientation towards the (physical) human body that was emphasised by practice theorists (Chapter 8), and, indeed, Bourdieu places equal emphasis on the physical surroundings and the physical body in his theory of *habitus*. This affinity suggests that the new *rapprochement* between anthropology and physical reality is taking place on very different terms than during the cultural ecology movement of the 1960s.

Finally, the general undermining of the concept of culture that had been going on since the 1960s, had, by the end of the 1990s, successfully discredited the old idea of 'a people' possessing 'a shared culture'. Thus, on the one hand, the idea of the social whole has been weakened, as 'society' is relativised and dissolves into dispersed and overlapping networks. On the other hand, as we pointed out above, the idea of the physical world (and the body) has attained greater prominence in anthropological thinking. This paradox might suggest a long-term drift away from Durkheimian notions of society as an autonomous system, and towards notions current in some of the natural sciences.

The latter trend is one of two that we have singled out for special consideration in this final chapter of our history of anthropology, along with the trend towards studies of globalisation and place. Our choice of these two particular subjects is more or less arbitrary. There are many other trends we might have discussed with equal justification. Thus, we have seen a marked growth in anthropological research on exchange, both in the traditional heartlands of the discipline (such as Melanesia; Barraud et al 1984; Strathern 1988; Weiner 1992; Godelier 1999) and 'at home' (such as a North London street; Miller 1998). There has also been much work done on symbolism, history and power, inspired in particular by the work of Marx, Gramsci and Foucault (Herzfeld 1992; Trouillot 1995; Gledhill 2000). We have seen a tendency towards a revival of economic anthropology, informed by post-structuralist theory, by the recently rediscovered work of Simmel, and by Marxism (Carrier 1997; Lutz and Nonini 1999). Important studies have been done on the anthropology of political violence (Malkki 1995; Nordstrom and Robben 1995; Tambiah 1996) and human rights (Wilson 1997); new research areas which may become decisive for the future of anthropology.

Our decision to focus on globalisation studies and studies of biology and culture, does not imply that we consider these fields more important than any of the above. We do, however, consider the two trends to be particularly interesting in the context of the history of the discipline – in part, because they both 'push the envelope' of mainstream anthropology in noticeable ways; in part, because both have been major growth industries in the 1990s. The two trends also present us with a number of interesting contrasts and overlaps. Roughly speaking, we might say that they respond to the present state of anthropology and the world in two very different ways – but ways which are, in both cases, faithful to the history of the discipline. The first trend seems to retreat from history and current complexities, to ask once again the old question 'What is a human being?' – thereby revitalising the nature/nurture controversy, which was in its day constitutive of modern anthropology. The second trend returns us once again to two other classical questions 'What is society?' and 'What is culture?' – but now in a context of global flow and flux.

BIOLOGY AND CULTURE

Two complementary questions can be asked about the nature of humanity (Ingold 1994): 'What is a human being?' (answer: 'A small twig on a branch of the great trunk of evolution'; 'A close relative of chimpanzees', etc.) and 'What does it mean to be a human being?' (a question that generates a whole range of different answers). In twentieth-century anthropology, as this book has shown, the latter question has predominated over the former. Grasping the native's point of view was essential for both Boas and Malinowski, and both Mauss and Radcliffe-Brown were concerned with the nature of society rather than the nature of *homo sapiens sapiens*. Causal explanations seeing human culture and society as a result of external forces, be they environmental or genetic, were always minority views, though sometimes influential ones. During the last two decades, however, we have seen a revitalisation of the relationship between anthropology and several of the natural sciences.

This movement is ultimately driven by the fact that the natural sciences are making use of increasingly complex models, that are able to provide realistic simulations of the behaviour of biological, and even, to some extent, mental processes. Though the direct application of such models to qualitative social science is obviously impossible (since the models are dependent on numerical input), nevertheless, we have previously seen (in our discussion of cybernetics) that models from natural science may profitably be used as metaphors of social process. Thus, Marilyn Strathern (1991) has used mathematical Chaos Theory as a metaphor of the kinds of differences that exist between social situations and arenas.

It is the complexity of the new models that is their prime attraction for many anthropologists. With complex systems theory, natural science itself seems to have abandoned the unilinear world of cause and effect in favour of a probabilistic, multi-stranded universe that seems far more familiar to social scientists – and which also increases understanding for the social sciences among many natural scientists. However, there is still substantial distrust between these two branches of academia, and misunderstandings are common, and impede the exchange of ideas. The problems may be illustrated with the following case.

In 1979, Bruno Latour and Steve Woolgar published the seminal monograph *Laboratory Life*. This was a traditional, single-sited field project, carried out in a high-tech biochemical laboratory in California. The authors are very careful, from the outset, to separate their task from that of the scientists they study. While the biochemists are unearthing knowledge about the physical world 'out there', Latour and Woolgar ask how such knowledge becomes a social fact: how does the experimenter recognise a 'result' when he sees it, how is that 'result' circulated within the laboratory collective, criticised or accepted, defended, related to other 'results' and published? In their answer to these questions, the authors develop the rudiments of what Latour (1991) would later refer to as Actor Network Theory, which links persons, objects and ideas in a network, in which constant 'translations' (person to object, object to idea, etc.) are taking place (see also p. 172). In the monograph's introductory chapter, by now a classic, the authors describe their entry into the laboratory, which is consciously exotified, to make it seem as 'unfamiliar' as a New Guinea tribe to the reader.

In the wake of this study, quite a number of sociological and anthropological studies of science, often referred to as 'STS' (Studies in Technology and Science) have appeared, ranging from general accounts of the embeddedness of science in large-scale economic and political processes to micro-studies of particular research milieux. However, the implicit critique of natural science that many of these studies conveyed, and their often poststructuralist concerns with knowledge regimes and ideology, did nothing to improve relations between anthropologists and natural scientists. Latour and Woolgar themselves generally avoided these pitfalls; nevertheless, their work was mostly either criticised or ignored by biologists and physicists.

More recently, the infamous Sokal affair demonstrated that tensions are still considerable. In 1996, physicist Alan Sokal published an article entitled 'Transgressing the boundaries: Toward a transformative hermeneutics of quantum gravity' in the journal *Social Text*, where he argued that theoretical physics should be seen as a social construction and not as 'objective truth' (Sokal 1996). Shortly afterwards, he announced that the article had been a hoax; an incoherent and incomprehensible argument full of postmodernist jargon and foggy thinking, and that the whole exercise had been an attempt to expose the vacuousness and anti-intellectualism of the postmodern cultural elite. While the Sokal affair did not involve anthropologists (his targets were chiefly literary theorists and philosophers), it offered an acute illustration of the continuing gap between humanistic and scientific approaches.

It is worth noting, however, that Latour has never argued a strongly social constructionist view. Indeed, in *We Have Never Been Modern* (1991) he asserts that it is as futile to seek to reduce physical science to social science as vice versa. Instead, one needs to develop an analytical language to describe the 'translations' that are constantly taking place between the two, ostensibly separate fields. On the one hand, Latour's theory thus constitutes a frontal attack on the axiomatic separation of society and nature that has been constitutive of *both* the natural and the human sciences since the 1600s. On the other hand, it calls attention to the *hybrid* nature of all scientific results, to the fact that knowledge is transformed as it moves out of the laboratory or the fieldwork situation and into a global network of translation and re-translation.

This view is worth keeping in mind in the following, where we will be discussing two broad families of anthropological approaches that engage more directly (often through interdisciplinary work) with the natural sciences. The first family of approaches is directly linked to the rapidly expanding interdisciplinary field of *cognitive science*. 'Cognition' (which we might briefly define as all mental processes associated with the acquisition and management of knowledge, including perception, memory, judgement, concept formation, language use, etc.) is an old interest in anthropology, which had taken many forms earlier in the century; ranging from the Sapir–Whorf hypothesis, the Rationality Debate and Lévi-Strauss' *La Pensée sauvage* to the speciality often simply called cognitive anthropology (D'Andrade 1995), which, in the 1950s and 1960s, developed new methods to analyse the relationships between concepts in a given culture. Thus, in a famous study of colour classification, Brent Berlin and Paul Kay (1969) offered evidence for the existence of universal colour categories. During the 1980s, several of these anthropological concerns converged with work being done in linguistics, psychology, neurology, evolutionary biology, artificial intelligence research and General Systems Theory, to form the new field of cognitive science.

Cognitive science is still a field in the process of formation, which utilises a wide variety of methods (from computer-assisted tomography to participant observation), and poses a large, and expanding, number of questions. The advent of new mathematical simulation models for complex systems has stimulated many branches of this research and, with programs becoming more complex and hardware more powerful day by day, this work may in the long run prove to have extraordinary potential. This piece of information has not been wasted on funding agencies world wide, who have invested heavily in several branches of cognitive science. A number of influential research institutes have been established, and extensive experimental and field-oriented research is being carried out. All of this means that cognitive science for the time being offers countless tantalising and suggestive questions, but mostly tentative and fragmentary results.

The long-term impact of cognitive science on anthropology is therefore hard to assess. However, it is bound to make an impression that the cognitive scientists consider it proven that the individual is not born as a cognitive *tabula rasa* (blank slate). Ever since Durkheim, anthropologists have tended to accept the *tabula rasa* postulate unquestioningly – human mental processes were universalistic and socially constructed, they could be adapted freely to an infinite variety of conditions. In contrast, the new research demonstrates that our mind and sensory apparatus are highly specialised instruments, with specific potentials and limitations. Clearly, if positive knowledge of how these instruments function is forthcoming, it will be of the greatest interest to anthropology.

The state of the art in anthropology itself is indicated by an influential study Scott Atran (1990), which develops themes from both Durkheimian sociology and ethnoscience in arguing that there are particular, inborn ways of classifying the natural world that are universally human. Otherwise, the anthropologists working within the framework of cognitive science represented a wide range of persuasions. On the one hand, Dan Sperber (a former student of Lévi-Strauss's) and Pascal Boyer were sympathetic to a Darwinist explanation of human cognition (Sperber 1996; Boyer 1999 – a similar argument was advanced by Bateson in 1979). On the other hand, a number of theorists suggested that neurology might contain clues to an understanding of universal aspects of human cognition (Turner 1987; Bloch 1991; Borofsky 1994). Finally, such scholars as Bradd Shore, Dorothy Holland and Naomi Quinn (Holland and Quinn 1987; Shore 1996) adhered to varieties of *schema theory* or *prototype theory* (originally developed in linguistics), which postulate that cognition is organised around a limited number of prototypical 'elementary meanings', which are composites of biological hardwiring and social construction ('up' and 'down' may be universal human categories, but their significance is obviously different on a Polynesian atoll and in the Andes).

A similar view is expressed in two books jointly written by a linguist and a philosopher, George Lakoff and Mark Johnson (1980; 1999), which have been hugely influential in establishing the view that cognition and human knowledge universally build on metaphors *based on* bodily experience. Bodily experience, which clearly has a universal component (we are all born with two hands), is also clearly particular to the individual and to societies. At the same time, bodily experience is intimately known to each of us, and is therefore a fruitful source of analogies with other experiential fields, which are thus imbued with some of the ambience the particular bodily experience invoked. Lakoff and Johnson's work, which reconciles a belief in universals with a concern for the particular, has been particularly important in subfields such as medical anthropology and the anthropology of knowledge.

A final example of the work in this genre is the Polish-American linguist Anna Wierzbicka's comparative work on concept formation in various European languages. In an influential comparison of Russian and English words for emotional states, she demonstrates that the two languages draw the conceptual division between mind (or soul) and body in different and incompatible ways (Wierzbicka 1989). Such work, which might seem to be no more than a revival of the Sapir–Whorf hypothesis (Chapter 4), and thus yet another contribution to cultural relativism, in fact has a strong universalistic component, in as much as Wierzbicka's long-term goal is to discover 'semantic universals'.

Indeed, all the above examples – and many others could have been cited – seem to suggest a tentative revival of universalism in anthropology and a reversal of the post-structuralist and postmodern trends, with their rejection (as some would have it) of anything reminiscent of scientific pretensions in anthropology. No matter how they stand on the nature–nurture issue, and here the new cognitive anthropologists differ, they consider cultural representations as 'enrichments of intuitive ontology' (Boyer 1999: 210) and are intent on revealing the exact nature of the hardwiring underlying the soft and shifting stuff of culture.

The universalism of the second approach we have chosen to highlight is far more pronounced. The attitudes of anthropologists towards evolutionary theory, or neo-Darwinism, were – and are – contentious and varied. Some see Darwinist accounts of society as de-humanising and scientifically irresponsible, as attempts to reduce the richness of experience and global sociocultural variation to genetics. Others see Darwinist theories of the human mind as poorly supported by evidence so far and therefore irrelevant – two prominent names here are Claude Lévi-Strauss and the famous linguist Noam Chomsky. Yet others see enormous explanatory potential in the fusion of Darwinism, cognitive psychology and detailed ethnographic research.

But clearly, the sceptics dominated the scene, and in this they had the support of a venerable lineage of anthropologists. Before the war, Boas, Malinowski and Radcliffe-Brown (whose critical views on racial segregation are little known, cf. Kuper 1999: xiii–xiv) had been relentless critics of biological determinism, eugenics and the often associated racist pseudo-science, which many Darwinian biologists, incidentally, supported (see Malik

2000). After the war, the orthodox view on both sides of the Atlantic was that biological accounts of human nature were either irrelevant or wrong when applied to the subject-matter of anthropology. Anthropologists who studied human nature saw it as infinitely malleable (with a few important exceptions, such as Lévi-Strauss), while those who primarily studied society and culture saw them as perfectly intelligible in terms of their historical development and internal dynamics. Biological accounts of human nature only re-emerged on the centre-stage of intellectual life in the mid-1970s (Chapter 7), and were then almost unanimously rejected by social and cultural anthropologists. Since the early 1990s, however, sociobiology has re-emerged in a new and more sophisticated form, with greater potential for coalitions with traditional social and cultural anthropology – but again, anthropologists have generally rejected their advances. Nevertheless, the debate has become less aggressive; perhaps because of the 'cognitive turn' in sociobiology, perhaps because anthropology itself has become more receptive to such issues.

Darwinist social science, which attempts to account for human society in terms of the evolutionary history of the human species, can roughly be divided into two clusters of research (Knight et al. 1999: 1–2): on the one hand, evolutionary anthropology, which takes as its point of departure advances in human genetics which seem to indicate that the degree of inter-personal solidarity is determined by kinship distance; the closer the biological relatedness, the more likely one is to make sacrifices.

The other cluster, increasingly known as evolutionary psychology, 'has focused less on the functional consequences of behaviour than on the cognitive mechanisms believed to underpin it' (Knight et al. 1999: 2). Unlike the first-generation sociobiologists, this school drew no simple inferences from the existence of a particular behaviour or set of beliefs to their immediate adaptive value. Put bluntly, it was more concerned with cognition and classification than with sex and violence. The benchmark publication for this new synthesis was the omnibus work *The Adapted Mind* (Barkow et al. 1992), and the most dedicated proponents of the theory have been a husband-and-wife team, anthropologist John Tooby and psychologist Leda Cosmides at the University of California at Santa Barbara. Deliberately avoiding the contentious label sociobiology, they – and others – developed a theory of the human mind which saw it as composed of specific domains that had originally evolved as an adaptive response to the Environment of Evo-lutionary Adaptation: the environment in which *homo sapiens sapiens* originated as a species (most likely the upland savannahs of the East African Rift Valley). The defining features of the human mind were thus originally adaptive (they enhanced the species' fitness or potential for survival), but in the contemporary context, they may well be maladaptive. Once again, there would seem to be good reason for anthropologists to welcome positive knowledge in this area – but so far the research of these scholars is too incon-clusive and too fragmented to be of use to anthropologists. Moreover, though several evolutionary psychologists have tried to account for the interrelationship between biological evolution and cultural change (Boyd and Richerson 1985; Durham 1991), the school has not yet developed a theory of cultural change, which makes it seem singularly inappropriate in today's rapidly changing world.

At the end of the day, and in spite of numerous refinements, evolutionary psychology was still seen by most anthropologists as a form of biological reductionism, and failed to make major inroads into the mainstream of social and cultural anthropology during the 1990s. Nevertheless, it seems safe to conclude that contacts between anthropologists and biologists were revitalised during the 1990s. The biologists increasingly realised that language, self-consciousness, myth and ritual were complex, uniquely human phenomena that could not simply be seen as elaborations on generic primate behaviour. The anthropologists, on the other hand, have largely admitted that the *tabula rasa* theory of human socialisation is untenable, and many have at least started to question the a priori separation of the natural and social sciences. Today, as very substantial investments are made in the biological sciences, and comprehensive research programmes are carried out, it is perhaps only a matter of time before the traditional interdisciplinary boundaries are further challenged.

GLOBALISATION AND THE PRODUCTION OF LOCALITY

For a while during the 1990s, it seemed that hardly any major conference in the social sciences failed to include the word 'globalisation' in its title. Before the late 1980s, the term had hardly been used (Robertson 1992: 8); then, suddenly, it was on everybody's lips. Many anthropologists were active in defining the field and developing new research agendas, new journals were inaugurated (such as the Chicago-based *Public Culture*), and a flurry of books were published, often with words like 'Global', 'Culture', 'Modernity' and 'Identity' in their titles. The most influential edited volume was Mike Featherstone's *Global Culture* (1990), which was followed by Scott Lash and Jonathan Friedman's *Modernity and Identity* (1991), sociologist Anthony Giddens' *Modernity and Self-Identity* (1991), Ulf Hannerz's *Cultural Complexity* (1992), Friedman's *Global Identity and Cultural Process* (1994) and Arjun Appadurai's *Modernity at Large* (1996), to mention a few of the most widely read books.

Globalisation could be provisionally defined as any process that renders the geographical distance between locations irrelevant. The spread of, say, human rights concepts, consumption patterns, information technologies, pop music and nationalist ideologies across the world may be described as processes of globalisation, as may international capital flows, the AIDS pandemic, the illegal drug and arms trade, the growth of transnational academic networks in anthropology, or the migratory movements through which, for example, Caribbean communities are established in Britain. Such processes are clearly dependent on the development of global-scale infrastructures (long-distance transportation networks, modern communication technologies, etc.), though anthropologists are quick to point out that the socio-cultural effects of, say, inexpensive plane tickets, satellite television or the Internet, are unpredictable and highly diverse.

The newness of globalisation has been debated both within and outside anthropology. Some have argued that wide-ranging economic, political and religious networks on a regional or even continental scale have existed for centuries, while others hold that phenomena such as the emergence of polyethnic urban societies in the West, the spread of modern educational systems in the Third World, the global dissemination of Western lifestyles and political ideals, or the growing politicisation of essentialised ethnic identities, deserve to be regarded as truly new, setting new agendas for theory and method in anthropology. To the present writers it seems beyond doubt that the *speed and volume* of modern flows of information, people and goods are unprecedented in human history; though long-distance networks of trade, kinship, ritual exchange and political conflict have probably existed – on a much smaller scale – as long as society itself.

Although it may seem trivial, we also feel the need to emphasise the distinction between *globalisation itself* – a complex of actually occurring socio-cultural processes with historical roots stretching back to colonialism and beyond, and *globalisation studies* – a family of anthropological approaches to these processes that attained prominence during the 1990s. As regards 'globalisation itself', the most prominent event of the postwar period was undoubtedly the fall of the Iron Curtain. For anthropology this had wide-ranging repercussions. First, as mentioned above, Western and Eastern anthropologists were soon rubbing shoulders at conferences, trying to make sense of each others' conception of the discipline. Second, and even more fundamentally, an entire new ethnographic region was 'opened up' to anthropological inquiry. Its recent shared past had established a measure of commonality throughout this region (embodied, for example, in bureaucratic, educational and scientific conventions, ideology and social memory), overlying a patchwork of local traditions of the most diverse extraction, which asserted themselves with renewed force upon the sudden collapse of central authority. To the Western anthropologists who were soon engaged in fieldwork in the 'post-socialist region', these conditions seemed sufficiently unique to prompt the development of a set of innovative theoretical and methodological approaches. Thus, in 1991, the American anthropologist Katherine Verdery published the highly influential article 'Theorizing Socialism: A Prologue to the "Transition"'. Drawing on the research of a handful of Western anthropologists who had done fieldwork in the region prior to 1989 (see Halpern and Kideckel 1983 for an overview), on the work of Eastern European scholars (such as the Hungarian economist János Kornai), and (surprisingly) on the theories of Karl Polanyi (Chapter 5),

Verdery here develops a holistic model of pre-1989, 'socialist' society, which describes it as a distinct historical social type, with certain similarities to feudalism. Later research has in part followed up Verdery's model (see Humphrey 1996/97), in part developed along different paths (see Ries 1997). Nevertheless, her perspective remains dominant in studies of the region.

This example may serve to illustrate several points, and at the same time to introduce us to the anthropological study of globalisation. On the one hand, we see a socio-economic globalisation process that leads to the collapse of a regional political system. On the other hand, we see anthropologists (themselves agents of globalisation) penetrating into a new, pristine 'field', defining it as an 'ethnographic region', forging alliances with local scholars, and attempting to establish a respectable 'regional tradition of ethnographic writing' (see p. 145 above). Thus, a globalising process has erased the barriers around the region, but anthropologists are busy localising themselves in it, proclaiming its uniqueness, and developing theory specifically tailored to it. Paradoxically, however, the theory that has thus developed is not itself much concerned with globalisation. Indeed, its emphasis on typologies and mechanisms of social integration harks back to the 1970s and earlier. Of course, this typological bent further strengthens the argument that the region is indeed distinct, and thus the legitimate object of study for a new sub-group of anthropologists.

As we see, globalisation has local effects, which are unpredictable, and may be autonomous to the extent that they directly oppose globalisation. This realisation was an important point of departure for the globalisation studies that emerged in anthropology during the 1990s.

The anthropological interest in globalisation did not emerge in a vacuum. The studies of ethnicity and nationalism that emerged during the 1980s (Chapter 8) clearly anticipated the globalisation school, in as much as nationalism was by definition a phenomenon associated with modernity and the state, and ethnic movements were also largely associated with change and modernisation. Likewise, there are clear continuities with the 1970s interest in Political Economy (Chapter 7). Indeed, two of the grand old men of this school, Eric Wolf (Steward's student) and Peter Worsley (Gluckman's student), had published major books in the early 1980s (Wolf 1982; Worsley 1984) dealing with cultural aspects of global capitalism and – especially in Worsley's case – the universalisation of modernity. Going even further back, there are continuities with the Marxian-Leninist theory of imperialism, with the peasant studies tradition pioneered by the Chicago school and Steward, and with the modernisation studies of the Manchester school.

In the influential work of the Swedish anthropologist Ulf Hannerz, such continuities are clearly reflected: while his first monograph (1969) was a study of American ghetto life largely in the Chicago tradition, and his first major theoretical work (1980) was an appraisal of urban anthropology, his most important contribution in the 1990s was a discussion of the field, methods and potentials of globalisation studies (Hannerz 1992). In the latter volume, the concept of culture was redefined to signify flow, process and partial integration rather than stable, bounded systems of meaning. This concept of culture was compatible with the still-dominant postmodernist sensibilities, as was Hannerz's definition of globalisation – as global aspects of modernity, rather than a monolithic 'global village'. Such adjustments made globalisation studies more palatable than traditional anthropology, but were also tailored to make sense of a world where bounded, stable cultural wholes were patently not predominant. Hannerz coined the term 'cultural creolisation' to describe the intermingling of two or several formerly discrete traditions; another term often used to denote the same phenomenon was 'cultural hybridity' (Modood and Werbner 1997).

Finally, like nearly every anthropologist writing in this field, Hannerz stresses that general global processes have specific local consequences. Globalisation does not necessarily entail the disappearance of local cultural differences; instead, a battle is waged with unpredictable, and often highly creative, outcome. Indeed, the neologism *glocalisation* has been proposed to stress the local component in globalisation processes. Nevertheless, the pattern of cultural variation in an era of intensified flow and contact across boundaries becomes radically different from the 'archipelago of cultures' envisaged in classic cultural anthropology (cf. Eriksen 1993b).

For anthropologists like Hannerz, globalisation studies were therefore simply an extension of existing research, into a new empirical context of global telecommunications and increased migration. For others, globalisation seemed to pose a number of new questions, to which they responded with innovative theoretical formulations.

An example of the latter kind is the 'actor-network theory' proposed by Bruno Latour (see p. 164). Originally developed in a study of scientific practice, this theory's emphasis on 'hybrids', and on the processes of 'translation' that occur when persons, objects or ideas flow from context to context, seemed ideally suited to a globalised world. When deployed methodically along the lines suggested by classical network theory (Chapter 5), and inspired theoretically by the burgeoning discussions of exchange theory that emerged during the 1990s, actor-network theory becomes a formidable tool for analysis of global processes.

Arjun Appadurai is another anthropologist who has contributed substantially to a dedicated theory of globalisation. In his edited volume on economic anthropology from 1986, he develops ideas of value transformation in global networks that are reminiscent of Latour's, and, as in Latour's case, ultimately inspired by phenomenological concerns. Then, in 1995, Appadurai published the article 'The production of locality', which proposes that human societies have always experienced tensions between local and global processes, in as much as any society necessarily must interact with its context. 'Producing locals', whose loyalty will ensure that the local community will not be swallowed by its context, thus becomes a prime concern of all societies, just as the tension between local and global concerns becomes a prime concern of all individuals. On this basis, Appadurai proposes a radical revision of anthropological studies of ritual, in which ritual is seen to function, first and foremost, as an instrument for 'producing locality'. Here we see yet another example of a theoretical construction that connects a potentially marginal subfield in anthropology to classical questions of anthropological inquiry, such as exchange or ritual.

Though globalisation research was largely an Anglophone speciality (as if in oblique confirmation of allegations that 'cultural globalisation' was tantamount to Americanisation), some of the most important contributions to the field were made by the French anthropologist Marc Augé, who had studied ritual and politics in West Africa, largely in a structural Marxist mode, during the 1960s. In small ethnographic studies of the Paris metro and the Luxembourg Gardens (Augé 1986, 1985), and most influentially, in his later theoretical books, including *Non-lieux* (1991; *Non-Places*, 1995), Augé discussed the fate of the classic anthropological notions of place, culture, society and community in the postmodern era of flux and change. Arguing that the stability of 'place' could no longer be taken for granted in this disembedded world, Augé parallels many of Appadurai's concerns (see Appadurai 1996). In a work reminiscent of that of his postmodern countryman, Jean Baudrillard, Augé discusses dreams and imagination under different informational regimes, drawing on his earlier West African research as well as recent global developments (Augé 1999).

The kinship between globalisation studies and postmodernist deconstructionism was evident in the work of several anthropologists, perhaps most poignantly in Strathern's *Partial Connections* (1991). Strathern argued that neither societies nor symbolic systems are coherent wholes, and cited globalisation research (notably Hannerz) approvingly in support. The multiplicity of voices, the erasure of clear distinctions between 'cultures' or 'societies', the eclectic attitude to research method, and the insistence that the world was inhabited by hybrids (objects, people or concepts, as the case might be), were some of the shared notions. Some of the leading postmodern anthropologists, most notably George Marcus, advocated comparative studies of modernity as an appropriate framework for an updated, reflexive anthropology. To some, the studies of the global–local interface, the paradoxes of widespread cultural reflexivity and the global spreading of the icons and institutions of modernity, gave a solid empirical grounding to the lofty and often purely theoretical claims of the postmodernists.

In spite of the many continuities with already existing research traditions, the emergence of globalisation studies (or comparative studies of modernity) may signify the final demise of the classical anthropological notions of 'culture' and 'society', that have shown remarkable tenacity in the face of near-continuous criticism ever since the 1960s. The reason for this is not even so much the intrinsic value of the globalisation theories themselves, as the fact that these theories direct our attention to an empirical reality, where even the ideal type of the stable, isolated, 'authentic' society or culture, seems increasingly anachronistic. The actor-network models briefly reviewed above may perhaps be a preview of the kind of concepts that will in the end replace the classical ones. They portray a world of 'partial connections', of ever-changing and hybridising 'discursive objects' employed and deployed by human carriers with reflexive ideas of their own identity, in which ideas of 'culture', derived from anthropology, may figure prominently. Indigenous peoples like the Sami of northern Scandinavia and many Native North American groups actively debate the relative merits of ethnographic studies of their cultures; people in Trinidad may be familiar with M.G. Smith's (1965) theory of cultural pluralism; Australian aborigines actively draw on classic ethnography in presenting their 'culture' to the authorities; Pacific Islanders copyright their rituals, to stop anthropologists from broadcasting video recordings of them. In this era of widespread cultural reflexivity, anthropologists may end up in the typically 'hybrid' situation of studying not other people's culture, but other people's quasi-anthropological representations of their culture.

The sudden enthusiasm for globalisation studies was not shared by all in the discipline. For some, it was a case of the emperor's new clothes: globalisation was merely a fancy name for neo-imperialism, cleansed of its political dimension. But while it is true that the concern with power relations has been variable in research on globalisation, it has not been absent. Power is a major issue in Appadurai's work, as well as in the influential body of research work on comparative modernities that has been produced or stimulated by John and Jean Comaroff at the University of Chicago (see, for instance, Comaroff and Comaroff 1993). Inspired by work on power and 'resistance' (Chapter 7) by such authors as James C. Scott (1985), Anthony Giddens (1979), Eric Wolf (1969) and ultimately Marx, the Comaroffs have argued, *inter alia*, that traditional rituals, such as witchcraft, may – under the impact of the extreme stresses inherent in global processes – mutate into virulent forms, that encourage mass violence.

Other objections levelled at globalisation studies were that anthropology should continue to emphasise the local and the unique, and that the prophets of globalisation exaggerated the reach of modernity. However, as we pointed out above, a recognition of global interconnectedness does not preclude a concern with the local – indeed, the fragmented local cultures of the globalised world seem to invite a particularist, or even Boasian approach. Indeed, the most famous anthropologists associated with the tradition of cultural relativism in the last decades of the twentieth century, namely Geertz and Sahlins, both wrote essays that judiciously placed the onslaught or, at least, impact of modernity on formerly tribal and traditional societies, in the larger framework of their respective projects. Sahlins wrote about the ironies of identity politics in Melanesia; 'as the New Guinean said to the anthropologist: if we didn't have *kastom* [custom], we would be just like white men' (1994: 378). He also described the commercialisation and politicisation of identity in the Pacific, decrying the commercial 'Hawaiian' culture presented to tourists by Hawaiians recreating themselves 'in the image others have made of them' (p. 379). However, he then emphasised, in continuity with his earlier work, that 'what needs to be studied ethnographically is the indigenization of modernity – through time and in all its dialectical ups and downs' (p. 390). Geertz, in a somewhat similar vein, wrote that difference 'will doubtless remain – the French will never eat salted butter. But the good old days of widow burning and cannibalism are gone forever' (1994: 454). He nevertheless saw no contradiction between the emergence of a seamless world of connections (as opposed to a discontinuous world of autonomous cultures), and his overall research programme, which he summarised, in one place, as 'grasping an alien turn of mind' (p. 462).

Both of these essays conveyed a distinct sense of discomfort, indirectly revealed through the extensive use of irony. Both Geertz and Sahlins admitted that an era was gone, speaking of the contemporary age as 'postmodern', using the term descriptively to denote fragmentation, reflexive modernity and blurred boundaries.

POSTSCRIPT

One of the most popular undergraduate monographs in anthropology during the last decades of the twentieth century was Napoleon Chagnon's slim volume on the Yanomamö of the dense rainforests of the Brazilian-Venezuelan borderlands. *The Fierce People* (1968; 5th edition, 1997) depicted a violence-ridden, warlike, 'Neolithic' culture, whose social organisation (kin-based villages prone to fission) and warfare were explained with reference to Darwinian theories of natural selection: villages split apart when they grew too big to be effectively united by genetic proximity, and warfare, caused by male competition for women, selected directly for the fittest.

In the autumn of 2000, another specialist on Amazonian peoples, Terence Turner, read the proofs of a forthcoming book on the Yanomamö, written by investigative journalist Patrick Tierney (Tierney 2000). In the book, Tierney presented some very serious criticism of researchers working among the Yanomamö, targeting in particular Chagnon and the team he had cooperated with in the late 1960s. Some of his points continue to be debated at the time of writing, but the very heated controversy engendered in American anthropology reveals the continued existence of some of the important faultlines that have defined the discipline at least since Boas.

Turner, whose work on the Kayapó was informed by postmodern sensibilities and tried to situate them historically, as well as discussing – in his most widely read articles – their emergent modern identity politics, reacted immediately to Tierney's allegations. He wrote to the president of the AAA, warning her that a major scandal affecting the entire discipline was under way. As it happened, his e-mail to the AAA was leaked, and in a matter of days, it was common knowledge to thousands of anthropologists. Although some of Tierney's allegations, notably that geneticist James Neel, Chagnon and other members of their team had more or less deliberately spread measles among the Yanomamö, turned out to be mistaken, he had other charges as well. He claimed, among other things, that Chagnon had blackmailed Yanomamö into giving him secret information about kinship, and that he had actively encouraged some of the violent acts that he then filmed as part of his documentation for their 'fierceness'. For some time Chagnon's Yanomamö research had been controversial among specialists who had pointed out methodological weaknesses (Ferguson 1995) or emphasised other aspects of Yanomamö society than he (Lizot 1984), but the intimations that he had virtually fabricated some of his data, as well as acting deeply unethically in the field, led to massive outrage, comparable to the hostility encountered by another biologically oriented anthropologist nearly two decades earlier, namely Derek Freeman. When, in November 2000, the AAA organised a special panel on the Tierney book during its annual conference, Chagnon declined to attend because he suspected the meeting would amount to a public lynching.

In this, he may have been right. The AAA was dominated by cultural relativists, most of whom were probably distrustful not only of Chagnon's field ethics, but of his Darwinian universalism, and who would have been glad to cheer his castigation (not to say professional castration) for either or both of these reasons. Be this as it may – and the dust has not yet settled at the time of writing – the affair, and especially the profiles of its main protagonists, highlighted two tensions that seem perennial in twentieth-century anthropology. First, there was the question of nature versus nurture. Chagnon saw cultural behaviour as closely linked with genetic programming; Turner saw it as largely autonomous and irreducible to biology. Their conflict seemed a re-enactment of the age-old dispute between relativism and universalism, with Turner in the role of the Boasian knight, subduing the evil dragon of Darwinism, whose slick talk of genes and natural selection concealed a heart blackened by eugenics, racism and ethnic cleansing. Second, there was the question of cultural authenticity and its relationship to professional ethics – which replaces the fiery dragon with the mad scientist, willing to obtain his data at any price. The popularity of Chagnon's book was in no small measure due to its depiction of a 'pristine' culture uncontaminated by modernity. During the 1990s, the Yanomamö negotiated for land rights with the Brazilian and Venezuelan authorities, were marginalised by the influx of goldminers, and presented their cause on prime-time television worldwide. However, Chagnon did not see it as his job to help them make the transition to a semi-modern way of life. On the contrary, his view of 'the tribal world' was at least in part that it was a laboratory for scientific research. Thus, in the debate, much was made of the fact that when Chagnon collected genealogies, he inscribed numbers on people's arms with indelible ink, a practice that recalled the treatment of prisoners in Hitler's death camps. Turner's work on the Kayapó, in contrast, described their culture as a dynamic, hybrid mix. His view was that in order to survive as a group, they needed to adapt to modern circumstances, and – paradoxically – that their modernisation was a precondition for their cultural survival. Among other things, he had encouraged them to learn Portuguese and taught them to use video cameras to bring their cause to the attention of the world.

This heated debate, which took place almost exclusively in cyberspace in the final months of 2000, revealed an anthropological community that was deeply divided on questions of theory, methods and professional ethics. With the 'Chagnon affair', the anthropology of the twentieth century had come to an inconclusive end.

Methods, conceptualisations and research agendas change. The boundaries between anthropology and other disciplines are extremely fuzzy in places; both of the broad families of approaches discussed in this final chapter, for example, are distinctly interdisciplinary; globalisation studies link up with political theory, human geography, macrosociology and history; evolutionary approaches with psychology, biology and neurology. Eclecticism in theory and method, moreover, has been characteristic of the last two decades of the twentieth century. Yet it can still be said that some of the classic tensions of anthropology, differences that have made a difference (Bateson's phrase) and that have defined the space within which anthropology has taken place, are still intact.

First of all, it still makes sense to distinguish between anthropology as a generalising science (prototypes: Harris, Gellner) and anthropology as one of the humanities, which aims for interpretive richness rather than accuracy (prototypes: Clifford, Strathern). Second, it also makes sense (although there are a lot of crossover studies) to distinguish between anthropologists of society focusing on agency, social structure, politics (prototypes: Barth, Wolf) and anthropologists of culture focusing on symbols, mental structures, meaning (prototypes: Lévi-Strauss, Geertz). Here, we have deliberately avoided the terms 'social' and 'cultural' anthropology, which generally refer to the American–European divide, which only partly overlaps with this distinction. Third, as not least the Chagnon affair suggests, it is still perfectly reasonable to distinguish between approaches that primarily see society and culture as historical phenomena (like globalisation studies) and approaches that primarily search for timeless, unchanging structures and patterns (like neo-Darwinism).

Many, if not most, actual anthropologists place themselves at the crossroads of one, two or all three of these polarities, but most feel the magnetism of the poles and are occasionally forced to take a stance. Boas himself oscillated between scientific and humanistic ambitions on the discipline's behalf, and his cultural relativism is often highlighted to the extent that it overshadows his strong beliefs in the scientific pretensions of anthropology.

Further dualities that define the boundaries of the subject could also be proposed: primitivism (modernist anthropology) versus comparative studies of modernities; neo-Darwinism and other materialist approaches versus phenomenology and reflexive anthropology; quests for the unique versus quests for the universal. In a famous controversy in the mid-1990s, Sahlins and Sri Lankan-born anthropologist Gananath Obeyesekere debated universality and relativity in agency. Sahlins, in his work on Hawaiian history (Sahlins 1981, 1985), had argued that Captain Cook was killed, on that fateful day in 1779, because the Hawaiians had incorporated him in a myth, and that he ultimately failed to follow the script of that myth. Obeyesekere, protesting this 'exoticism', wrote an entire book where he claimed that Sahlins exaggerated the 'otherness' of the Hawaiians, who were probably driven by the same universal, pragmatic and ultimately psychological motivations as everybody else (Obeyesekere 1992). Sahlins eventually responded with another book where he defended his view in great detail (Sahlins 1995). A much less personalised and aggressive debate than some of the other recent controversies in anthropology (such as Gellner vs. Said, Freeman vs. Mead, Turner vs. Chagnon), the nuanced and unsensationalist exchange between the highly regarded professors revealed that, even at the centre of American cultural anthropology, there are profound disagreements about the essence of humanity, worthy of book-length arguments.

In so far as the tensions outlined above have not been resolved, the intellectual space that defined anthropology in the first place is still intact, notwithstanding 'the end of modernism'. The idea of the primitive may be gone, and the notion of a world of discrete cultures may have been rendered obsolete; but the large questions – 'What is society?', 'What is culture?', 'What is a human being?' and 'What does it mean to be a human being?' – remain unanswered. Or rather: they are still being answered in conflicting ways. It is only if these conflicts are made sufficiently explicit that the discipline can continue to thrive, for as this book has hopefully shown, anthropology has throughout its history depended on controversy for its ability to develop new perspectives and new knowledge.

BIBLIOGRAPHY

Whenever available, English translations are listed in the Bibliography. When applicable, original dates of publication are placed in brackets.

Abu-Lughod, Lila. 1986. *Veiled Sentiments: Honor and Poetry in a Beduin Society*. Berkeley: University of California Press.

Althusser, Louis. 1979 [1965]. *For Marx*. London: Verso.

—— and Étienne Balibar. 1979 [1965]. *Reading Capital*. London: Verso.

American Anthropological Association. 1947. Statement on human rights. *American Anthropologist*, **49** (4): 539–43.

—— 1971. *Statement on Ethics*. Washington, DC: American Anthropological Association.

Anderson, Benedict. 1991. *Imagined Communities: An Inquiry into the Origins and Spread of Nationalism*, 2nd edition. London: Verso.

Anderson, Perry. 1974. *Lineages of the Absolutist State*. London: New Left Books.

Appadurai, Arjun, ed. 1986. *The Social Life of Things: Commodities in Cultural Perspective*. Cambridge: Cambridge University Press.

—— 1995. The production of locality. In Richard Fardon, ed., *Counterworks: Managing the Diversity of Knowledge*, pp. 204–23. London: Routledge.

—— 1996. *Modernity at Large: Cultural Dimensions of Globalization*. Minneapolis: University of Minnesota Press.

Ardener, Edwin. 1989. *The Voice of Prophecy and Other Essays*, ed. Malcolm Chapman. Oxford: Blackwell.

Ardener, Shirley, ed. 1975. *Perceiving Women*. London: Dent.

—— ed. 1978. *Defining Females: The Nature of Women in Society*. London: Routledge.

Asad, Talal. 1972. Market model, class structure, and consent: a reconsideration of Swat political organization. *Man* **7** (1): 74–94.

—— ed. 1973. *Anthropology and the Colonial Encounter*. London: Ithaca.

Atran, Scott. 1990. *Cognitive Foundations of Natural History: Towards an Anthropology of Science*. Cambridge: Cambridge University Press.

Augé, Marc. 1985. *La Traversée du Luxembourg, Paris: 20 juillet 1984: ethno-roman d'une journée française considérée sous l'angle des moeurs, de la théorie et du bonheur*. Paris: Hachette.

—— 1986. *Un ethnologue dans le métro*. Paris: Hachette.

—— 1995 [1991]. *Non-Places: Introduction to an Anthropology of Supermodernity*. London: Verso.

—— 1999. *The War of Dreams*. London: Pluto.

Bachofen, J.J. 1968 [1861]. *Myth, Religion, and Mother Right: Selected Writings of J.J. Bachofen*. London: Routledge & Kegan Paul.

Bailey, F.G. 1960. *Tribe, Caste and Nation: A Study of Political Activity and Political Change in Highland Orissa*. Manchester: Manchester University Press.

Balandier, Georges. 1967. *Anthropologie politique*. Paris: Presses Universitaires Françaises.

Bamberger, Joan. 1974. The myth of matriarchy: why men rule in primitive society. In Michelle Z. Rosaldo and Louise Lamphere, eds, *Woman, Culture, Society*, pp. 263–80. Stanford, CA: Stanford University Press.

Banks, Marcus. 1996. *Ethnicity: Anthropological Constructions*. London: Routledge.

Barkow, John, Leda Cosmides and John Tooby, eds. 1992. *The Adapted Mind: Evolutionary Psychology and the Generation of Culture*. Oxford: Oxford University Press.

Barnard, Alan. 2000. *History and Theory in Anthropology*. Cambridge: Cambridge University Press.

Barnes, John A. 1990 [1954]. *Models and Interpretations*. Cambridge: Cambridge University Press.

Barraud, Cécile, Daniel de Coppet, André Iteanu and Raymond Jamous. 1994. Exchanges, wholes, comparisons. In C. Barraud et al., *On Relations and the Dead: Four Societies Viewed from the Angle of their Exchanges*, pp. 101–22. Oxford: Berg.

Barth, Fredrik. 1959. *Political Leadership among Swat Pathans*. London: Athlone Press.

—— 1966. *Models of Social Organization*. London: Royal Anthropological Institute, Occasional Papers, **23**.

—— 1967. Economic spheres in Darfur. In *Themes in Economic Anthropology*, pp. 149–74. London: Tavistock.

—— ed. 1969. *Ethnic Groups and Boundaries: The Social Organization of Culture Difference*. Oslo: Scandinavian University Press.

—— 1987. *Cosmologies in the Making: A Generative Approach to Cultural Variation in Inner New Guinea*. Cambridge: Cambridge University Press.

—— 1993. *Balinese Worlds*. Chicago: University of Chicago Press.

Bateson, Gregory. 1958 [1936]. *Naven*, 2nd edition. Stanford, CA: Stanford University Press.

—— 1971. The cybernetics of 'self': a theory of alcoholism. In G. Bateson, *Steps to an Ecology of Mind*, pp. 309–37. New York: Ballantine.

—— 1972. *Steps to an Ecology of Mind*. New York: Ballantine.

—— 1979. *Mind and Nature*. Glasgow: Fontana.

—— and Margaret Mead. 1942. *Balinese Character: A Photographic Analysis*. New York: The New York Academy of Sciences.

Bateson, Mary Catherine. 1984. *With a Daughter's Eye: A Memoir of Margaret Mead and Gregory Bateson*. New York: Harper.

Benedict, Ruth. 1970 [1934]. *Patterns of Culture*. Boston, MA: Houghton Mifflin.

—— 1974 [1946]. *The Chrysanthemum and the Sword*. Boston, MA: Houghton Mifflin.

Berlin, Brent and Paul Kay. 1969. *Basic Color Terms: Their Universality and Evolution*. Berkeley: University of California Press.

Berman, Marshall. 1982. *All That is Solid Melts Into Air: The Experience of Modernity*. New York: Simon & Schuster.

Bloch, Maurice, ed. 1975. *Marxist Analyses and Social Anthropology*. London: Malaby.

—— 1986. *From Blessing to Violence*. Cambridge: Cambridge University Press.

—— 1991. Language, anthropology and cognitive science. *Man*, **26**: 183–98.

—— and Jonathan Parry, eds. 1989. *Money and the Morality of Exchange*. Cambridge: Cambridge University Press.

Boas, Franz. 1927. *Primitive Art*. New York: Dover.

—— 1940 [1896]. *Race, Language and Culture*. New York: Macmillan.

Borofsky, Robert. 1994. On the knowledge and knowing of cultural activities. In Robert Borofsky, ed., *Assessing Cultural Anthropology*, pp. 331–46. New York: McGraw-Hill.

Bourdieu, Pierre. 1977 [1972]. *Outline of a Theory of Practice*. Cambridge: Cambridge University Press.

—— 1990 [1980]. *The Logic of Practice*. Cambridge: Polity.

Bowen, Elenor Smith (Laura Bohannan). 1954. *Return to Laughter*. London: Gollancz.

Boyd, Robert and Peter J. Richerson. 1985. *Culture and the Evolutionary Process*. Chicago: University of Chicago Press.

Boyer, Pascal. 1999. Human cognition and cultural evolution. In Henrietta Moore, ed., *Anthropological Theory Today*, pp. 206–33. Cambridge: Polity.

Briggs, Jean. 1970. *Never in Anger: Portrait of an Eskimo Family*. Cambridge, MA.: Harvard University Press.

Burnham, P.C. and Roy F. Ellen, eds. 1979. *Social and Ecological Systems*. London: Academic Press.

Carrier, James, ed. 1995. *Occidentalism: Images of the West*. Oxford: Oxford University Press.

—— ed. 1997. *Meanings of the Market: The Free Market in Western Culture*. Oxford: Berg.

Carrithers, Michael, Steven Collins and Steven Lukes, eds. 1985. *The Category of the Person: Anthropology, Philosophy, History*. Cambridge: Cambridge University Press.

Chagnon, Napoleon A. 1997 [1968]. *Yanomamö: The Fierce People*, 5th edition. New York: Holt, Rinehart & Winston.

Clifford, James. 1988. *The Predicament of Culture*. Berkeley: University of California Press.

—— and George Marcus, eds. 1986. *Writing Culture: The Poetics and Politics of Ethnography*. Berkeley: University of California Press.

Cohen, Abner. 1969. *Custom and Politics in Urban Africa*. London: Routledge.

—— 1974a. *Two-Dimensional Man*. London: Tavistock.

—— ed. 1974b. *Urban Ethnicity*. London: Tavistock.

Cohen, Anthony P. 1985. *The Symbolic Construction of Community*. London: Routledge.

Comaroff, Jean and John Comaroff, eds. 1993. *Modernity and its Malcontents: Ritual and Power in Postcolonial Africa*. Chicago: University of Chicago Press.

Condee, Nancy. 1995. *Soviet Hieroglyphics: Visual Culture in Late Twentieth-Century Russia*. Bloomington, IN: Indiana University Press.

Dahlberg, Frances, ed. 1981. *Woman the Gatherer*. New Haven, CT: Yale University Press.

DaMatta, Roberto 1991. *Carnivals, Rogues, and Heroes: An Interpretation of the Brazilian Dilemma*. Notre Dame, IN: University of Notre Dame Press.

—— 1995. *On the Brazilian Urban Poor: An Anthropological Report*. Notre Dame, IN: University of Notre Dame Press.

D'Andrade, Roy. 1995. *The Rise of Cognitive Anthropology*. Cambridge: Cambridge University Press.

Darwin, Charles. 1859. *On the Origin of Species by Natural Selection*. London: John Murray.

Dawkins, Richard. 1983 [1976]. *The Selfish Gene*, 2nd edition. Oxford: Oxford University Press.

Deloria, Vine Jr. 1970. *Custer Died for Your Sins*. New York: Avon.

Dennett, Daniel. 1995. *Darwin's Dangerous Idea: Evolution and the Meanings of Life*. New York: Simon & Schuster.

Descola, Philippe and Gisli Pálsson, eds. 1996. *Nature and Society: Anthropological Approaches*. London: Routledge.

DeVos, George and Lola Romanucci-Ross, eds. 1975. *Ethnic Identity: Cultural Continuities and Change*. Palo Alto, CA: Mayfield.

Douglas, Mary. 1966. *Purity and Danger*. London: Routledge & Kegan Paul.

—— 1970. *Natural Symbols*. London: Barrie & Rockliff.

—— 1978. *Cultural Bias*. London: Royal Anthropological Institute.

—— 1980. *Evans-Pritchard*. Glasgow: Fontana.

—— 1987. *How Institutions Think*. London: Routledge.

—— and Baron Isherwood. 1979. *The World of Goods*. New York: Basic Books.

Dumont, Louis. 1980. *Homo Hierarchicus. The Caste System and its Implications*, 2nd edition (revised). Chicago: University of Chicago Press. (Orig. French edn 1968, 1st English edn 1970.)

—— 1983. *Essais sur l'individualisme*. Paris: Seuil.

—— 1986 [1983]. *Essays on Individualism: Modern Ideology in Anthropological Perspective*. Chicago: University of Chicago Press.

Dunbar, Robin, Chris Knight and Camilla Power, eds. 1999. *The Evolution of Culture*. Edinburgh: Edinburgh University Press.

Dunn, Stephen P. and Ethel Dunn. 1974. *Introduction to Soviet Ethnography*. Berkeley: University of California Press.

Durham, William. 1991. *Coevolution: Genes, Culture, and Human Diversity*. Berkeley: University of California Press.

Durkheim, Émile 1951 [1897]. *Suicide: A Study in Sociology*. New York: Free Press.

—— 1964 [1893]. *The Division of Labor in Society*. New York: Free Press.

—— 1982 [1895]. *Rules of Sociological Method*, ed. Steven Lukes. New York: Free Press.

—— 1995 [1915]. *The Elementary Forms of Religious Life*. New York: Free Press.

—— and Marcel Mauss. 1963 [1900]. *Primitive Classification*. London: Routledge & Kegan Paul.

Engels, Friedrich. 1972 [1884]. *The Origin of the Family, Private Property and the State, in the Light of the Researches of Lewis H. Morgan*. New York: International Publishers.

Epstein, A.L. 1958. *Politics in an Urban African Community*. Manchester: Manchester University Press.

—— 1978. *Ethos and Identity*. London: Tavistock.

Eribon, Didier and Claude Lévi-Strauss. 1988. *De près et de loin*. Paris: Odile Jacob.

Eriksen, Thomas H. 1993a. *Ethnicity and Nationalism: Anthropological Perspectives*. London: Pluto.

—— 1993b. Do cultural islands exist? *Social Anthropology*, **1** (3): 133–47.

—— 2001. *Small Places – Large Issues: An Introduction to Social and Cultural Anthropology*, 2nd edition. London: Pluto.

Evans-Pritchard, E.E. 1940. *The Nuer*. Oxford: Clarendon.

—— 1951a. *Social Anthropology*. London: Cohen & West.

—— 1951b. *Kinship and Marriage among the Nuer*. Oxford: Clarendon.

—— 1956. *Nuer Religion*. Oxford: Clarendon.

—— 1983 [1937]. *Witchcraft, Magic and Oracles among the Azande*, ed. Eva Gillies. Oxford: Oxford University Press.

Fabian, Johannes. 1983. *Time and the Other: How Anthropology Makes its Object*. New York: Columbia University Press.

Fanon, Frantz.1967 [1960]. *The Wretched of the Earth*. Harmondsworth: Penguin.

—— 1986 [1956]. *Black Skin, White Masks*. London: Pluto.

Fardon, Richard. 1990. Introduction. In R. Fardon, ed., *Localising Strategies: Regional Traditions in Ethnographic Writing*. Edinburgh: Scottish Academic Press.

Featherstone, Mike, ed. 1990. *Global Culture: Nationalism, Globalization and Modernity*. London: Sage.

Feld, Steven. 1982. *Sound and Sentiment: Birds, Weeping, Poetics, and Song in Kaluli Expression*. Philadelphia, PA: University of Pennsylvania Press.

Ferguson, Brian. 1995. *Yanomami Warfare: A Political History*. Santa Fe: School of American Research Press.

Feyerabend, Paul. 1975. *Against Method*. London: Verso.

Finley, Moses I. 1973. *The Ancient Economy*. London: Chatto & Windus.

Firth, Raymond. 1929. *Primitive Economics of the New Zealand Maori*. New York: Dutton.

—— 1937. *We, the Tikopia: A Sociological Study of Kinship in Primitive Polynesia*. London: Allen & Unwin.

—— 1939. *Primitive Polynesian Economy*. London: Routledge.

—— 1951. *Elements of Social Organization*. London: Watts.

—— 1957. *Man and Culture: An Evaluation of the Work of Bronislaw Malinowski*. London: Routledge & Kegan Paul.

—— ed. 1967. *Themes in Economic Anthropology*. London: Tavistock.

Fortes, Meyer. 1945. *The Dynamics of Clanship among the Tallensi*. London: Oxford University Press.

—— 1949. Time and the social structure: an Ashanti case study. In Meyer Fortes, ed., *Social Structure: Studies Presented to A.R. Radcliffe-Brown*. Oxford: Clarendon.

—— and E.E. Evans-Pritchard, eds. 1940. *African Political Systems*. Oxford: Oxford University Press.

Fortune, Reo. 1932. *Sorcerers of Dobu: The Social Anthropology of the Dobu Islanders of the Western Pacific*. London: Routledge.

Foster, George M., Thayer Scudder, Elizabeth Colson and Robert V. Kemper. 1979. *Long-Term Field Research in Social Anthropology*. London: Academic Press.

Foucault, Michel. 1972. *The Archaeology of Knowledge*. London: Tavistock.

—— 1975a. *Surveiller et punir: naissance de la prison*. Paris: Gallimard.

—— 1975b. *The Birth of the Clinic*. New York: Norton.

—— 1991 [1966]. *The Order of Things: An Archaeology of the Human Sciences*. London: Routledge.

Frankenberg, Ronald. 1967. Economic anthropology: one anthropologist's view. In Raymond Firth, ed., *Themes in Economic Anthropology*, pp. 47–90. London: Tavistock.

—— 1980. Medical anthropology and development: a theoretical perspective. *Social Science and Medicine* **14B**: 197–207.

Frazer, James. 1996 [1890]. *The Golden Bough*, abridged edition. Harmondsworth: Penguin.

Freeman, Derek. 1983. *Margaret Mead and Samoa: The Making and Unmaking of an Anthropological Myth*. Cambridge, MA: Harvard University Press.

Friedman, Jonathan. 1979. Hegelian ecology: between Rousseau and the World Spirit. In P.C. Burnham and R.F. Ellen, eds, *Social and Ecological Systems*, pp. 253–70. London: Academic Press.

—— 1994. *Cultural Identity and Global Process*. London: Sage.

Galtung, Johan. 1971. A structural theory of imperialism. *Journal of Peace Research*, **8**.

Geana, Georghita. 1995. Discovering the whole of humankind: the genesis of anthropology through the Hegelian looking-glass. In Han Vermeulen and Arturo Alvarez Roldán, eds, *Fieldwork and Footnotes: Studies in the History of European Anthropology*, pp. 64–74. London: Routledge.

Geertz, Clifford. 1960. *The Religion of Java*. New York: The Free Press.

—— 1963a. *Agricultural Involution: The Processes of Ecological Change in Indonesia*. Berkeley: University of California Press.

—— 1963b. *Peddlers and Princes: Social Change and Economic Modernization in Two Indonesian Towns*. Chicago: University of Chicago Press.

—— 1973. *The Interpretation of Cultures*. New York: Basic Books.

—— 1983. *Local Knowledge: Further Essays in Interpretive Anthropology*. New York: Basic Books.

—— 1988. *Works and Lives: The Anthropologist as Author*. Cambridge: Polity.

—— 1994. The uses of diversity. In Robert Borofsky, ed., *Assessing Cultural Anthropology*, pp. 454–65. New York: McGraw-Hill.

Gellner, Ernest. 1969. *Saints of the Atlas*. Chicago: University of Chicago Press.

—— 1983. *Nations and Nationalism*. Oxford: Blackwell.

—— 1991. *Reason and Culture: The Historical Role of Rationality and Rationalism*. Oxford: Blackwell.

—— 1992. *Postmodernism, Reason and Religion*. London: Routledge.

—— 1993. The mightier pen? Edward Said and the double standards of inside-out colonialism. *TLS*, 19 February 1993.

Gennep, Arnold van. 1960 [1909]. *The Rites of Passage*. London: Routledge.

Giddens, Anthony. 1979. *Central Problems in Social Theory*. London: Macmillan.

—— 1984. *The Constitution of Society*. Cambridge: Polity.

—— 1991. *Modernity and Self-Identity* . Cambridge: Polity.

Giglioli, Pier Paolo, ed. 1976. *Language and Social Context: Selected Readings*. Harmondsworth: Penguin.

Givens, David B. and Timothy Jablonski. 1995. *1995 Survey of Anthropology PhDs*, http://www.aaanet.org/surveys/95survey.htm

Gledhill, John. 2000. *Power and its Disguises: Anthropological Perspectives on Politics*, 2nd edition. London: Pluto.

Gluckman, Max. 1956. *Custom and Conflict in Africa*. Oxford: Blackwell.

—— 1965. *Politics, Law and Ritual in Tribal Society*. Oxford: Blackwell.

Godelier, Maurice. 1975. Infrastructures, societies and history. *Current Anthropology*, **19** (4): 763–71.

—— 1977. *Perspectives in Marxist Anthropology*. Cambridge: Cambridge University Press.

—— 1999. *The Enigma of the Gift*. Cambridge: Polity.

Goffman, Erving. 1967. *Interaction Ritual: Essays in Face-to-Face Interaction*. Chicago: Aldine.

—— 1978 [1959]. *The Presentation of Self in Everyday Life*. Harmondsworth: Penguin.

Golde, Peggy, ed. 1970. *Women in the Field: Anthropological Experiences*. Chicago: Aldine.

Goody, Jack ed. 1958. *The Developmental Cycle in Domestic Groups*. Cambridge: Cambridge University Press.

—— ed. 1968. *Literacy in Traditional Societies*. Cambridge: Cambridge University Press.

—— 1977. *The Domestication of the Savage Mind*. Cambridge: Cambridge University Press.

—— 1995. *The Expansive Moment: The Rise of Social Anthropology in Britain and Africa, 1918–1970*. Cambridge: Cambridge University Press.

—— and Ian Watt. 1963. The consequences of literacy. *Comparative Studies in Society and History*, **5**: 304–45.

Griaule, Marcel. 1938. *Masques dogons*. Paris: Institut d'Ethnologie.

—— 1948. *Dieu d'eau: Entretiens avec Ogotemmli*. Paris: PUF.

Grillo, Ralph and Alan Rew, eds. 1985. *Social Anthropology and Development Policy*. London: Routledge.

Gullestad, Marianne. 1984. *Kitchen-Table Society*. Oslo: Scandinavian University Press.

Gupta, Akhil and James Ferguson, eds. 1997. *Anthropological Locations: Boundaries and Grounds of a Field Science*. Berkeley: University of California Press.

Halpern, Joel Martin and David A. Kideckel. 1983. Anthropology of Eastern Europe. *Annual Review of Anthropology*, **19** (2): 70–92.

Handler, Richard. 1988. *Nationalism and the Politics of Culture in Quebec*. Madison, WI: Wisconsin University Press.

Hannerz, Ulf. 1969. *Soulside: Inquiries into Ghetto Culture and Community*. New York: Columbia University Press.

—— 1980. *Exploring the City: Inquiries toward an Urban Anthropology*. New York: Columbia University Press.

—— 1992. *Cultural Complexity*. New York: Columbia University Press.

Harries-Jones, Peter. 1995. *A Recursive Vision: Ecological Understanding and Gregory Bateson*. Toronto: University of Toronto Press.

Harris, Marvin. 1968. *The Rise of Anthropological Theory: A History of Theories of Culture*. New York: Thomas Crowell.

—— 1979. *Cultural Materialism: The Struggle for a Science of Culture*. New York: Random House.

—— 1994. Cultural materialism is alive and well and won't go away until something better comes along. In Robert Borofsky, ed., *Assessing Cultural Anthropology*, pp. 62–76. New York: MacGraw-Hill.

Hart, Keith 1998. The place of the 1898 Cambridge Anthropological Expedition to the Torres Straits (CAETS) in the history of British social anthropology. Lecture given at conference Anthropology and Psychology: The Legacy of the Torres Strait Expedition, 1898–1998, Cambridge, 10–12 August 1998.

Hastrup, Kirsten. 1995. *A Passage to Anthropology: Between Experience and Theory*. London: Routledge.

Herder, Johann Gottfried. 1993 [1764– c. 1803]. *Against Pure Reason: Writings on Religion, Language, and History*. Minneapolis: Fortress Press.

Herdt, Gilbert. 1982. *Rituals of Manhood: Male Initiation in Papua New Guinea*. Berkeley: University of California Press.

Herzfeld, Michael. 1992. *The Social Production of Indifference: Exploring the Symbolic Roots of Western Bureaucracy*. Chicago: University of Chicago Press.

Hobsbawm, Eric and Terence Ranger, eds. 1983. *The Invention of Tradition*. Cambridge: Cambridge University Press.

Hocart, A.M. 1938. *Les Castes*. Paris: Musée Gimet.

Holland, Dorothy and Naomi Quinn, eds. 1987. *Cultural Models in Language and Thought*. Cambridge: Cambridge University Press.

Hollis, Martin and Steven Lukes, eds. 1982. *Rationality and Relativism*. Oxford: Blackwell.

Holmes, Lowell. 1987. *Quest for the Real Samoa: The Mead/Freeman Controversy and Beyond*. South Hadley, MA: Bergin & Garvey.

Holy, Ladislav. 1996. *Anthropological Perspectives on Kinship*. London: Pluto.

Hubert, Henri and Marcel Mauss. 1964 [1898]. *Sacrifice: Its Nature and Functions*. Chicago: University of Chicago Press.

Humphrey, Caroline. 1996–97. Myth-making, narratives and the dispossessed in Russia. *Current Anthropology*, **19** (2): 70–92.

Hynes, Nancy 1999. Culture comes home. *Prospect*, March. Downloaded from: http://www.prospect-magazine.co.uk/highlights/culture_home

Inden, Ronald. 1990. *Imagining India*. Oxford: Blackwell.

Ingold, Tim. 1976. *The Skolt Lapps today* . Cambridge: Cambridge University Press.

—— 1986. *Evolution and Social Life*. Cambridge: Cambridge University Press.

—— ed. 1994. *Companion Encyclopedia of Anthropology: Humanity, Culture and Social Life*. London: Routledge.

—— 2000. *The Perception of the Environment: Essays on Livelihood, Dwelling and Skill*. London: Routledge.

Josselin de Jong, J.P.B. 1952. *Lévi-Strauss's theory of kinship and marriage*. Meedelingen Rijksmuseum voor Volkenkunde, **10**. Leiden: E. J. Brill.

Kahn, Joel and Josip Llobera. 1980. French Marxist anthropology: twenty years after. *Journal of Peasant Studies*, **7**: 81–100

Kant, Immanuel. 1991 [1781]. *Critique of Pure Reason*. London: J.M. Dent.

Kapferer, Bruce. 1988. *Legends of People, Myths of State*. Baltimore, MD: Smithsonian Institution Press.

Kardiner, Abraham and Ralph Linton. 1949. *The Individual and His Society*. New York: Columbia University Press.

Keesing, Roger M. 1989. Exotic readings of cultural texts. *Current Anthropology*, **30**: 1–42.

—— 1994. Theories of culture revisited. In Robert Borofsky, ed., *Assessing Cultural Anthropology*, pp. 301–12. New York: McGraw-Hill.

Kleinman, Arthur. 1980. *Patients and Healer in the Context of Culture: An Exploration of the Borderland between Anthropology, Medicine, and Psychiatry*. Berkeley: University of California Press.

—— 1988. *Rethinking Psychiatry: From Cultural Category to Personal Experience*. Berkeley: University of California Press.

—— and Byron Good, eds. 1985. *Culture and Depression: Studies in Anthropology and Cross-Cultural Psychiatry of Affect and Disorder*. Berkeley: University of California Press.

—— Veena Das and Margaret Lock, eds. 1997. *Social Suffering*. Berkeley: University of California Press.

Kluckhohn, Clyde. 1944. *Navaho Witchcraft*. Cambridge, MA: Harvard University Press.

—— and Alfred E. Kroeber. 1952. *Culture: A Critical Review of Concepts and Definitions*. Cambridge, MA: Harvard University Press.

Knauft, Bruce M. 1996. *Genealogies for the Present in Cultural Anthropology*. London and New York: Routledge.

Knight, Chris, Robin Dunbar and Camilla Powers. 1999. An evolutionary approach to human culture. In Robin Dunbar, Chris Knight and Camilla Powers, eds., *The Evolution of Culture*. Edinburgh: Edinburgh University Press.

Koepping, Klaus-Peter. 1983. *Adolf Bastian and the Psychic Unity of Mankind: The Foundations of Anthropology in Nineteenth-Century Germany*. New York: University of Queensland Press.

Kroeber, Alfred. 1925. _Handbook of the Indians of California_. Washington, DC: Government Print Office.

—— 1939. _Cultural and Natural Areas of Native North America_. Berkeley: University of California Press.

—— 1952. _The Nature of Culture_. Chicago: University of Chicago Press.

—— ed. 1953. _Anthropology Today: An Encyclopedic Inventory_. Chicago: University of Chicago Press.

Kuper, Adam. 1988. _The Invention of Primitive Society: Transformations of an Illusion_. London: Routledge.

—— 1996. _Anthropology and Anthropologists: The Modern British School_, 3rd edition. London: Routledge & Kegan Paul.

—— 1999. _Culture: The Anthropologists' Account_. Cambridge, MA: Harvard University Press.

Lakoff, George and Mark Johnson. 1980. _Metaphors We Live By_. Chicago: University of Chicago Press.

—— 1999. _Philosophy in the Flesh: The Embodied Mind and its Challenge to Western Thought_. New York: Basic Books.

Lash, Scott and Jonathan Friedman, eds. 1991. _Modernity and Identity_. London: Routledge.

Latour, Bruno. 1991. _We have Never Been Modern_. Cambridge, MA: Harvard University Press.

—— and Steve Woolgar. 1979. _Laboratory Life: The Social Construction of Scientific Facts_. London: Sage.

Layton, Robert. 1997. _Introduction to Theory in Anthropology_. Cambridge: Cambridge University Press.

Leach, Edmund R. 1954. _Political Systems of Highland Burma_. London: Athlone.

—— 1968. Ritual. _Encyclopedia of the Social Sciences_. New York: Free Press

—— 1970. _Lévi-Strauss_. London: Fontana.

—— 1984. Glimpses of the unmentionable in the history of British social anthropology. _Annual Review of Anthropology_, **13**: 1–22.

LeClair, Edward E. and Harold K. Schneider, eds. 1968. _Economic Anthropology: Readings in Theory and Analysis_. New York: Holt, Rinehart & Winston.

Lee, Richard and Irven DeVore, eds, (1968) _Man the Hunter_. Chicago: Aldine.

Leenhardt, Maurice. 1937. _Gens de la Grande Terre_. Paris: Gallimard.

Leiris, Michel. 1981 [1934]. _L'Afrique fantôme_. Paris: Gallimard.

Lévi-Strauss, Claude. 1963a [1958]. _Structural Anthropology_. New York: Basic Books.

—— 1963b [1961]. _Totemism_. Boston, MA: Beacon.

—— 1966 [1962]. _The Savage Mind_. Chicago: University of Chicago Press.

—— 1969 [1949]. _The Elementary Structures of Kinship_. London: Tavistock.

—— 1976 [1955]. _Tristes tropiques_. Harmondsworth: Penguin.

—— 1985 [1983]. _The View from Afar_. New York: Basic Books.

—— 1987a [1950]. _Introduction to the Work of Marcel Mauss_. London: Routledge.

—— 1987b The concept of 'house'. In C. Lévi-Strauss, _Anthropology and Myth_, pp. 151–2. Oxford: Blackwell.

Lévy-Bruhl, Lucien. 1978 [1922]. _Primitive Mentality_. New York: AMS Press.

Lewis, Oscar. 1951. _Life in a Mexican Village: Tepoztlán Restudied_. Urbana: University of Illinois Press.

—— 1960. _Tepotzlán, a Mexican Village_. New York: Holt.

Lienhardt, Godfrey. 1961. _Divinity and Experience: The Religion of the Dinka_. Oxford: Oxford University Press.

Linton, Ralph. 1937. _The Study of Man: An Introduction_. New York: Appleton-Century-Crofts.

Lipset, David. 1982. _Gregory Bateson: The Legacy of a Scientist_. Boston, MA: Beacon.

Lizot, Jacques. 1984. _Les Yanomami Centraux_. Paris: Éditions de l'École des Hautes Études en Sciences Sociales.

Lowie, Robert H. 1920. _Primitive Society_. New York: Liveright.

Lutz, Catherine and Donald Nonini. 1999. The economies of violence and the violence of economies. In Henrietta Moore, ed., *Anthropological Theory Today*, pp. 73–113. Oxford: Blackwell.

Lyotard, Jean-François. 1984 [1979]. *The Postmodern Condition: A Report on Knowledge*. Manchester: Manchester University Press.

Maine, Henry. 1931 [1861]. *Ancient Law, Its Connection with the Early History of Society, and its Relation to Modern Ideas*. London: J.M. Dent.

Malik, Kenan. 2000. *Man, Beast, or Zombie: What Science Can and Cannot Tell Us About Human Nature*. London: Weidenfeld & Nicolson.

Malinowski, Bronislaw. 1967. *A Diary in the Strict Sense of the Term*. London: Routledge & Kegan Paul.

—— 1974 [1948]. *Magic, Science and Religion and Other Essays*. London: Souvenir.

—— 1984 [1922]. *Argonauts of the Western Pacific*. Prospect Heights, IL: Waveland.

Malkki, Liisa H. 1995. *Purity and Exile: Violence, Memory, and National Cosmology among Hutu Refugees in Tanzania*. Chicago: University of Chicago Press.

Marcus, George and Michael Fischer. 1986. *Anthropology as a Cultural Critique: An Experimental Moment in the Human Sciences*. Chicago: University of Chicago Press.

Marx, Karl. 1906 [1867–1894]. *Capital: A Critique of Political Economy*. New York: Modern Library.

Mauss, Marcel. 1954 [1924]. *The Gift*. London: Cohen & West.

—— 1979 [1934]. Body techniques. In M. Mauss, *Sociology and Psychology*, pp. 97–122. London: Routledge.

Mayer, Philip. 1960. *Townsmen or Tribesmen? Conservatism and the Process of Urbanization in a South African City*. Cape Town: Oxford University Press.

Mead, Margaret. 1975 [1930]. *Growing Up in New Guinea: A Comparative Study of Primitive Education*. New York: Morrow.

—— 1978 [1928]. *Coming of Age in Samoa*. Harmondsworth: Penguin.

—— 1980 [1935]. *Sex and Temperament in Three Primitive Societies*. New York: Morrow.

Meillassoux, Claude. 1960. Essai d'interprétation du phénomène économique dans les sociétés traditionelles d'autosubsistance. *Cahiers d'Etudes Africaines*, **4**: 38–67.

—— 1981. *Maidens, Meal and Money: Capitalism and the Domestic Community*. Cambridge: Cambridge University Press.

Melhuus, Marit. 1993. Pursuits of knowledge – pursuit of justice: a Marxist dilemma. *Social Anthropology* **1** (3): 265–75.

Miller, Daniel. 1998. *A Theory of Shopping*. Cambridge: Polity.

—— and Don Slater. 2000. *The Internet: An Ethnographic Approach*. Oxford: Berg.

Mintz, Sidney. 1974. *Caribbean Transformations*. Chicago: Aldine.

—— 1985. *Sweetness and Power: The Place of Sugar in Modern History*. New York: Viking.

Mitchell, J. Clyde. 1956. *The Kalela Dance: Aspects of Social Relationships among Urban Africans in Northern Rhodesia*. Livingstone: Rhodes-Livingstone Papers, **27**.

Modood, Tariq and Pnina Werbner, eds. 1997. *Debating Cultural Hybridity: Multi-cultural Identities and the Politics of Anti-Racism*. London: Zed.

Montaigne, Michel de. 1580. *Essays*. Translated by Charles Cotton. Downloaded from the Internet at: http://www.orst.edu/instruct/phl302/texts/montaigne/m-essays_contents.html

Montesquieu, Charles de Secondat. 1973 [1722]. *Persian Letters*. Harmondsworth: Penguin.

—— 1977 [1748]. *Spirit of Laws*. Berkeley: University of California Press.

Moore, Henrietta L. 1986. *Space, Text and Gender: An Anthropological Study of the Marakwet of Kenya*. Cambridge: Cambridge University Press.

—— 1999. Introduction, in Henrietta Moore, ed., *Anthropological Theory Today*. Cambridge: Polity.

Moore, Jerry W. 1997. *Visions of Culture: An Introduction to Anthropological Theories and Theorists*. London: Alta Mira Press.

Morgan, Lewis Henry. 1870. *Systems of Consanguinity and Affinity of the Human Family*. Washington, DC: Smithsonian Institution.

—— 1976 [1877]. *Ancient Society*. New York: Gordon Press.

Murphy, Yolanda and Robert Murphy. 1985. *Women of the Forest*. New York: Columbia University Press.

Needham, Rodney. 1962. *Structure and Sentiment: A Test Case in Anthropology*. Chicago: University of Chicago Press.

Newman, Katherine. 1988. *Falling from Grace: The Experience of Downward Mobility in the American Middle Class*. New York: Vintage.

Nordstrom, Carolyn and Antonius C.G.M. Robben, eds. 1995. *Fieldwork under Fire: Contemporary Studies of Violence and Survival*. Berkeley: University of California Press.

Obeyesekere, Gananath. 1981. *Medusa's Hair*. Chicago: University of Chicago Press.

—— 1992. *The Apotheosis of Captain Cook: European Mythmaking in the Pacific*. Princeton, NJ: Princeton University Press.

Okely, Judith. 1975. The self and scientism. *Journal of the Anthropological Society of Oxford (JASO)*, **6** (3): 171–88.

—— and Helen Calloway, eds. 1992. *Anthropology and Autobiography*. London: Routledge.

O'Laughlin, Bridget. 1974. Mediation of contradiction: why Mbum women do not eat chicken. In Michelle Z. Rosaldo and Louise Lamphere, eds, *Woman, Culture & Society*, pp. 301–42. Stanford, CA: Stanford University Press.

Ortner, Sherry B. 1974. Is female to male as nature is to culture? In Michelle Z. Rosaldo and Louise Lamphere, eds, *Woman, Culture & Society*, pp. 67–87. Stanford, CA: Stanford University Press.

—— 1984. Theory in anthropology since the sixties. *Comparative Studies in Society and History*, **26**: 126–66.

—— ed. 1999. *The Fate of 'Culture': Geertz and Beyond*. Berkeley: University of California Press.

Overing, Joanna, ed. 1985. *Reason and Morality*. London: Tavistock.

Parkin, David. 1969. *Neighbours and Nationals in an African City Ward*. London: Routledge & Kegan Paul.

Plotkin, Vladimir and Jovan E. Howe. 1985. The unknown tradition: continuity and innovation in Soviet ethnography. *Dialectical Anthropology*, **9** (1–4): 257–312.

Polanyi, Karl. 1957 [1944]. *The Great Transformation: The Political and Economic Origins of our Time*. Boston, MA: Beacon.

Powdermaker, Hortense. 1966. *Stranger and Friend: The Way of an Anthropologist*. New York: Norton.

Rabinow, Paul. 1989. *French Modern: Norms and Forms of the Social Environment*. Cambridge, MA: MIT Press.

Radcliffe-Brown, A.R. 1922. *Andaman Islanders: A Study in Social Organization*. Cambridge: Cambridge University Press.

—— 1952. *Structure and Function in Primitive Society*. London: Cohen & West.

—— 1957. *A Natural Science of Society*. Glencoe: Free Press.

—— and Daryll Forde, eds. 1950. *African Systems of Kinship and Marriage*. London: Oxford University Press.

Rappaport, Roy A. 1984 [1967]. *Pigs for the Ancestors: Ritual in the Ecology of a New Guinea People*, 2nd edition. New Haven, CT: Yale University Press.

Redfield, Robert. 1930. *Tepotzlán: A Mexican Village*. Chicago: University of Chicago Press.

—— 1955. *The Little Community: Viewpoints for the Study of a Human Whole*. Chicago: University of Chicago Press.

Richards, Audrey. 1939. *Land, Labour and Diet in Northern Rhodesia: An Economic Study of the Bemba Tribe*. London: Oxford University Press.

—— 1956. *Chisungu: A Girls' Initiation Ceremony Among the Bemba of Northern Rhodesia*. New York: Grove Press.

—— 1964 [1932]. *Hunger and Work in a Savage Tribe: A Functional Study of Nutrition among the Southern Bantu*. Cleveland: World Publishing Co.

Ricoeur, Paul. 1971. The model of the text: meaningful action considered as text. *Social Research*, **38**: 529–62.

Ries, Nancy. 1997. *Russian talk, Culture and Conversation during Perestroika*. Ithaca, NY: Cornell University Press.

Rivers, W.H.R. 1914. *The History of Melanesian Society*. Cambridge: Cambridge University Press.

—— 1967 [1908]. *The Todas*. Oosterhout: Anthropological Publications.

Robertson, Roland. 1992. *Globalization*. London: Sage.

Rosaldo, Michelle Z. 1974. Woman, culture and society: a theoretical overview. In Michelle Z. Rosaldo and Louise Lamphere, eds, *Woman, Culture and Society*, pp. 17–43. Stanford, CA: Stanford University Press.

—— 1980. *Knowledge and Passion: Ilongot Notions of Self and Social Life*. Cambridge: Cambridge University Press.

—— and Louise Lamphere, eds. 1974. *Woman, Culture and Society*. Stanford, CA: Stanford University Press.

Rousseau, Jean-Jacques. 1978 [1762]. *On the Social Contract*. New York: St Martin's Press.

Sahlins, Marshall D. 1968. *Tribesmen*. New York: Prentice-Hall.

—— 1972. *Stone Age Economics*. Chicago: Aldine.

—— 1976. *Culture and Practical Reason*. Chicago: Aldine.

—— 1977. *The Use and Abuse of Biology*. Chicago: University of Chicago Press.

—— 1981. *Historical Metaphors and Mythical Realities*. Ann Arbor: University of Michigan Press.

—— 1985. *Islands of History*. Chicago: University of Chicago Press.

—— 1994. Goodbye to tristes tropes: ethnography in the context of modern world history. In Robert Borofsky, ed., *Assessing Cultural Anthropology*, pp. 377–94. New York: McGraw-Hill.

—— 1995. *How 'Natives' Think: About Captain Cook, For Example*. Chicago: University of Chicago Press.

Said, Edward A. 1978. *Orientalism*. New York: Pantheon.

—— 1993. *Culture and Imperialism*. New York: Knopf.

Sangren, Steven. 1988. Rhetoric and the authority of ethnography: 'postmodernism' and the social reproduction of texts. *Current Anthropology*, **29** (3): 405–35.

Sapir, Edward. 1921. *Language, an Introduction to the Study of Speech*. New York: Harcourt, Brace & Co.

Scheper-Hughes, Nancy. 1979. *Saints, Scholars and Schizophrenics: Mental Illness in Rural Ireland*. Berkeley: University of California Press.

—— 1992. *Death Without Weeping: The Violence of Everyday Life in Brazil*. Berkeley: University of California Press.

—— 2000. Nancy Scheper-Hughes Interview: conversations with history. Institute of International Studies, University of California, Berkeley, downloaded from http://globetrotter.berkeley.edu/people/Scheper-Hughes/sh-con0.html

—— and Margaret Lock. 1987. The mindful body: a prolegomenon to future work in medical anthropology. *Medical Anthropology Quarterly*, **1** (n.s.): 6–41

Schneider, David M. 1968. *American Kinship: A Cultural Account*. Englewood Cliffs, NJ: Prentice-Hall.

—— 1984. *A Critique of the Study of Kinship*. Ann Arbor: University of Michigan Press.

Scott, James C. 1985. *Weapons of the Weak: Everyday Forms of Peasant Resistance*. New Haven, CT: Yale University Press.

Seligman, C.P. and Brenda W. Seligman. 1932. *Pagan Tribes of the Nilotic Sudan*. London: Routledge.

Shore, Bradd. 1996. *Culture in Mind: Cognition, Culture and the Problem of Meaning*. New York: Oxford University Press.

Silverman, Sydel. 1981. *Totems and Teachers: Perspectives on the History of Anthropology*. New York: Columbia University Press.

Smith, M. G. 1965. *The Plural Society in the British West Indies.* Berkeley: University of California Press.

Sokal, Alan. 1996. Transgressing the boundaries: toward a transformative hermeneutics of quantum gravity. *Social Text* **14** (1–2).

Southall, Aidan, ed. 1973. *Introduction to Urban Anthropology.* London: Oxford University Press.

Spencer, Jonathan. 1989. Anthropology as a kind of writing. *Man,* **24** (2): 145–64.

—— 1996. Marxism and anthropology. In Alan Barnard and Jonathan Spencer, eds., *Encyclopedia of Social and Cultural Anthropology,* pp. 352–4. London: Routledge.

Sperber, Dan. 1996. *Explaining Culture: A Naturalist Account.* Oxford: Blackwell.

Steward, Julian. ed. 1946–50. *Handbook of South American Indians.* Washington, DC: US GPO.

—— 1955. *The Theory of Culture Change: The Methodology of Multilinear Evolution.* Urbana: University of Illinois Press.

Stocking, George W. 1995. *After Tylor: British Social Anthropology, 1888–1951.* Madison: University of Wisconsin Press.

—— ed. 1996. *Volksgeist as Method and Ethic: Essays on Boasian Ethnography and the German Anthropological Tradition.* Madison: University of Wisconsin Press.

Stoller, Paul. 1989. *The Taste of Ethnographic Things: The Senses in Anthropology.* Philadelphia: University of Pennsylvania Press.

Strathern, Marilyn. 1988. *The Gender of the Gift: Problems with Women and Problems with Society in Melanesia.* Berkeley: University of California Press.

—— 1991. *Partial Connections.* Savage, MD: Rowman & Littlefield.

—— 1992. *After Nature: English Kinship in the Late Twentieth Century.* Cambridge: Cambridge University Press.

Tambiah, Stanley J. 1996. *Leveling Crowds: Ethnonationalist Conflicts and Collective Violence in South Asia.* Berkeley: University of California Press.

Thomas, Nicholas. 1991. *Entangled Objects: Exchange, Material Culture and Colonialism in the Pacific.* Cambridge, MA: Harvard University Press.

Thomas, William and Florian W. Znaniecki. 1918–20. *The Polish Peasant in Europe and America: Monograph of an Immigrant Group,* vols I–V. Chicago: University of Chicago Press.

Tierney, Patrick. 2000. *Darkness in El Dorado: How Scientists and Journalists Devastated the Amazon.* New York: Norton.

Tishkov, Valery A. 1992. The crisis in Soviet ethnography. *Current Anthropology,* **33** (4): 371–93.

Todorov, Tzvetan. 1984. *The Conquest of America: The Conquest of the Other.* New York: Harper & Row.

Tönnies, Ferdinand. 1963 [1887]. *Community and Society.* New York: Harper & Row.

Tooby, John and Leda Cosmides. 1992. 'The psychological foundations of culture'. In Jerome Barkow, Leda Cosmides and John Tooby, eds, *The Adapted Mind: Evolutionary Psychology and the Generation of Culture,* pp. 19–136. Oxford: Oxford University Press.

Trouillot, Michel-Rolph. 1995. *Silencing the Past: Power and the Production of History.* Boston, MA: Beacon.

Turner, Victor. 1957. *Schism and Continuity in an African Society: A Study of a Ndembu Village.* Manchester: Manchester University Press.

—— 1967. *The Forest of Symbols: Aspects of Ndembu Ritual.* Ithaca, NY: Cornell University Press.

—— 1969. *The Ritual Process.* Chicago: Aldine.

—— 1974. *Dramas, Fields and Metaphors: Symbolic Action in Human Society.* Ithaca, NY: Cornell University Press.

—— 1987 [1988]. *The Anthropology of Performance.* New York: PAJ Publications.

—— and Edward Bruner, eds. 1986. *The Anthropology of Experience.* Urbana, IL: University of Illinois Press.

Tylor, Edward. 1964 [1865]. *Researches into the Early History of Mankind and the Development of Civilization.* Abridged edition. Chicago: University of Chicago Press.

—— 1958 [1871]. *Primitive Culture.* Abridged edition. New York: Harper.

Ulin, Robert C. 1984. *Understanding Cultures: Perspectives in Anthropology and Social Theory*. Austin: University of Texas Press.

Vayda, Andrew P. 1994. Actions, variations, and change: the emerging anti-essentialist view in anthropology. In Robert Borofsky, ed., *Assessing Cultural Anthropology*, pp. 320–30. New York: McGraw-Hill.

Velsen, Jaap van. 1967. The extended-case method and situational analysis. In A.L. Epstein, ed., *The Craft of Social Anthropology*, pp. 129–52. London: Tavistock.

Verdery, Katherine. 1983. *Transylvanian Villagers: Three Centuries of Political, Economic, and Ethnic Change*. Berkeley: University of California Press.

—— 1991. Theorizing socialism: A prologue to the 'transition'. *American Anthropologist*, **18** (3): 419–36.

Vermeulen, Han F. and Arturo Alvarez Roldán, eds. 1995. *Fieldwork and Footnotes: Studies in the History of European Anthropology*. London: Routledge.

Vico, Giambattista. 1999 [1725]. *The New Science*. London: Penguin.

Wagner, Roy. 1975. *The Invention of Culture*. Chicago: University of Chicago Press.

—— 1986. *Symbols That Stand for Themselves*. Chicago: University of Chicago Press.

Wallerstein, Immanuel. 1974–9. *The Modern World-System* (3 vols). New York: Academic Press.

Wax, Rosalie. 1971. *Doing Fieldwork: Warnings and Advice*. Chicago: University of Chicago Press.

Weber, Max. 1976 [1904–5] *The Protestant Ethic and the Spirit of Capitalism*. London: Allen & Unwin.

—— 1968 [1922] *Economy and Society: An Outline of Interpretive Sociology*. New York: Bedminster Press.

Wedel, Janine R. 1986. *The Private Poland*. New York: Facts on File.

Weiner, Annette B. 1976. *Women of Value, Men of Renown: New Perspectives in Trobriand Exchange*. Austin: University of Texas Press.

—— 1992. *Inalienable Possessions: The Paradox of Keeping-while-giving*. Berkeley: University of California Press.

Werbner, Pnina and Tariq Modood, eds. 1997. *Debating Cultural Hybridity: Multi-Cultural Identities and the Politics of Anti-Racism*. London: Zed.

White, Leslie A. 1949. *The Science of Culture: A Study of Man and Civilization*. New York: Grove Press.

Wiener, Norbert. 1948. *Cybernetics: or Control and Communication in the Animal and the Machine*. Cambridge, MA: Technology Press.

Wierzbicka, Anna. 1989. Soul and mind. Linguistic evidence for ethnopsychology and cultural history. *American Anthropologist*, **91** (1): 41–56.

Wilson, Bryan, ed. 1970. *Rationality*. Oxford: Blackwell.

Wilson, Edward O. 1975. *Sociobiology: The New Synthesis*. Cambridge, MA: Harvard University Press.

—— 1978. *On Human Nature*. Cambridge, MA: Harvard University Press.

Wilson, Godfrey. 1941–2. *An Essay on the Economics of Detribalization in Northern Rhodesia, Parts I–II*. Livingstone: Rhodes-Livingstone Institute.

Wilson, Richard, ed. 1997. *Human Rights, Culture and Context*. London: Pluto.

Winch, Peter. 1958. *The Idea of a Social Science and its Relation to Philosophy*. London: Routledge.

Wolf, Eric. 1966. *Peasants*. Englewood Cliffs, NJ: Prentice-Hall.

—— 1969. On peasant rebellions. *International Social Science Journal*, **21** (2): 286–94.

—— 1982. *Europe and the People without History*. Berkeley: University of California Press.

—— 1994. Facing power: old insights, new questions. In Robert Borofsky, ed., *Assessing Cultural Anthropology*, pp. 218–28. New York: McGraw-Hill.

Worsley, Peter. 1964. *The Third World*. London: Weidenfeld & Nicholson.

—— 1968 [1957]. *The Trumpet Shall Sound*, 2nd edition. New York: Schocken.

—— 1984. *The Three Worlds: Culture and World Development*. London: Weidenfeld & Nicolson.

INDEX

Compiled by Auriol Griffith-Jones